Last train from

Trent Station

A history of a celebrated Midland Railway interchange

1862-1968

by

Geoffrey Kingscott

Reprinted October 2007

Last train from Trent Station

Page layout: Roger Brandon

Printed by: Glenwood Printing, Unit 4, Baines Industrial Park, Woods Lane, Derby DE22 3UD.

Published by: Geoffrey Kingscott Consultants Limited, 23 Shaftesbury Avenue, Long Eaton, Nottingham NG10 3FG, **www.geoffreykingscott.co.uk**

ISBN: 978-0-9555016-0-9

Other railway books by Geoffrey Kingscott:

Lost Railways of Nottinghamshire, 2005.

Lost Railways of Leicestershire and Rutland, 2006.

Lost Railways of Derbyshire, in preparation, due October 2007.

These three books are published by Countryside Books, Newbury, Berkshire.

TABLE OF CONTENTS

Introduction 1

Chapter 1 - The Midland Railway 5

Chapter 2 - The Trent Triangle 9

Chapter 3 – The station is built 16

Chapter 4 – The Goose Fair Disaster 32

Chapter 5 – “The junction for everywhere” 36

Chapter 6 – Three cheers for Mr Gladstone 42

Chapter 7 – Platform tickets and station signs 48

Chapter 8 – Trent for Trent College 54

Chapter 9 – Memories of Trent Station 65

Chapter 10 – “The economic facts have to be faced”. 75

Chapter 11 – Turning out the lights 83

Chapter 12 – Relics and revivals 90

Works consulted 95

Introduction

Trent Station was an oddity in British railway history.

The oddity manifested itself in a number of ways.

It was a Nowhere Station. It was never intended to serve any local population, and never had a proper surfaced road leading to it.

For this reason it was not named after any local town, village or even hamlet. It was named after a river, which makes it unique in English railway history (I use the word 'English' advisedly, because there is one other example in Britain: Dyfy (Dovey) Junction in West Wales, where the Aberystwyth and Barmouth/Pwllhelli lines divide).

And yet, despite its remoteness, even to the end of its days Trent Station was a busy station.

This is because of its role as an interchange point. Trent Station was built at a junction, where lines coming down from the north, and lines coming up from the south, intersected with lines running west to east.

Over the 106 years of the station's history many people changed trains at Trent, without having any clear idea where they were. This particularly applied during the second world war, when servicemen making long journeys home often found themselves stranded for hours on its exposed platforms. It is recounted that some American servicemen, stranded on Trent Station during the war, said something like: "Let's go and find the night-life in this Trent place". A porter had to explain that Trent did not exist and they were a long way from anywhere.

The platforms were exposed because Trent was an island station. With the station buildings in the middle, there was nothing to shelter anyone on those platforms from the wind. And because the station was surrounded by open country, the wind whistled round it, and in and out of its five wide arches, adding to its reputation for bleakness and remoteness.

Those arches were part of what was architecturally a handsome station, built in the style known as Midland Gothic (of which St Pancras Station in London is the prime example). And here is another oddity about Trent Station: the buildings were hardly altered from start to finish. Even in the 1960s the station remained a determinedly Victorian structure.

Yet another peculiar feature was that Trent Station never had electric light or power. Even as long ago as 1967, its last full year of operation, this was highly unusual. There was no electricity for heating or lighting, even though electricity cables ran through the station. Trent remained lit only by the soft light of gas lamps until the moment it closed for ever.

And a further oddity was the confusion it engendered. This was because of its loops, which allowed trains to come in and leave in all directions. Thus it was possible to have two London-bound trains, an express and a stopping train, standing on the adjacent platforms, yet facing in opposite directions. We shall need to explain in chapter 3 the system of curves and junctions which created this confusing situation.

This confusion was always one of Trent's most notorious features.

In 1956, in an article in *Railway World*, W.A. Tuplin described the difficulties even railway staff had of reading London Midland region timetables.

> "…Of course, a railway system that has a junction like Trent can reasonably expect to be able to tie its patrons into knots with its timetables, and if the staff also become a bit dazed, why not?"

In its local area (the south-east corner of Derbyshire, the nearest town being Long Eaton) it was the subject of a number of sayings. A common expression of surprise was "Well, I'll go to Trent Station!". A variant of this, the exact significance of which escapes the author, was "Well, I'll go to Trent Station in an open boat!"

Another expression was a parody of the line in the Lord's Prayer about leading us not into temptation. In the Long Eaton area at school assembly, or anywhere where we were asked to repeat the Lord's Prayer, wicked youngsters that we were, we solemnly intoned the line as "Lead us not into Trent Station". It ceased almost to be a joke and became something we did as a matter of course.

A book of memories of a childhood in Long Eaton, written by local man Richard Guise, actually took the title of *Lead us not into Trent Station*.

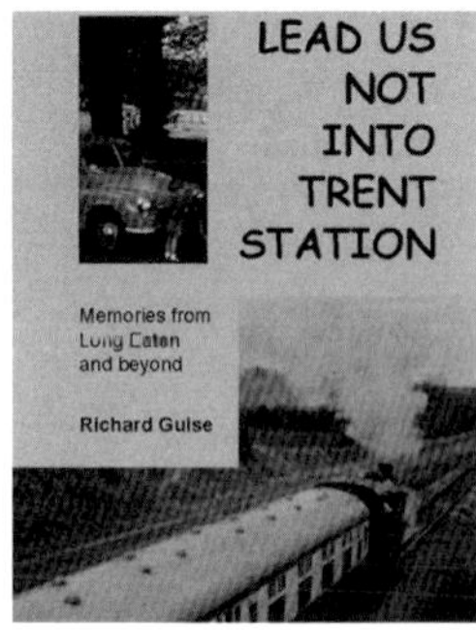

The cover of the Richard Guise book about his childhood in the area near Trent Station. The railway photograph is not actually taken at Trent. Photograph reproduced by permission of Richard Guise.

A similar parody involved those who lived near Exhall, a Warwickshire village which, pre-Beeching, had a station on the line between Coventry and Nuneaton. Invited at Christmastime to "Sing in Exultation" the words came out as "Sing in Exhall Station". Exhall Station, like Trent, is now closed but the sentiment has not been forgotten.

My own interest in Trent Station was, until I came to research a talk on the subject, a vague one. I am not a railway buff. I was born in 1936, and lived not far away from Trent Station, so up to the age of 31 I often used Trent, and always found it fascinating. My wife and I deliberately arranged to travel on the last train out of the station, in the first minutes of the year 1968.

Towards the end of 2001, as a committee member of the Sawley Historical Society, I felt it was time I offered to give a talk at one of the monthly meetings. The society is the local history group for the village to which I belong, Sawley, which is about a mile down the line from Trent Station.

I chose to do the station, and only then commenced the research. My research itself stimulated a lot of memories from those who had known Trent Station even after the nearly 40 years which had elapsed since its closure. And the more I researched, the more the fascination grew, until it turned into this book.

Another tinted Edwardian postcard, again looking north, but from an angle which can show the 'down' platform.

Photographs have been a problem. Because Trent is an island station, there are very few angles from which photographs can be taken. They tend to be taken from the ends of the platform, particularly the southern end, looking north, and therefore always to show the same view. And because of the peculiarity mentioned, that the station scarcely changed its appearance in its 106 years, the view looks the same whether the photograph was taken in 1906 or 1960.

Trent Station was oriented approximately in a direction north-north-east to south-south-west, but for simplicity's sake, and copying railway usage, I will refer to the directions as north (towards Nottingham) and south (towards Derby or London). In railway parlance 'up' is towards London and 'down' is away from London. Although, as we have seen, trains could leave Trent from any direction, the station did officially have an 'up' platform and a 'down' platform, the easterly and westerly sides respectively, and we shall occasionally use these designations. Only in its final years, it seems, were the platforms given numbers, 1 for the up platform and 2 for the down platform.

I have used only Imperial measurements, which were of course the only ones in use during the existence of Trent Station, and have made no attempt to give metric equivalents. For those unfamiliar with Imperial measures, most reference books have conversion tables. Also in use throughout Trent's existence was the pre-decimalisation money system, £sd, in which 12d (pennies) made 1s (shilling), and 20 shillings made £1 (one pound). Thus 5s 0d, the amount of the tip given to the porter by Norman Wisdom, mentioned in Chapter 6, is five shillings, or 25p in decimal currency. Younger readers may be puzzled by the references to two classes, "first" and "third", on trains and in station accommodation. There were three classes (first, second, third) on the railways only in the very early days, and in 1875 the Midland Railway took the lead in abolishing the second class, a lead quickly followed by the other companies. However, the term "third class" continued to be used – with no "second class" at all - until as late as 1956, when it was replaced by the modern term "standard class".

Some of the artefacts from Trent Station and its associated signalboxes were saved from destruction by Midland Railways expert Roy Burrows, and he kindly identified for us all the Trent-related items in his extensive collection, which has, since we visited him, been transferred from his home to the Derby Industrial Museum and the Midland Railway Centre at Butterley.

Roy Burrows. Photograph Judy Wheldon

I would also like to acknowledge the assistance I have received from a number of individuals, all of whom share with me an affection for, and an interest in, the story of Trent Station. Some of their contributions are mentioned in the text, while others have helped me with the research or pointed me in the right directions.

My wife Judy, being a trained librarian specialising in local studies, not only helped with research but also listened patiently to my enthusiastic recounting of every new discovery. My son Laurence helped with the scanning of photographs and layout. David Shaw, who saw the end of the station and recorded its demolition, has been the most valuable source of information about what it was like to be a member of the staff there in its final years, and his photographs of the demolition (Chapter 11) are remarkable for both their quality and their historical interest.

Other former members of staff whose memories are included in chapters six or eight include Frank Barber, David Panter and David Archer.

Brian Amos, a knowledgeable collector of railwayana, and another enthusiast for Trent Station, had the foresight to photograph the site in its later days, while it was still in existence (some of his photographs are featured in the covers to this book and elsewhere. He and his colleague Phil Burton were also kind enough to read the text in manuscript form.

Ian Mitchell, who is researching the history of the nearby Trent Sheet Stores, generously communicated information on Trent Station he had found in his investigations into old Midland Railway minute books kept in the Public Records Office at Kew.

My old friend Roy Talbot, son of Trent's last station foreman, has also long been interested in anything to do with the station. Invaluable assistance has also come from John Blackburn, Alan Bowler, Keith Breakwell, Judith Dakin, Hylton Holt, Laurence Knighton, Keith Reedman and Glynn Waite and others too numerous to mention.

Copyright remains strictly with the owners of each photograph wherever a photographer's name has been identified. Every effort has been the made to identify copyright ownership of other photographs, particularly old postcards.

One of Brian Amos's photographs, taken in March 1967, the last year of Trent Station's existence. This shows the south end.

Chapter 1

The Midland Railway

How do we get coal to Leicester?

It was solving that problem that led to the creation of what became the Midland Railway, and of a major railway junction called Trent.

To understand how and why the problem was tackled, we have to go back to the Canal Age.

It is difficult for us today, surrounded as we are by technology, to even imagine a world where motive power was measured by how much a horse could pull.

This is why canals were such a revolution. A horse pulling a barge or narrow boat on a level waterway, where the water supported the load, could pull 20 times or more the weight it could manage on a road.

The Canal Age lasted only 75 years or so (1755-1830) before it was supplanted by the Railway Age, but in that short time it changed the landscape of Britain and revolutionised the transport of freight.

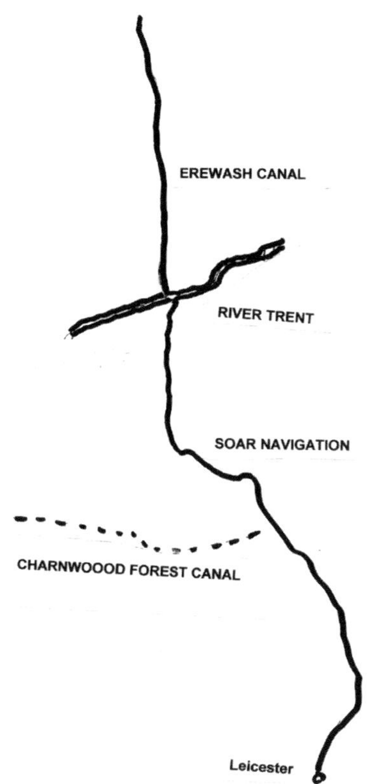

An approximate diagram of the river and canal navigation system for supplying coal to Leicester.

In the 18th century the city of Leicester was already a major market for coal. Traditionally it had been supplied by the coalfields in the Charnwood Hills of Leicestershire, only ten miles away, with the coal being transported by packhorses. But as demand grew because of early industrialisation, so this method of supply was proving inadequate: too slow, too laborious, and too expensive.

The solution was to bring coal, wherever it came from, into Leicester by water. The River Soar did flow northwards right through the centre of the city, so in the 1770s local merchants set about making it navigable downstream to its confluence with the River Trent. They did this by dredging out some stretches, and by making short canal 'cuts' to bypass the stretches where the river was too shallow to permit boats to pass.

Some ten miles north of the River Trent lay the Erewash Valley coalfield. There was no way the little River Erewash (which flows south to the Trent) could be made navigable, but the valley could be utilised for a canal. This Erewash Canal opened in 1779, joining the Trent almost opposite the mouth of the River Soar. At a stroke Erewash Valley coal could be transported to Leicester in quantities and at prices which the Leicestershire coalowners could not match.

By 1808 the Erewash Canal was carrying 270,000 tons of coal a year, and the mine owners and the owners of shares in the canal were able to sit back and enjoy some very handsome profits.

The Charnwood Forest coal-owners were at their wits' end wondering how to compete. At great expense they began to build, in 1794, the Charnwood Forest Canal. However, canals across hills are more difficult to engineer than canals along valleys, and barely had the new waterway become operational than it was wrecked by a period of severe weather in the winter of 1799. The thaw which came after the heavy winter snowfalls caused the Blackbrook reservoir, which fed the canal, to burst, an aqueduct was destroyed, and embankments damaged.

Efforts were made to carry out repairs and bring it back into operation, but eventually these were abandoned. So for the next 30 years Erewash Valley coal ruled the roost.

Then a farmer who had interests in the Charnwood Forest pits, William Stenson of Whitwick, visited the north-east in 1827 and happened to see the building of the Stockton and Darlington line, the world's first public railway. It was if a light bulb had lit up in Stenson's head. Here was the solution to making the Leicestershire coalfields the main supplier to their own county town. When he got back to Leicestershire he talked to his friend John Ellis, a wealthy Quaker involved with Leicester's textile industry. Ellis got in touch with the "father of the railways", George Stephenson himself, and went to see him.

Stephenson, with his son Robert, took time off from building his second pioneering venture, the Liverpool and Manchester Railway, to make a quick visit to Leicester and decided the project for a Leicestershire coalfield railway was feasible. Robert Stephenson was appointed its engineer.

Ellis persuaded the Charnwood Forest coalowners to take up the new invention, and – they moved fast in those days - on May 5, 1832, the first stretch of a railway between Swannington (in the heart of the Charnwood Forest coalfields) and Leicester was opened. It was only the fifth long-distance railway line authorised in England, and the first in the Midlands. These were very early days indeed in the history of steam locomotives pulling trains on iron rails.

But Charnwood Forest coal could now be transported to Leicester and sold at prices well below that of Erewash Valley coal.

The Erewash Valley coal proprietors were not going to take this new and dangerous competition lying down. They also moved quickly. Some time in the summer of 1832 they held an exploratory meeting at the Bulls Head & Anchor Hotel, Loughborough. Presumably Loughborough was chosen because they were talking to their friends in the Soar Navigation. The upshot of this meeting was a decision on the lines of "If you can't beat them, join them".

So, at a more formal meeting held on August 16, 1832, at the Sun Inn in Eastwood, followed by another at the George Inn, Alfreton, on August 27, 1832, they decided they would have their own railway, a single line running from Pinxton, in the heart of the Erewash Valley coalfield, direct to Leicester.

The reason Pinxton was chosen was that it would there join up with the Mansfield and Pinxton [horse-drawn] Railway, which previously had brought coal from the Mansfield pits to the canal system. A further meeting was held at the Sun Inn, Eastwood, on September 14, 1832, at which the coal-owners considered reports of surveys. They now calculated that with a railway they would be able to move coal to Leicester at a conveyance charge of 3s 0d a ton instead of 7s 6d a ton by canal.

The September meeting also decided – and it was a crucial decision for the subject of our book - to go for markets in Derby and Nottingham by making east-west branches from its north-south Pinxton to Leicester line. The branches would leave the north-south line at a point just north of the river Trent, near the then hamlet of Long Eaton. The meeting also decided on a name for the new venture – the Midland Counties Railway.

But the Erewash Valley coalowners found they could not raise enough capital by themselves, and had to take on board outside investors from Liverpool. It was these investors who changed the whole emphasis of the line, by insisting on exploiting also the potential for passenger traffic. The Railway Age was beginning, and such investors were now looking at much wider horizons. The biggest attraction of all was a link to London, and this they planned to achieve by extending the north-south line to Rugby, where there would be a link with the London and Birmingham Railway.

The finalised plans, for a railway from Pinxton to Rugby, with branches to Derby and Nottingham, were presented to Parliament in 1835. At this time all railways needed an Act of Parliament before they could be constructed.

Canal owners, as was only to be expected, registered objections to the new line but, more importantly, so did two other railway companies.

This was because someone had incautiously mentioned the possibility of eventually taking the Pinxton line north beyond Pinxton to Clay

Cross or Chesterfield. This idea came to the attention of the North Midland Railway (NMR), which was already entrenched in that very area, and also to the attention of the NMR's allies, the Birmingham and Derby Junction Railway, which was wanting to link up with the NMR to provide a continuation of it southward.

To get the bill through Parliament the Liverpool investors - to the fury and indignation of the coal-owners who had originated the whole enterprise - insisted on dropping the Pinxton line, whereupon these other railway companies withdrew their objections.

All that was now proposed was one line between Nottingham and Derby, and another line from this at Trent Junction to Leicester and Rugby (for the London connection), a total of 57 ¾ miles.

As Frederick Williams, the earliest historian of the Midland Railway, put it: "the substantial assistance of moneyed men of the North, whose only anxiety was to secure a great through route to the South, and who cared little for the solicitude of a few coal-owners in a remote Nottinghamshire valley...forced the abandonment of the entire Erewash Valley section of the MCR".

The Midland Counties Railway Act became law (i.e. received Royal Assent) on June 21, 1836.

The engineer selected to survey and plan the line was Charles Blacker Vignoles. During the first week of September 1835 he was instructed to re-survey the line (there had been an earlier survey). Again note how quickly they moved in those days. By November 12 Vignoles had completed the re-survey, by November 28 he had submitted the plans, and these were formally deposited on November 30.

Vignoles, then 42 years old and at the height of his powers, was one of the great Victorian engineers. Though others, such as Brunel, Telford or Stephenson, are today better known, Vignoles had a long and just as successful a career. Born at Wexford in Ireland in 1793, he was an army engineering officer as a young man. Leaving the army in 1816 he went out to America to work for the next seven years on the surveying of South Carolina.

Charles Blacker Vignoles, surveyor and engineer for the Midland Counties Railway. Picture reproduced by permission of the British Library.

Returning to England he quickly became interested in the new railway phenomenon, an interest he retained for the rest of his life. He had kept up contact with friends and surveyors in America, and through them he heard of a new type of rail profile being pioneered over there. He introduced it and popularised it in Europe. This profile, similar to the one still in use today, is sometimes (particularly in continental countries) known as the Vignoles rail.

Vignoles always remained a civil engineer rather than a professional railway engineer, and in 1841 he became Professor of Civil Engineering at the recently formed University College London. Some 15 years after the Midland Counties railway line project Vignoles went to Russia, where he was commissioned by the Tsar to build a major bridge over the River Dnieper. He became a Fellow of the Royal Society. He died in 1875.

The survey completed and approved, the first contract for construction of the new railway was let to John Taylor, Thomas Johnson and Henry Sharp of Long Eaton on May 22, 1837 for the section of line between Nottingham and Long Eaton (£35,236). The contractor for the Derby to Long Eaton section, and also from Long Eaton to Loughborough (including all three curves at Sawley and Long Eaton and the three-span bridge over the River Trent) was William McKenzie of Leyland in Lancashire, who earlier in his career had been an assistant to Thomas Telford.

Between July and September 1837, 423 men were employed on construction work between Derby and Nottingham. The figure reached a peak of 922, with 76 horses, by the end of the year. In early 1838 there were two months of severe frost, which delayed progress.

In 1838 the contracts for laying the rails were given to the same people who had earlier obtained the contracts for laying out the route, building the embankments etc.

The rails were to be laid on stone blocks. The ceremonial first block (for bedding the actual rails) was laid at Chilwell on August 13, 1838 before a large crowd.

The railway had arrived.

Chapter 2

The Trent Triangle

As the Nottingham to Derby line was nearing completion, work was started on the line south towards Leicester, together with the creation of the triangle of lines called Trent Junction. No station was planned at this stage, and it was to be another 22 years before Trent Station itself came into being.

The first railway bridge over the River Trent was a construction with three equal-sized arches with a 100-feet span. The cast iron for the arches was supplied by the Butterley Company .

That first bridge was regarded as one of the engineering wonders of the early railway age. It was the subject of a special article in *The Engineer* in 1840. The author of the article reserved particular praise for the arches.

"These arches are remarkable for the great simplicity in the mode of structure; each entire rib consisting only of three castings, which comprehend the spandril and upper bearing on which the platform rests, and they are fitted accurately to each other and joined together by diagonal braces which also connect them to the adjoining ribs".

That original 1840 bridge was replaced by the present girder structure in 1902-1903.

The first Midland Counties Railway bridge over the River Trent, a structure in cast iron far surpassing in elegance anything which succeeded it.

The castellated portals of the Red Hill tunnels. When the second (goods lines) tunnel was made in the 1890s, it was given an equivalent treatment. This picture, from an old postcard, also shows the 1902 bridge with its ugly girder construction.

When the replacement bridge was put in place the armorial device of the Midland Counties Railway was transferred from the piers of the old bridge to the parapet of the new one. Note, this was the device of the Midland Counties Railway, which only lasted seven years, and not its successor company the Midland Railway, so is really a piece of early railway history.

South of the river is the sandstone ridge known as Red Hill, and this required a 154-yard tunnel. The teams tunnelling from each side of Red Hill met on February 9, 1839, and a celebration was held at the Navigation Inn, Trent Lock (not the present Navigation Inn, but the public house now known as The Steamboat). The tunnel entrance was subsequently given a castellated portal, which it has preserved to this day.

In April 1839 the first of the locomotives intended for passenger service had been delivered, and soon locomotives pulling coaches were making trial runs from Nottingham to Long Eaton and back.

These trial runs, we are told, were " witnessed by large crowds at the lineside".

The first test train to go all the way to Derby ran on May 29, 1839.

The author remembers as a boy seeing the first diesel locomotives, 10,000 (pictured in chapter 9, below) and 10,001, running on trial from Derby -where they were built - on the line to Nottingham, and the excitement they caused. So he can imagine some of the greater excitement there must have been 163 years ago. Because steam-powered locomotives running on parallel metal tracks were the most dramatic element in the movement which ushered in the modern world, the Industrial Revolution.

All this excitement was building up to the great ceremonial opening of the Nottingham-Derby line on June 4, 1839, when the directors of the Midland Counties Railway, and 300 guests (it was a ticket-only affair) travelled from Nottingham to Derby in four trains drawn by the locomotives Ariel, Hawk, Sunbeam and Wizard.

The special guests were conveyed by a horse-drawn omnibus belonging to the railway company.

The omnibus, named the *British Queen*, all newly painted, started its journey at the White Lion in Clumber-street, Nottingham, and its passage through the city itself made quite a stir. Once at the station the guests showed their "tickets of admission, bearing the arms of the company, most splendidly emblazoned in gold".

The Midland Counties locomotives set off from Nottingham station which, like a modern airport, had separate platforms for arrivals and departures. It was a beautiful sunny day. They were played out by the band of the 5th Dragoon Guards (the National Anthem was played for each departure), and to the extra sound of the bells of St Mary's Church in Nottingham. All four engines had four wheels, or were 2-2-0 in railway parlance. The first three trains had six carriages, the fourth train two. Each carriage had the painted arms of the three Midland counties – Derbyshire, Nottinghamshire, and Leicestershire – and each train had a flag flying.

The first train, pulled by *Sunbeam* (the locomotive had cost £1,300) departed at 12.33 prompt, followed ten minutes later by *Ariel* (a slightly smaller engine). Later, when engine numbering was introduced, *Ariel* became Midland Railway engine no. 1, though it was subsequently re-numbered to 136, and renamed *Bee*. A reserve engine, *Mersey* (one of those used for track laying), had steam up in case anything went wrong, but in fact everything went very well. Signalling was done by flags handled manually by railway policemen.

The journey to Derby took 44 minutes. On the return journey the train "flew at tremendous speed" and arrived, in 42 minutes, to the tune of "See the conquering hero comes". During this latter journey the then stupendous speed of 40 mph was reached.

After the excitement of this opening day a regular service was established between Nottingham and Derby, with three trains (two on Sundays) in each direction. The three trains a day on weekdays quickly became four trains a day.

At the time of opening the line was only single-track, but within a year it had been made double-track.

The Trent to Leicester section was formally opened on May 4, 1840, and opened to normal traffic the following day.

Again there was a ceremonial first train to Leicester, pulled by the engine *Leopard*, with a stop so passengers could get out to look at the Red Hill bridge and tunnel.

The only people who were not happy with all these developments were the Erewash Valley coal owners, who still could not transport their coal all the way by rail to the most lucrative markets. In June 1836 there was created the provisional committee of the Sheffield and Midland Junction Railway, to create a railway from Sheffield to the Trent Junction. But events were now moving fast, and on May 10, 1844 the former rivals the Midland Counties Railway, the North Midland Railway, and the Derby and Birmingham Junction Railway, came together to form the Midland Railway.

Drawn by the locomotive Sunbeam, the first railway train from Nottingham to Derby crosses The Meadows at Nottingham on June 4, 1839.

This was the very first of the major railway amalgamations which were to mark the second stage of the 19th century railway mania, and it was masterminded by the man who became known as the "Railway King", George Hudson.

TRENT COMPLEX 1840-1847

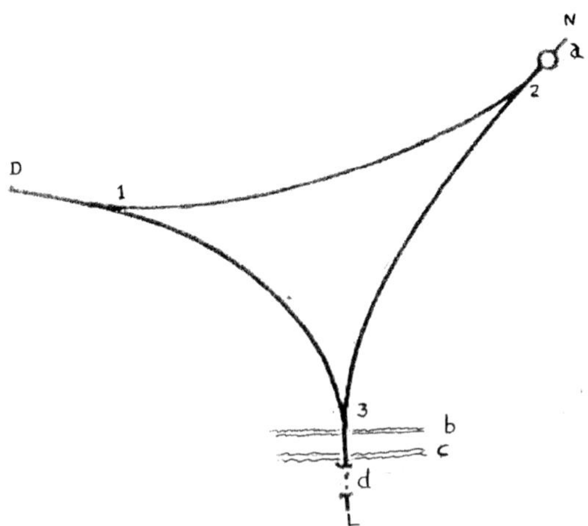

Directions:

D = Towards Derby
N = Towards Nottingham
L = Towards Leicester

Rail Junctions:

1 = Sawley Junction
2 = Long Eaton Junction
3 = Trent Junction

Other features:

a = Long Eaton's first station,
at Meadow Lane
b = Cranfleet Cut
c = River Trent
d = Redhill Tunnel

The first simple layout at Trent Junction. The Derby to Nottingham line, opened in 1839, runs across the top of the picture, with Long Eaton station (at Meadow Lane) shown top right. On this line were two railway junctions, Sawley Junction and Long Eaton Junction, with lines (opened in 1840) running south towards Leicester, and converging at a point shortly before the River Trent. The convergence point became known as Trent Junction. This layout continued until 1847.

Hudson had begun his working life as a draper in York, and as an alderman of that city had become involved with a committee formed to build a railway from York to London. That line was over-ambitious for its time, but a new railway company was formed to build a section from York to South Milford. There it joined the Leeds to Selby railway and the growing general railway network.

Hudson had become chairman of this company, and now threw himself into railway affairs. His dynamic and financially dubious career is too complex to be summarised here, but suffice it to say that he eventually gained control of the North Midland Railway. Then, after secret negotiations with the Birmingham and Derby Junction railway directors, he was able to force the Midland Counties on the defensive, and convince the MCR shareholders over the heads of their board to accept amalgamation.

The Midland Railway, thus formed, was incorporated by Act of Parliament on May 10, 1844, and at 170 miles it was then the longest railway in England. The new company made its headquarters at Derby. Hudson became chairman, and John Ellis deputy chairman.

John Ellis we have previously met, as the man who had interested George Stephenson in creating the Leicester to Swannington Railway. Ellis was a Quaker, and he made sure that the Midland Railway was run to strict business ethics. This was fortunate, for it meant that the Midland was to survive more or less intact when Hudson's huge business empire, built on less ethical methods which he was free to practise elsewhere, collapsed.

Hudson's antics, and even Ellis's inspired stewardship of the Midland Railway (he succeeded Hudson as chairman after the latter's disgrace) belong to the general railway histories, and cannot detain us here.

But what the formation of the Midland Railway did – by bringing all the competitors together – was to remove all obstacles to the construction of a line from Pinxton to Trent Junction, so opening up at long last the Erewash Valley coalfields to rail traffic. On September 6, 1847 the Erewash Valley line was opened as far as Codnor Park. The old Mansfield to Pinxton horse railway was upgraded to take steam locomotives in 1849.

One-third of the coal Britain produced in the mid-19th century was used for iron production, and the iron industry underwent rapid expansion, as the Industrial Revolution got into full swing. In the 1840s the Nottinghamshire coalfields were producing an extra 25,000 tons a year. However, after the opening of the new line they increased production to an astonishing extra half million tons a year.

TRENT COMPLEX 1847-1862

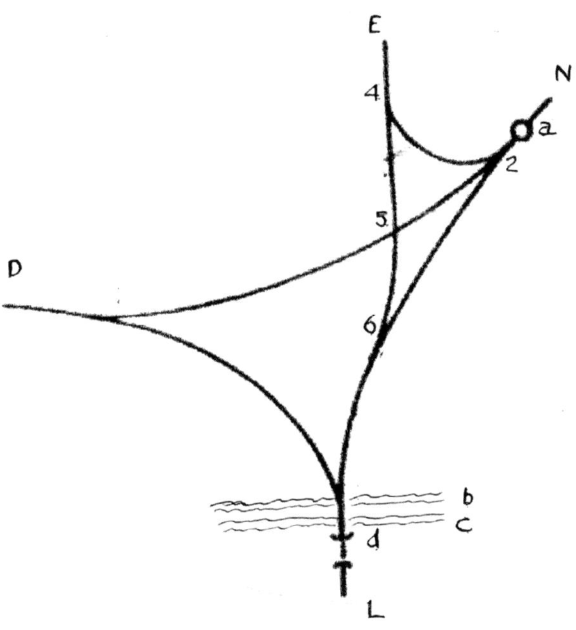

Directions:

D = Towards Derby
E = Erewash Valley line towards Codnor Park
N = Towards Nottingham
L = Towards Leicester

Rail Junctions:

1 = Sawley Junction
2 = Long Eaton Junction
3 = Trent Junction
4 = North Erewash Junction
5 = Platts Crossing
6 = South Erewash Junction

Other features:

a = Long Eaton Station
b = Cranfleet Cut
c = River Trent
d = Red Hill Tunnel

The addition of the Erewash Valley line in 1847 made the Trent Triangle a much more complicated network. In particular Platts Crossing was a source of considerable congestion.

By 1860 the Midland Railway was carrying 12 per cent of the country's mineral output. Two iron industries started up along the Erewash Valley line. One was the Butterley Company at Ripley. The Butterley name can still be seen on the supports of the great engine shed of St Pancras station in London, St Pancras having been created as the Midland Railway's own London terminus.

The other local ironworks was at Stanton.

Three new blast furnaces were constructed in 1846 at Stanton Ironworks, and by 1848 these were producing 10,400 tons of iron per annum, with the three new blast furnaces of the Butterley company, only a few miles away at Codnor Park, producing 10,920 tons. In 1849 there was still more coal moving by canal than by rail, but only four years later that trend had been completely reversed. One of the reasons for extending the Erewash Valley line through to Clay Cross in 1861 was to ease the supply of Northamptonshire iron ore to the furnaces of north-east Derbyshire, since the quarrying of local ore had declined.

It does appear that, long before there was a station there, Trent Junction was a place for dividing and combining trains, and even for passengers to change trains.

It quickly became the custom for through trains from the south to run to Derby rather than Nottingham, Nottingham at this time being something of a dead end as far as railway routes are concerned. Passengers could change at Leicester, but some passengers for Nottingham may have been put down at the Trent Junction itself to wait for a connection.

At that time coaches had sufficient steps to make climbing down to ground level feasible (think of American trains as portrayed in Westerns). But it is doubtful whether there was any shelter of any kind.

The lines from Nottingham and Derby converging on the junction do run on embankments above the flood plain, but at the junction itself there was, and still is, in the actual fork of the junction, an area of flat ground at the level of the rails.

In a Midland Railway bill of 1848 plans submitted indicated a very small platform just north of the junction at Trent.

There was a reference to cottages in the minutes of the Midland Railway Way and Works Committee No.2 in February 1853:

> "The following tenders for the erection of a stationary engine house and 4 cottages at the Trent Junction, partly using old materials in their construction was laid before the

Committee: *6 tenders between £407 and £1187.* Resolved that the tender of George Thompson be accepted *(lowest)."*

These cottages, constructed in the fork of the junction but further inland from the flat ground in the fork itself, were below the level of the embankment. These particular cottages survived until the 1940s, and careful examination of the site (now fenced off) still shows evidence of the footings for these buildings. They were in the trough of the V, at ground level, with railway embankments on two sides, hardly a desirable position.

The line from Codnor Park (quickly extended to Pinxton) was at first used mainly for coal and iron rather than passengers, although there were three passenger trains a day in each direction during the week. As there was no direct link from the Erewash Valley line to Derby, passengers changed at Long Eaton [Junction] Station.

Then, at the beginning of the 1860s, two separate trends combined to give greater importance to Trent Junction, and led to the creation of both Trent Station and the complex of surrounding lines which characterised it.

The first trend was started by a demand in the great city of Sheffield for a more direct railway connection. Sheffield residents had only a branch line, and if they wanted to go to London or other mainline destinations they had to journey to a junction at Masborough. By 1867 the town council was clamouring for more direct access, and the Midland Railway responded by promising a direct line up from Chesterfield. But the Sheffield councillors had already embarked on a mad scheme of their own to strike across the Peak District (a difficult engineering enterprise) to join up with the London and North-Western Railway at Stafford. This enterprise had the bizarre name (considered unwieldy even in those days of long railway company names) of the Sheffield, Chesterfield, Bakewell, Ashbourne, Stafford and Uttoxeter Junction Railway. But the ill-advised nature of the scheme soon became apparent, and the Midland Railway was then free to drive its own line from Chesterfield via Dronfield and Totley right into the heart of Sheffield at Pond Street. The Pond Street station survives today as Sheffield Midland. Chesterfield was already on the mainline, the old George Stephenson-built North Midland Railway line from Derby which is still the mainline today.

The second trend was one already noted, the ever-increasing demand for Erewash Valley coal. What had once been a small coalfield was turning into one of the largest coal-producing regions in Britain.

In a very short time the Erewash Valley line had become a very lucrative and vital mineral artery for the Midland Railway. In the year 1856 alone 867,288 tons of coal were carried by rail from the collieries in the valley, and to deal with this amount of traffic – bearing in mind that contemporary rail wagons would hold little more than six tons each and that therefore hundreds of them were needed - sidings were laid out at Toton. This was in addition to the iron ore being brought in, and finished iron being produced, at the Stanton Ironworks and the Butterley works at Codnor Park.

The coal and iron traffic had become so important it was decided to open up markets to the north as well as the south, so in 1862 the line had been extended as far as Chesterfield, where it joined up with the old North Midland Derby to Chesterfield line.

Until the 1840s and 1850s the population of the coalfield had been insignificant, but with the large new mines and the recruitment from far and wide of men to work them, hamlets were becoming villages, villages were becoming small towns, and the whole area was becoming a major conurbation, and remains so to the present day.

And people mean passengers for the railway, so the line which had been conceived and built primarily for minerals traffic was creating a demand for stations and regular passenger trains. The Great Exhibition of 1851 had proved a huge stimulus to railway passenger travel and had inculcated the train-using habit in many middle-class families.

Near Trent Junction itself the increasingly frequent coal trains had to cross the Derby-Nottingham line at a place which was called Platt's Crossing (John Platt was a veteran railwayman who had a house nearby). This was what was known as a level crossing, a term later used only for a place where the railway crossed a road. Rail/rail level crossings were not unknown in the early days of railways, but where they occurred on busy lines the dangers of congestion and delays at best, and collision at worst, were only too obvious.

And there was no way for trains running out of Derby to access the Erewash Valley line. The existing Erewash Valley line at Long Eaton Junction allowed trains to run only in the direction of Nottingham.

In 1857 the Midland Railway had linked up with the Great Northern at Hitchin and began to run its London trains to and from King's Cross instead of over LNWR lines into Euston. At the same time they began planning their own terminus at St Pancras. The Midland then looked to shorten the distance between London and Leeds and presented a bill in the Parliamentary session of 1859 for an extension of the Erewash Valley line from Pye Bridge to Clay Cross where it would join the former NMR main line. In the 1860s there were considerable advantages to be gained from shorter routes, with savings on time, savings on coal, and the ability to offer cheaper prices to passengers and freight forwarders – ticket prices and freight costs were based on mileage. This short extension opened for goods traffic on 1 November 1861 and to passengers on May 1, 1862. After that date through expresses formerly travelling via Derby were diverted to the shorter route.

It had already occurred to the Midland Railway chiefs at Derby that now they were going to have both a London terminus and a new more direct through route to the north via the Erewash Valley line, what they needed to do was to find ways of exploiting these advantages. And their eyes turned to that crucial place where the north-south and east-west lines met, Trent Junction.

Chapter 3

The station is built

After the opening of the Erewash Valley line in 1847 the directors and planners of the Midland Railway had to decide what to do about the problems at Trent Junction.

Problem no. 1 was that of arranging for passengers coming from Nottingham to gain access to the through trains.

These through trains ignored Nottingham and ran directly to or from Derby. The idea of changing trains at Trent Junction itself (the southerly point of the triangle), without any platform facilities, was obviously impractical as a long term solution, though it seems to have been tried. Normally, however, passengers from Nottingham were first taken to Derby and either changed trains there or had their 'through carriage' from Nottingham detached at Derby and then attached to the main London train. Later another arrangement was tried, where a carriage or carriages from Nottingham were formed into a short train and taken south as far as Kegworth, then shunted into a siding until the train from Derby arrived, and then attached to that train for the onward journey to London.

Problem no. 2 was that there was no way for Erewash Valley line trains - passenger or freight - to go to Derby or vice versa.

As early as 1848 the Midland Railway had acquired powers to create a new westwards curve off the Erewash Valley line to join the Nottingham to Derby line, but these powers had never been taken up. Passengers who had joined a train at stations in the Erewash Valley (from 1847 to 1862 there were three weekday trains each way between Codnor Park and Nottingham), and who wanted to go to Derby or Leicester, had to change at Long Eaton Junction station, which was on the Nottingham to Derby line.

Problem no. 3 was Platts Crossing.

The new Erewash Valley line had very quickly generated an enormous amount of mineral freight.

Much of this mineral freight was made up of very long coal trains snaking down and crossing the Derby to Nottingham line.

The place the two lines intersected, as mentioned in the previous chapter, was called Platts Crossing. It was an obvious danger spot, with the large numbers of those coal trains, or returning goods trains with empty wagons, crossing in the path of the Nottingham to Derby trains. Platts Crossing had been in use since September 6, 1847, and the congestion, and the potential danger, were getting worse every year.

The Midland Railway might have made its mind up eventually to solve these problems, but what really impelled it into action was what was seen as a new marketing advantage.

The railway's Board of Directors became really excited at the chance to steal a march on their competitors by having the shortest route between London and Leeds (with future eyes on a line between London and Scotland). As previously mentioned, in 1857 the Midland Railway had already completed its link with the Great Northern at Hitchin and had over-running rights on GN lines into Kings Cross, which was more convenient than Euston. And already the Midland was thinking of its own London terminus.

To achieve a shorter link the Erewash Valley line needed to be extended from Codnor to Clay Cross, where it would join the old North Midland line, with its direct link to the north of England.

This was explained at the ordinary half-yearly meeting of shareholders held at Derby Station on Wednesday, February 16, 1859. The chairman (Samuel Beale MP) told the meeting that the Midland Railway board "originally took powers to extend their railway from the Erewash line to Clay Cross, but they were not exercised at the time as they could not then afford to spend the money.

"It was proposed now to complete their system, by which they would save many miles of running, and open up another valuable mineral district, besides avoiding one of three tunnels on the present line, which would be a means of greatly facilitating the traffic. The landowners had asked them over and over again to make the line, and the directors had bound themselves not to go to Parliament without applying for the necessary powers.

"They wished now to redeem that promise, and he doubted not it would be a source of great advantage to the Midland Company."

The actual route became seven miles shorter, so, by the methods of charging in force at the time, the Midland Railway could lower its fares.

By the next half-yearly meeting, on August 16 1859, Mr Beale could announce that the Erewash Valley bill had passed through Parliament.

The first thoughts were to adapt the existing Long Eaton Junction station, but this did not solve any of the three problems mentioned above, so it was decided to obtain Parliamentary powers to build a new station nearer to the Trent Junction. An Act for this, and the complex re-arrangements of lines, was obtained in May 1860. To get rid of Platts Crossing and avoid any direct crossing of lines, the railway engineers had come up with the idea of what were called the north and south curves. These curves, laid out in 1862, ran in to the north and south ends of the brand-new interchange station. This station, after some early references in the plans to Trent Junction Station, quickly became simplified to Trent Station.

The John Platt (occupation: railway ticket collector) whose name had been given to the crossing continued to live in the adjacent house, as is shown in the 1871 census return, when the other occupant was John Dawkins, a station clerk.

The new curves became known as North Curve and South Curve. North Curve (which was about ¾ mile in length) also acquired the name among locals of Squeaky Bend, from the noise made by the wheels as they negotiated its very tight curve (one of the tightest on the whole railway system). But this system of curves which the railway planners had designed meant that trains from London or Leicester to Derby could call at Trent without having to reverse. Also, in emergencies they could be used for one train to overtake another going in the same general direction. However, a much more common use was to hold goods trains until there was a clear line.

THE TRENT STATION COMPLEX

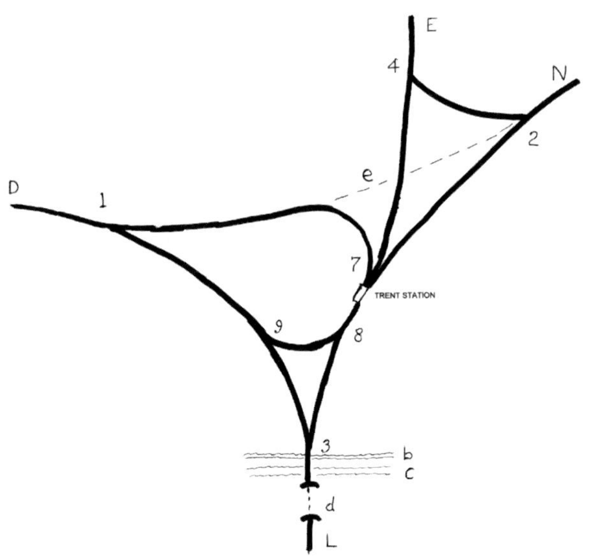

Directions:

D = Towards Derby
E = Erewash Valley line towards Codnor Park
N = Towards Nottingham
L = Towards Leicester

Rail Junctions:

1 = Sawley Junction
2 = Long Eaton Junction
3 = Trent Junction
4 = North Erewash Junction
7 = Trent Station North Junction
8 = Trent Station South Junction
9 = Sheet Stores Junction

Other features:

b = Cranfleet Cut
c = River Trent
d = Red Hill Tunnel
e = Former Midland Counties line, now Girder Yard sidings.

The re-organisation of lines which allowed for the construction of Trent Station. A section of the original direct Midland Counties line between Derby and Nottingham was removed (dotted line) and the North and South curves established to allow movement in any direction.

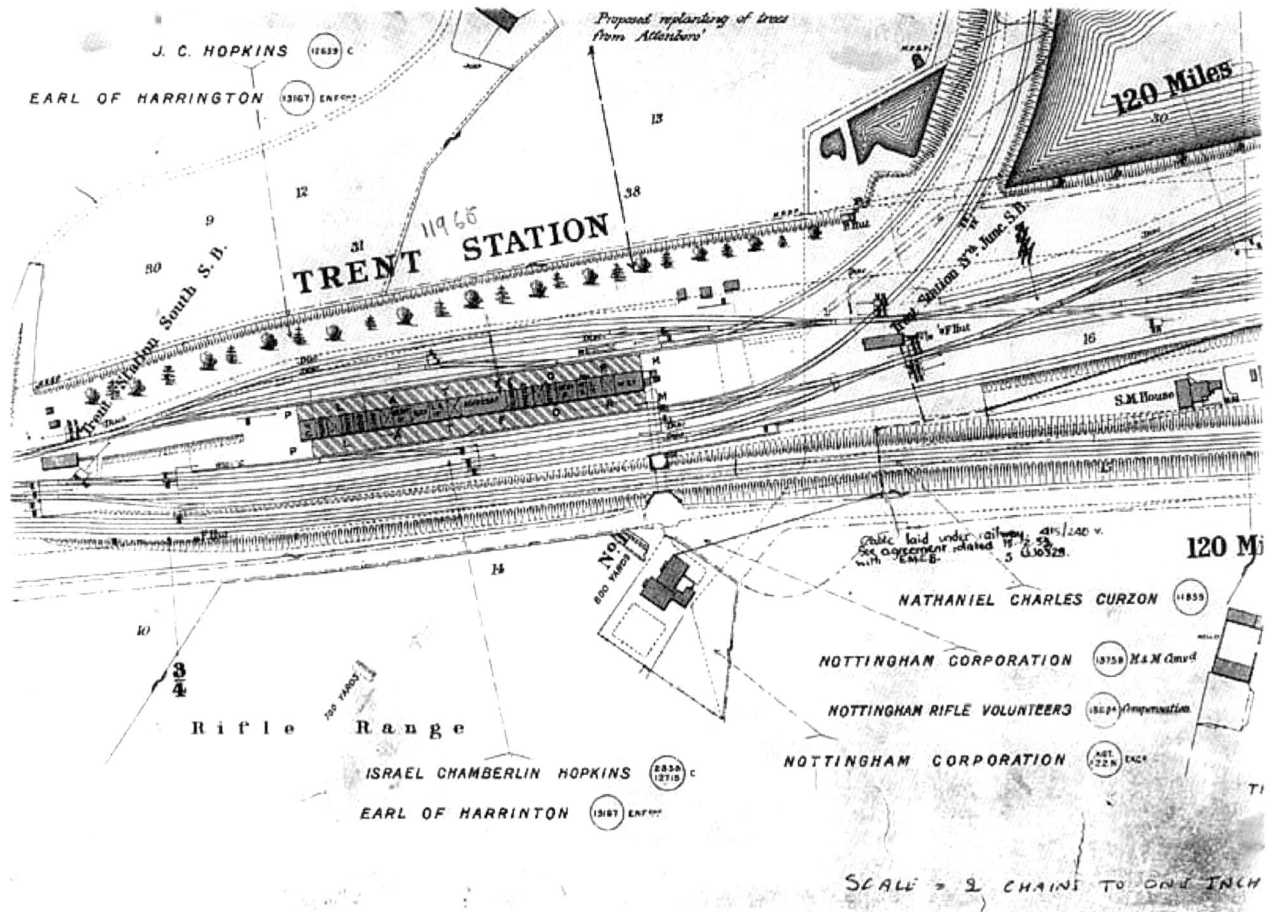

Early plan of Trent Station with indication of local landowners involved. This, the most detailed plan we have found, does compartmentalise the station. The compartments, reading from left to right, were apparently: WC, Guards' room, Archway, Store, Lamp Room, Gentlemen's waiting room, W.C., Ladies' waiting room, Archway, Refreshment Rooms, Telegraph Office, Parcels Office, Archway, Office, General waiting room, WC, Ladies' room, Archway, WCs. Calculations from this plan indicate platforms 143 yards in length, and refreshment rooms 78 feet x 16 ½ feet.

Even after parliamentary approval had been obtained, there were hold-ups in creating Trent Station because of difficulty coming to an agreement on the price for land owned by a Mr Howitt. It was not until April 1861 that plans could be finalised, and a month later the contract for building the station was given to Thomas Smith of Leicester, who had built Leicester's Midland Railway station in 1840.

In September 1861 approval was given to build a gas works at Sheet Stores Junction to supply the stores, the new station and junction signal boxes, and by the end of the year the station and the new north and south junctions were almost complete.

The Erewash Valley line extension to Clay Cross and the junction with the North Midland line opened for goods traffic on November 1, 1861.

Eventually all was ready for the opening of the new arrangements to passengers on May 1, 1862. This was done without any formal ceremony. According to the earliest history of the Midland Railway (Frederick Williams, 1876) although the station was opened on the due date, "it was not completed in some details till some time afterwards". But the essential part of the new system – curves and junctions - came into operation on that May 1st date, which was also the first day of the 1862 Midland Railway's summer timetable. On that same day, too, the old Long Eaton Junction station (at Meadow Lane) closed. In December 1862 plans were approved for a new Long Eaton station on the Erewash Valley line, at first known as 'Toton for Long Eaton', but soon to be relocated to a more central site on Tithe Barn Lane (which became Station Road) in Long Eaton.

This engraving, possibly made in the 1870s, is the earliest known picture of Trent Station. Picture reproduced by permission of Railway Magazine.

To complete the story of Long Eaton Station, This town centre location is where it remained (as 'Long Eaton') until its closure in 1967. The Long Eaton name was then transferred to a station on the Nottingham to Derby line previously called Sawley Junction.

Trent Station was built in the same architectural style – known as Midland Gothic - as the comparatively new stations on the London extension between Wigston and Bedford.

However, instead of platforms on either side of the rails, Trent Station just had one broad island platform. A major architectural feature was the canopy, which had 27 triangular section roof gables on each side, with at each end a canopy running right across. Glass roofs were a characteristic of the Midland Railway, perhaps because Joseph Paxton, the man who designed the Crystal Palace, was a director. Other examples can be seen at Market Harborough, Wellingborough and Kettering. The canopy was supported by light iron columns. These were painted in a warm brown colour, changing to cream at the upper levels.

Access from one platform side to the other was through five large archways, which were notorious for their draughts.

There are no reports of anything unusual on that first day of operation. All that seemed to have happened was that the Midland Railway placed advertisements in local newspapers.

One read:

MIDLAND RAILWAY

Opening of EREWASH VALLEY EXTENSION RAILWAY from PYE BRIDGE to CLAY CROSS

THE PUBLIC is informed that this Railway will be OPENED for Passenger traffic on Thursday, May 1st, and that trains for local accommodation will run between Nottingham, Clay Cross and Chesterfield, in connection with through Main Line trains, as follows:-

Down		Week-days			Sundays	
		A.M.	P.M.		A.M.	P.M.
Nottingham	dep.	7.15	4.15	.	6.20	3.0
Clay Cross	arr.	8.40	5.45	.	7.50	4.30
Chesterfield	"	-	6.0		-	-
Up		Week-days			Sundays	
		A.M.	P.M.		A.M.	P.M.
Chesterfield	dep.	-	6.25	.	-	-
Clay Cross	"	9.20	6.35		9.55	6.0
Nottingham	arr.	10.45	8.10	.	11.20	7.25

For times of arrival at and departure from intermediate stations, and further particulars, see Time Tables published by the Company.

The Passenger Fares on the Erewash Valley Branch will be revised and First and Second-Class Day Tickets will be issued between all stations.

From the same date the present LONG EATON STATION will be CLOSED and the new TRENT STATION OPENED, to which station the interchange of traffic now effected at Long Eaton and Kegworth respectively, will be transferred.

JAMES ALLPORT, General Manager. Derby, April, 1862.

The second advertisement, issued on April 24, 1862, and published in the *Nottingham Journal* of May 2, 1862, placed its emphasis on the shorter route now available.

MIDLAND RAILWAY

ALTERATIONS OF TRAINS, MAY, 1862

In consequence of the opening of the new and shorter route to Yorkshire and the North of England via the Erewash Valley Extension Railway to Clay Cross, the passenger fares between Nottingham and all stations north of Clay Cross will be reduced. An improved communication will be given between Nottingham and the North of England by trains running to or from the New Trent Station in connection with the several main line trains.

Considerable alterations will be made in the trains running between Nottingham and Derby; Nottingham and Mansfield; and Nottingham and Codnor Park.

On the same day, perhaps taking its cue from this advertisement, the same paper reported in its news columns:

TRAVELLERS on the MIDLAND LINE will do well to notice that the company have closed their old station at Long Eaton, and have opened another about a quarter of a mile nearer the Red Hill Tunnel. The new "Trent Station" is a handsome and commodious structure, and was chiefly built to accommodate travellers taking the route via Pye Bridge and Clay Cross, from Chesterfield, and other towns northward. Various alterations have been made in the times at which trains arrive and depart from the stations at Derby, Nottingham, and other towns in this locality. Several minutes are allowed for the retention of trains at the Trent Station, therefore our travelling readers will do well to study the new time tables of the Midland Company, before trusting to their supposed knowledge of railway matters.

On May 9, 1862, the *Nottingham Journal* reported as follows:

OPENING of the NEW BRANCH LINE from PYE BRIDGE TO CLAY CROSS

On Thursday, the 1st instant, this newly completed railway, connecting the branch line of the Erewash Valley with the main line of the Midland Railway Company, was opened for passenger and general traffic. There was no opening ceremony on this occasion. The line has been completed five or six months, but the opening of it was postponed until the erection of the Trent station and the commencement of the summer traffic. The work, which comprises eleven and a quarter miles of railway, has been accomplished without any obstacle of importance, owing to the level nature of the country through which it passes. Owing to the formation of this connecting line, the route northward will be shortened by about eight miles, and in consequence of this the company have reduced the scale of fares. There will be two trains stop at the Trent station daily – the Scotch express and another fast train, besides various other advantages offered by the opening of this line to the passengers on the Midland Railway.

The Trent Station buildings remained virtually unaltered until the station was demolished 106 years later. An example of this was the two enamel drinking fountains on each platform, installed within four years of the opening, and which were still there at the end of the station's life, clearly showing the embossed date "1865".

Cast iron drinking fountains were a feature of Trent Station's platforms for over 100 years. This one was still here when the station was demolished, yet another indication of how unchanged Trent Station was over its 106-year history. Photograph reproduced by permission of National Railway Museum, reference OP01468.

The signals at the station were always distinctive, with impressive gantries at both ends of the station. Originally these were Midland Railway semaphore signals, lower quadrants with wooden arms on wooden posts, in a particular concentration.

Until 1876 all expresses (including through trains to Leeds which formerly went via Derby but which now used the Erewash Valley route) and all local trains stopped at Trent, and Nottingham immediately benefited from an improved London service. In 1852 the fastest trip to the capital had taken 3h 45 min and the slowest 7hr 20 min with a return service of exactly 4 hr or by an exceptionally slow 7 p.m train from Euston which took 9 hr 30 min.

Now it was possible to reach London Kings Cross from Nottingham in 3 hr 5 min and return in exactly 3 hours. Between Nottingham and Derby, after Trent Station opened, there were nine trains a day from Derby, the first leaving at 3.14 a.m. (arriving at Nottingham at 3.44) and the last, at 9.20 p.m., reaching Nottingham at 10.10. There were eight in the opposite direction, between 6.25 a.m. and 9.20 p.m.

A London-bound train from Derby would leave the main line at Sawley Junction to negotiate the North Curve, bringing it then on to the up platform facing London.

Because Trent Station was built to serve as a transference point for passengers, complete with refreshment facilities and waiting rooms, and because it was not intended to attract local custom, it did not have its own road connection until much later. From the time it was opened until 1876 every Midland passenger and express train stopped at Trent, the expresses often for 30 minutes. This was to allow passengers to use the toilets and get something to eat and drink, for at that time trains were without toilet or refreshment facilities.

At each end the platforms ran down to track level with the usual wedge-shaped ramp.

There was a clock on each platform.

We assume that there were already toilets in the original construction, but there is a Midland Railway minute from May 1873, "resolved that Mr Griffith's tender of £24 be accepted for the construction of a lavatory at Trent Station".

Still known even today as Trent Cottages, these were built at the same time as the station. They have become desirable residences. Photograph by Barry Cope.

The Stationmaster's house and a row of ten semi-detached dwellings, called Trent Cottages, built at the same time as the station, are still there. The first-class workmanship that went into their construction, and the elegant Midland Railway style, have made them desirable residences.

Another view of the Trent Railway Cottages. Photograph by Barry Cope.

An examination of the deeds for these cottages showed that they remained as one unit in the possession of the Midland Railway and its successors, the London Midland and Scottish Railway (LMS) and the British Railways Board, until they were sold off in 1983-1984. The deeds were then split so that the individual properties could be sold off separately. Before they were sold off the British Railways Board carried out a number of improvements, with the help of local government grants. For example, internal bathrooms were installed, and wooden floors replaced the previous solid floors on the ground level. The tenanted cottages were at first offered to the sitting tenants, who were of course railway employees, and three empty cottages auctioned off.

The current residents of the cottages are interested in the association with Trent Station and the Midland Railway, as some of the outside decoration shows.

Sign outside one of the Trent Station railway cottages. Photograph by Barry Cope.

The Stationmaster's House, now a private residence known as Station House, still has its original Station Master sign.

The Trent Station Master's house today. Photograph by Judy Wheldon, by courtesy of the present owners.

Detail of the original sign next to the front door. Photograph by Judy Wheldon.

From the beginning it was intended that the station was to be lit by gas, and that the Trent Station and the nearby Trent Sheet Stores complex should have their own gas works. The Midland Railway ordered in September 1861 that the gas works be erected at the "sheet stores or at the engine house as may be found most convenient for the supply of the sheet stores, new station and the junction signals". It was decided to build the works on land adjoining the station, on the northern side. In November 1862 the Midland Railway Way and Works Committee went on an inspection visit to Trent Station. They found that the new gas works was nearing completion, and that one bank of retorts was ready for the manufacture of gas. An early manager of the gas works was William Burns, who was to play a leading part in local government in Long Eaton and was also the driving force behind the formation of the Long Eaton Co-operative Society.

The lack of any direct access caused some anxiety in Long Eaton about their rail connections, and a letter was sent by some of the townspeople to the Midland Railway, asking for a footpath to Trent Station.

The Midland Railway were able to assure the good people of Long Eaton that the "Toton for Long Eaton" station at Nottingham-road was going to be replaced by a new Long Eaton station in the centre of the town. As already mentioned this station, in what became Station-street, was opened on June 1, 1865. There it remained until it was closed, along with other Erewash Valley stations in January 1967.

Figure 21 – The earliest known photograph of Trent Station, unfortunately rather grainy. It may have been taken in the 1870s. An unidentified Midland Railway 2-4-0 locomotive with a short train of four coaches stands at the down platform. Photograph reproduced by permission of V.R. Webster / Kidderminster Railway Museum.

The residents of the nearby village of Sawley were also anxious to get a connection to the new Trent Station, since Sawley station itself was some two miles from the centre of the village (it was to be another 26 years before the more conveniently-located station, Sawley Junction, was provided). Their spokesman was the Rector of Sawley, the Rev. Samuel Hey, and within three weeks of the station opening he was asking for a footpath from Sawley to the new station, to run alongside the railway line from no. 9 bridge, This was the bridge which carried the Nottingham to Derby line over the Nottingham to Tamworth road at Sawley. The Midland Railway discussed the application, but "resolved that the path proposed, being alongside the line, is objectionable, and that the application cannot therefore be entertained".

For additional safety at Trent a small fire engine was suggested. In January 1863 the Midland Railway agreed to have one constructed, together with a suitable lurry (hand-propelled truck) on which to move it along the line. The unit was kept at the Sheet Stores, in a special small siding.

Communications were gradually developed. In May 1868 the Midland Railway ordered that the block system of telegraph be adopted between Sheet Stores Junction and Trent Junction and Trent Station South Junction so as to ensure the safety of engines whilst taking water. In February 1870 a single needle telegraph communication was provided between Trent North Junction and Trent Sawley Junction.

TRENT STATION COMPLEX 1869-1899

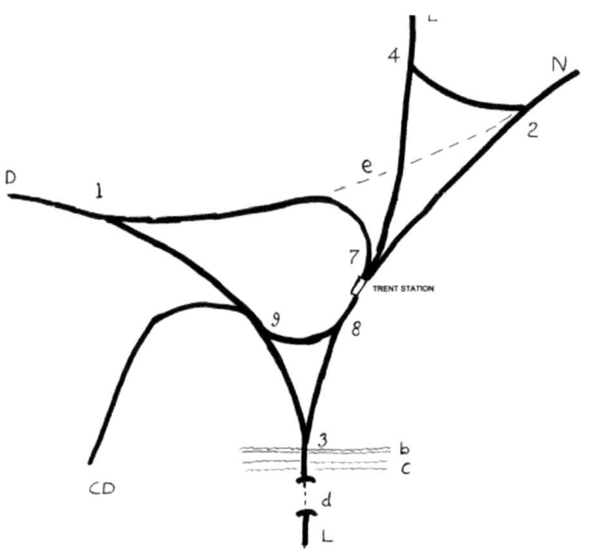

Figure 22 - The Trent Station complex of lines after the addition in 1869 of the Stenson Junction line via Castle Donington (shown as CD on the plan).

Directions:

CD = Towards Castle Donington

D = Towards Derby
E = Erewash Valley line towards Codnor Park
N = Towards Nottingham
L = Towards Leicester

Rail Junctions:

1 = Sawley Junction
2 = Long Eaton Junction
3 = Trent Junction
4 = North Erewash Junction
7 = Trent Station North Junction

8 = Trent Station South Junction

9 = Sheet Stores Junction

Other features:

b = Cranfleet Cut
c = River Trent
d = Red Hill Tunnel

e = Former Midland Counties line, now Girder Yard sidings.

In March 1870 it was ordered that a single stroke bell communication be made between the north & south signal boxes at Trent Station to facilitate the passage of trains through that place.

There seem to have been refreshment rooms at Trent from the start, and separate ones for each class of passenger, seeing that in June 1880 the Midland Railway decided, "in view of the altered train arrangements at this place, it was agreed that the third class refreshment room at Trent be abolished". In 1882 the former 3rd class refreshment room was converted into telegraph stores, and later to a parcels office.

In 1869 the already complicated track layout around Trent became even more complex, when the branch to Stenson Junction via Castle Donington was opened, giving yet another route out from Trent for both passenger and goods trains. There was then a regular passenger service throughout the day between Trent and Derby on this alternative route calling at four intermediate stations: Castle Donington & Shardlow, Aston-on-Trent, Chellaston & Swarkestone and Pear Tree & Normanton. All these intermediate stations except Pear Tree (which survives as an unmanned halt on the Derby to Birmingham line) disappeared in the 1960s.

Separate tracks reserved for freight traffic were put in by the Midland Railway over 55 miles between Wellingborough and Trent in the years 1873 – 1893. Between 1899-1901 these were extended past Trent Station, with the creation of the "high level" goods to Toton marshalling yard. A new tunnel had been bored through Red Hill and given a castellated entrance to match the portal of the passenger tunnel, and an additional bridge erected over the River Trent.

The higher level allowed the trains to climb to a bridge which took them over the Nottingham to Trent Station passenger line, and pass through Long Eaton on an embankment, bridging the roads, instead of having to negotiate three busy level crossings in the centre of the town. In the 60 years since the coming of the railway Long Eaton had grown from a rural hamlet into an industrial town.

TRENT STATION COMPLEX 1899 - 1967

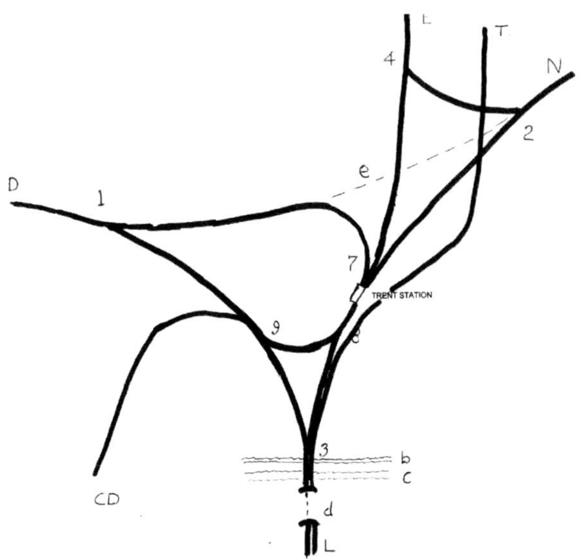

The Trent Station complex of lines in its form following the addition of the High Level goods line (T). It was to retain this layout for the next 68 years.

Directions:

CD = Towards Castle Donington

D = Towards Derby
E = Erewash Valley line towards Codnor Park
N = Towards Nottingham
L = Towards Leicester

Rail Junctions:

1 = Sawley Junction
2 = Long Eaton Junction
3 = Trent Junction
4 = North Erewash Junction
7 = Trent Station North Junction
8 = Trent Station South Junction
9 = Sheet Stores Junction

Other features:

b = Cranfleet Cut
c = River Trent
d = Red Hill Tunnel
e = Former Midland Counties line, now Girder Yard sidings.

An early 20th century postcard of Trent Station showing the new high level goods line in the foreground, running past the up platform.

Although back in 1862 the station itself had commenced operations without any fuss, this new high level line was given a ceremonial opening. The local newspaper, the *Long Eaton Advertiser*, reported as follows:

"The new goods line, which the Midland Railway have constructed from Toton Sidings to Trent Station, was formally opened on Saturday last [June 1, 1901] in the presence of a large number of officials and servants of the company.

"Between 5 and 6 o'clock a light engine, on which were Chief Inspector A.H. Lovatt, Inspector E. Jackson and the resident engineers started at Toton, and after running to Trent, a distance of a mile and a half, proceeded to Attenborough Junction, a distance of three quarters of a mile."

The line opened for normal traffic the following Monday (June 3).

The construction of new lines through Long Eaton led to an argument with the Long Eaton Recreation Ground Co Ltd, owners of what later became known as Long Eaton Stadium. The recreation ground company claimed £1000 damages (a large sum in those days) for injury to their property by the railway embankment etc. of the new Trent and Toton lines. The case was submitted to a Sheriff's Jury who found a verdict for £650, which was upheld by Mr Justice Lawrence at the Derby Spring Assizes, and on appeal the decision of the Court of Appeal was against the Midland Railway.

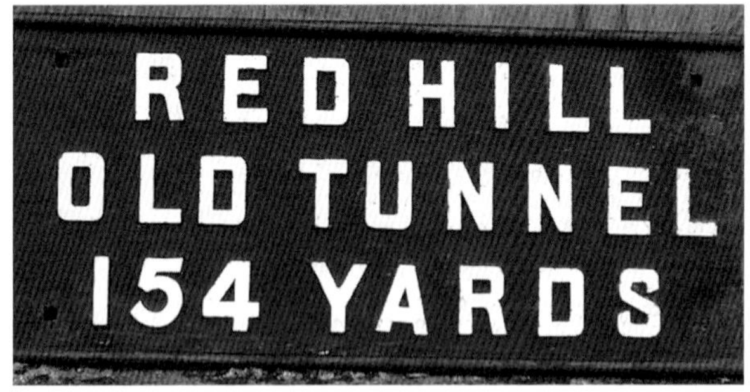

After the new goods line tunnel had been bored through Red Hill, south of Trent Station, the existing passenger tunnel became known as the Old Tunnel, as shown by this approach notice, now in the Burrows collection. Photograph by Judy Wheldon.

By this time Toton had become one of the biggest marshalling yards in the world. The reason for its importance was coal. At this time the country, by now fully industrialised after a century of the Industrial Revolution, ran on coal. Huge amounts of coal were devoured by workplaces and private homes. The Erewash Valley coalfield, on the Derbyshire-Nottinghamshire border, and the Leen Valley coalfield in central Nottinghamshire, were both major producers. The prize was so valuable that several railway companies had sent their lines snaking into the coalfields, but the Midland Railway was there first, and still shifted the lion's share of the coal. And most of the Midland Railway coal traffic went to Toton to be sorted into long coal trains to go north and south, but mainly south.

"In its goods traffic the Midland provided one of the sights of the shires – the immense coal trains snaking south from Toton", comments Hamilton Ellis in his history of the Midland Railway.

Goods trains on the high level line, drawn by British Rail 2-10-0 locomotive 92049. Photograph reproduced by permission of Brian Amos.

The bridges over the Trent had curved girders as late as October 1953, but by May 1955 these had been replaced by less elegant angular beams.

The latest version of the bridges over the River Trent, with angular beams. Photograph by Judy Wheldon.

In its early years Trent Station got its water from its own wells. The stationmaster's house and cottages also had their own wells (the one in the stationmaster's house is still there), but in 1878 a Midland Railway committee decided that "water be laid on to the cottages at Trent from the Locomotive Tank in lieu of the supply from wells as at present and that a filter be constructed to intercept any muddy matter being conveyed from the tank, the estimated cost being £60".

Water pump at Trent Station down platform. Photograph reproduced by permission of Frank Nixon Collection / Derby Museums & Art Gallery.

Although records seem to indicate that Trent Station, the cottages, and the stationmaster's house, were connected to the Long Eaton Urban District Council mains from 1899, porter David Shaw recalls that even in the latter days, the 1960s, water for Trent came from a natural source, and was often of a reddish colour. People who used the water in the toilets often complained of this.

A 1940s picture of a LMS 2-6-2T tank locomotive taking on water at Trent Station up platform. Note the brazier to stop the pump freezing in cold weather, a feature retained until Trent Station's final days. Compare Brian Amos's picture on page 4. Photograph reproduced by permission of Transport Treasury.

The Trent complex in the 19th century had a locomotive turntable, though this disappeared later. It was adjacent to the London line, just south of the South Junction.

Despite the Midland Railway originally envisaging Trent as solely an interchange station, eventually they had to concede that some communication had to be established with the outside world. Despite their initial reservations a footpath was eventually established to Long Eaton, at first reserved for railway staff, but later opened to the public and in 1888 illuminated with gas lamps supplied from the station's gas works. This footpath no longer exists (except for a short overgrown stretch running parallel with New Tythe Street, near the centre of Long Eaton, and a short section in the Forbes Hole nature reserve), but in Trent Station days it ran from Long Eaton's Station Road, crossed the Erewash Valley line at the level crossing at the top of Meadow-lane, where the North Erewash Crossing Box stood, and then ran alongside that line all the way to Trent Station. It finally crossed the line again at an open boarded crossing point near the Trent North signal box. A wooden fence protected it from the railway, possibly dating from 1880, when the Midland Railway Ways committee was told by its Engineer, "that the necessary improvement required to the Footpath at Long Eaton to render it safe for public traffic had been completed".

The author negotiates the overgrown footpath parallel with New Tythe Street, Long Eaton. This is the last remaining section of the footpath which once ran all the way to Trent Station. Photograph by Barry Cope.

The next demand was for a road. On February 23, 1884, the *Long Eaton Advertiser* mused as follows:

> "We have often thought it strange that there has been no continuation of the Main-street to Trent Station. The ease with which such a road could be made, the convenience it would afford to those who use the Trent Station, and the value of the land for building purposes if such an improvement were made make us conclude that we may yet see it."

But it was not until 1889 that the road access was constructed, after some initial difficulties, largely involving negotiations with Long Eaton Urban District Council over easements over railway land. The road was made from compacted cinders and led to an underpass which gave pedestrian access under the up platform to a flight of steps. A similar arrangement to that of Trent can still be seen at Hellifield in Yorkshire. Hellifield, another interchange station, escaped destruction and is now a Grade II listed building, and is worth a visit, since it shares many of the features which Trent used to have, such as an island position, glass canopies over the platforms, and a small suite of first floor rooms.

The entrance to the underpass at Hellifield Station today, which was similar to the arrangement at Trent Station – no photograph of the Trent access is known to exist. Photograph by Judy Wheldon.

The Trent Station footpath, and the flight of steps from the underpass, both came out at the ticket collector's box, a wooden construction akin to a sentry box. Because Trent served hardly any local population, the ticket collector's job, like that of the booking office clerk, was hardly an onerous one.

In the thinking of the Midland Railway, Trent was a whole complex rather than a single station, and Trent included the Trent Sheet and Sack Works even though these were about a mile away from the station, next to the Erewash Canal. In 1874 the two works were linked by telegraph, and in 1886 telephonic communication was established with the north and south junction signal boxes. In 1889 this was extended to the Trent Junction box. When the building of Sawley Junction station was first mooted in the late 1880s it was referred to in the Midland Railway board minutes as Trent Sawley Junction.

The Sheet and Sack Works were built at what later became known as Sheet Stores basin on the Erewash Canal. This was originally for a rail/canal interchange, in the very early days, in order to get coal to Leicester by rail without using the North Midland Railway. Although they later combined to form the Midland Railway, in those early days the Midland Counties Railway and the North Midland were bitter rivals. The coal was shipped down the Cromford and Erewash canals and trans-shipped to rail at Sheet Stores basin. The first building on the site was known as the Coke Store. Coke was manufactured at Riddings and brought down by canal boat. It was used as fuel by the railway locomotives because they were originally prohibited from using coal owing the large amount of smoke emitted. Eventually this restriction was lifted when firebox design reduced the quantity of smoke being given off.

The Sheet Stores (some of the original buildings are still there) lie between the Nottingham-Derby line and the Derby-Leicester line where they cross, at a short distance from one another, the Erewash Canal on 26 foot span bridges, allowing for 20 ft of waterway and 6 ft of towing path. There was an inclined siding down from the embankment into the Sheet Stores yard.

View of the Trent Sheet and Sack Works complex in Midland Railway days seen from near Trent Station, with Sheet Stores Junction in the foreground. The Stenson Junction (Castle Donington) line goes off to the left and the Derby line is straight ahead, with a one-coach train approaching Trent along this line. Trucks stand on the works siding, while another, ramped, siding runs down into the centre of the works complex. Photograph reproduced by permission and courtesy of the National Railway Museum, reference 13667.

Sheet Stores produced tarpaulin and waterproof sheets for the wagons and drays used by the Midland Railway. Some 10,000 tarpaulins were made annually at the works, and 90,000 repaired. The Trent Sack Depot was established on the same site, adjacent to the railway, in order to maintain the 450,000 grain sacks used on the railway, with 12 women (some of whom are shown in the photograph below) permanently employed on sewing up any holes which had appeared. Six cats were always kept on the 'staff' at the stores to keep down mice and rats which might be attracted by the residues of grain. Originally the stores and depot were set up by a private firm of contractors – Halcombe and Company, London, but the Midland Railway Company took control in 1877. Before long some 200 people were working at the Trent Sheet and Sack works.

Where did some of these people come from? I can give one example. A sailmaker working in West Country ports such as Gloucester, Bristol and Cardiff must have started to worry that the new steamships were taking over from sail and there was no telling how long his livelihood would last. But he heard that there were openings for skilled workers in canvas on the railways, making up the canvas and tarpaulin sheets to cover railway wagons. And one of the key places was the Trent Sheet Stores. So in 1856 he uprooted his family and came to live in Sawley, and found work there. His name was Alfred Kingscott and he was the author's great-grandfather. At least three of his sons followed him in the same trade, and 35 years later, in the 1891 census, Alfred was still calling himself a sailmaker. However, on his sons' wedding certificates, while he is still the 'sailmaker' (probably he had served an apprenticeship as such) his sons described themselves as 'railway sheet makers'.

Women workers using sewing machines to repair sacks at the Trent Sheet and Sack Works. Photograph reproduced by permission and courtesy of the National Railway Museum, reference 13674.

Figure34. Railway sheetmakers at work at Trent Sheet and Sack Works. Photograph reproduced by permission and courtesy of the National Railway Museum, reference1367.

Sawley resident Ian Mitchell is working on a separate history of the Trent Sheet and Sack Works, and would be glad of any new information (ihmitchell@ukonline.co.uk).

Girder Yard, on the other side of the Erewash Valley line and the high level goods line, and once part of the now discontinued 1839 original line between Nottingham and Derby, was often associated with Trent and was called the Way and Works Yard. It had several railway sidings, used over the years for various purposes.

It was probably the Girder Yard sidings which were referred to in Frederick Williams's 1876 history of the Midland Railway:

"At the Nottingham end of Trent station are sidings set apart for the use of men who have charge of the asphalting of station platforms between Lincoln and Derby, Trent, Syston and Peterborough. The materials consist of engine cinders and gas tar, riddled out into three sorts, and then mixed together hot, the heat being produced by the burning of a little coal.

"Some small white stone, obtained from Trent river-ballast, is sprinkled over the work when it is nearly finished."

Former railwayman Alan Bowler remembers when a couple of old Pullman bogies were 'grounded' on the east side of the site, facing the Trent North to Long Eaton Junction line.

According to Midland Railway board minutes a new "Engine House etc at Trent Junction" was established in 1898, but it is not clear what this refers to.

But what is certain is that in 1862 Trent Station had come to life as a fully functioning complex, an essential component of one of the super-companies of the Victorian age, the Midland Railway.

Figure 35 - No taking a short cut across the tracks. These railings made sure you used the underpass if you were approaching the station from the south. The path was probably used by residents of the Trent Cottages, seen in faint outline in the background. Photograph reproduced by permission of Frank Nixon Collection / Derby Museums & Art Gallery.

Chapter 4

The Goose Fair Disaster

One foggy night, just seven and a half years after it opened, Trent Station became the centre of a major rescue operation, an operation which followed one of the biggest disasters in the history of the Midland Railway.

It was Goose Fair time in Nottingham.

Goose Fair was then, as it still is today, Britain's largest travelling fair. It had its origin in the Middle Ages when flocks of geese were walked to Nottingham to be sold at a special fair in early September. Their purchasers would then be able to fatten them up for the Michaelmas feast. Michaelmas is on September 29, and a goose was the traditional centrepiece of the feast - it was only in later centuries that the goose became associated with Christmas. But as time went on Nottingham's Goose Fair became a more general fair for agricultural produce, such as cheeses, and also a popular meeting place for all sections of the population. In 1752 its date was moved from early September to early October.

By mid-Victorian times Goose Fair had become what it is today, first and foremost an amusement fair. There were carousels and hot pie stalls, boxing booths and fortune tellers, and altogether a gaiety and animation which made a wonderful contrast to the hard-working lives and limited horizons of the working people of Nottinghamshire and surrounding counties. In those days when the concept of holidays for working people was virtually unknown, an outing to Nottingham for Goose Fair was a pleasure to be looked forward to for weeks.

So the people flocked to Nottingham in their thousands, and they came by train.

The date was October 9, 1869. It was getting late on the Saturday night of Goose Fair when the drama unfolded. Many excursion trains had already left Nottingham that night, but there were still crowds milling around in Nottingham's Midland Station at 11 p.m., and extra trains were being put on.

Large numbers joined a special excursion train to Leicester, and this was to follow another special train travelling to Burton-on-Trent. The Leicester special left Nottingham at 11.35 bound for Loughborough and Leicester. The regular service mail train followed 15 minutes later, scheduled to stop at Beeston and Trent.

In Victorian times crowds thronged to Nottingham's annual Goose Fair. In those days the fair was held in the Market Square and surrounding streets in the centre of the city. These days it has grown so big it has been moved to the large area of open ground known as The Forest. Photograph reproduced by permission of Nottingham City Council Local Studies Library.

The Leicester-bound excursion train was a very long one, and, the reports stated "the carriages filled by a light-hearted and almost jovial crowd".

So, you have, following each other on the same line, the Burton-bound special, the Leicester-bound special, and the mail train.

But the fog was getting worse. As the Burton train was approaching Trent Station, the driver decided that the very limited visibility was getting dangerous, so he would have to proceed at a slow speed. But first, following procedures, he stopped so that his guard could put fog signals on to the line, small cracker-like exploding devices which were a recognised warning. The Burton train then resumed its progress at its slow speed.

Along next came the Leicester-bound special, and its driver heard the fog signals. It too slowed to a crawl, walking pace at first, but then speeded up slightly to 6-8 mph, though some had the impression it was at a standstill.

Unfortunately coming up behind was the mail train. One newspaper, later criticised for sensationalism, said it was travelling at a "terrific speed, probably 25 miles an hour", but at the inquest the speed was stated to have been about 16-18 mph.

A Mr Elliott, driver of the mail train, and his fireman, saw the lights of the excursion train emerge suddenly in front of them out of the fog. They sounded the whistle and applied the brakes, in time to have some effect, but too late to prevent a major collision. The engine of the mail train ploughed into the rear of the excursion train, and the last three carriages of the excursion train were turned into a heap of scrap metal and splintered planking. The force of the impact derailed the locomotive of the mail train.

The most fortunate man that night was the guard (also known as the brakeman) who was in his guard's van at the rear of the excursion train. He heard the warning whistle of the mail train and with astonishing quickness of mind leapt clear of his van down to the trackside. Just in time. His guard's van was demolished by the impact. Next to it, in the rearmost passenger carriage, six people, two of them children, were killed instantly. A seventh man, a workman called Richard Cuffling, died on the way to hospital.

Driver Elliott jumped clear from the engine of the mail train and fell into a hedge bottom. There is no information on what happened to his fireman, but he was not among the injured.

The guard of the excursion train, slightly stunned, stumbled back to the wrecked trains, and, according to the report in the *Nottingham Daily Guardian*, "the first thing he stepped against was the dead body of a woman, and almost the next thing that met his view was the body of a dead child."

The news of the crash was carried to Trent Station, which immediately became a centre of activity.

Passengers worked hard to free the trapped and wounded and tended the injured till doctors could arrive. Fires were lit to provide some illumination.

Trent Station's telegraph office busied itself sending morse-code telegrams to Nottingham and Derby, calling for doctors. A party made up from station staff was sent to the scene to give what help it could and to start clearing the line for rescue trains.

As soon as other traffic could be cleared and the line declared open as far as the crash site, the rescue trains were brought to the scene, bringing doctors from miles around, as well as rail workers and lifting equipment. The darkness and the fog made rescue work a nightmare. The seriously injured were conveyed to Derby in one of the special trains. There was one exception. Mrs Rebecca Poole, of Northampton, had such severe internal injuries that she was removed by a fly (horse-drawn light cab) to Mr Burton's at the Blue Bell Inn in Long Eaton, where she remained for some days in a very dangerous condition, under the care of Mr Ewart and Dr Lory Marsh.

But by 5 a.m. – and this is astonishing to us today – the lines were clear, and normal operations were resumed. The wreckage was carried away to Derby for the public enquiry.

A reporter from another newspaper, the *Nottingham and Midland Counties Daily Express* (whose headline was "Dreadful Railway Catastrophe near Trent") visited the crash site later in the morning, and reported that he could observe little to indicate that an accident of such a terrible character had happened.

> "The rails were quite straight and uninjured, and all the carriages and debris had been removed. Here and there were splinters of wood and pieces of glass, and we were informed that early in the morning traces of blood were perceptible, but, at the time we arrived, all these had disappeared. The evidence of a fire however still remained. This was made immediately after the accident to assist in discovering the bodies."

The bodies were taken to the Trent Sheet Stores, "where a large crowd clamoured all day long for a sight of the mangled bodies". But the police sergeant in charge of the bodies only allowed relatives of the dead, and the Press, to view them.

The *Nottingham Daily Guardian* took full advantage of this privilege, and reported that the bodies "presented a horrid spectacle" adding for good measure that one woman's stays had been 'crushed into her side'. A rival paper, the *Derby Mercury*, reproached the Nottingham paper for its sensationalist reporting.

> "During most of the day crowds of persons were present – attracted by curiosity to see all that could be seen. Prominent amongst them were the boys from Trent College, accompanied by several of the masters. Many of the visitors picked up and carried away pieces of the remains as mementoes."

The dead were two small children, John Thomas Parrott (18 months) and Mary Parrott (five), and adults Elizabeth Wright, Alice Henson, George Gilks, Richard Cuffling and Joseph Day, all from Leicester. The mother of the two children was among the seriously injured.

The bodies of the seven dead were removed in coffins made of the best oak, at the expense of the Midland Railway Company, from Trent on Monday (October 11) night, and were conveyed to the homes of their respective relations.

The collision occurred between 80 and 100 yards after where the line crosses the River Erewash. This river forms the county boundary between Nottingham and Derbyshire, so it fell to the Derbyshire coroner to organise and conduct the inquest.

The crash site today. Photograph by Barry Cope

The jury returned a verdict of accidental death, but suggested (presumably at some expert prompting) the adoption of the block system of signalling. The Midland Railway agreed to this. The block system was a means of not allowing a train to proceed until the line in the next section had become signalled 'clear'. Signalling was then of course in its infancy, although wire-operated signals were already in use.

.By 1870 there was a 'single needle' telegraph communication between Trent North Junction and Sawley Junction signal boxes, and a single stroke bell communication between the north and south boxes at Trent Station. In 1874 a telegraph instrument was put in at the Sheet Stores to facilitate communication with Trent Station. By 1884 the system known as electric interlocking was being introduced in the Trent area. In 1886 telephones were being put in, and there was telephonic communication provided between the passenger station and the north and south signal boxes at Trent, at an estimated cost of £42.

The telephone circuit was extended in 1889 to the Trent Junction box, with intermediate instruments at the Sheet Stores Junction and Trent Junction. At the same time the signalbox at the Sheet Stores Junction was renewed.

Some form of block arrangement continued on the railways up to the introduction of electronic controls. Lines were divided up into sections, and a common arrangement was for passenger lines to have absolute block arrangement (no two trains going in the same direction on the same section at any one time), and goods trains to have permissive block arrangements, where more than one train could be allowed in a section under controlled conditions.

The platform lines at stations with major traffic movements such as Trent came under a special regime, what was called station yard working arrangements. This meant that under very closely regulated conditions more than one passenger train could be permitted in a section at one time.

These arrangements, pioneered in the 1870s, were to form the basis for railway signalling for nearly 100 years.

Otherwise, throughout its 106 year history, Trent remained reasonably accident-free.

On January 3, 1867 a John Daykin had been killed near Trent Station, in what circumstances we do not know, but on February 5 the Midland Railway approved a donation of £5 to his widow

On February 13, 1885 the 8.40 a.m. train from Nottingham to Derby was just pulling out of Trent Station when the cylinder of the engine burst. "Luckily", states a report in the local newspaper (*Long Eaton Advertiser*) "there was a goods train standing on the Leicester line and the engine belonging thereto was at once detached and placed in front of the passenger train". The train then continued its journey, and the passengers arrived safely at Derby, only ten minutes late.

Here again what is impressive about the incident is the speed with which railway personnel could react.

Chapter 5

"The junction for everywhere"

"Trent is the first important station on the line to the south, commonly described as the 'junction for everywhere', as lines from all points of the compass converge there."

This phrase is taken from a booklet published by the Midland Railway in Victorian times, which was provided free to first-class travellers.

Another early history of the Midland Railway refers to Trent Station as a *ganglion*, a word from anatomy meaning a place where a lot of nerves come together .

Trent Station was one of the few stations built purely as an interchange, with no thought of serving any local population.

If you were travelling from London to the Midlands (or vice versa) to any station other than on the direct north-south route you would very likely find yourself having to change at Trent. At Trent you could catch your connection eastbound to Nottingham and Lincoln, or westbound to Derby and Stoke-on-Trent, and anywhere in between. Trent Station was the transfer point from mainline expresses to local stations between Nottingham and Derby:

> Beeston, Attenborough, Sawley Junction, Sawley, Breaston & Draycott, Borrowash, and Spondon,

or to stations on the Erewash Valley line:

> Stapleford & Sandiacre, Stanton Gate, Trowell, Ilkeston Junction, Langley Mill & Eastwood, Codnor Park & Ironville, Pye Bridge, Alfreton & South Normanton, Westhouses & Blackwell, Doe Hill and Clay Cross,

or to stations on the southern route into Derby, the Castle Donington line:

> Castle Donington & Shardlow, Weston-on-Trent, Chellaston & Swarkestone, and Pear Tree & Normanton.

A passenger train crossing a viaduct over the River Trent floodplain on the Castle Donington line. But this is a modern picture. The locomotive is GWR 4-6-0 4965 Rood Ashton Hall, and the occasion was a special rail enthusiasts' excursion in 2006. The train had just come down the Erewash Valley line and had passed through the site of where Trent Station used to be.

Travelling habits have changed so much within a generation or two that it is difficult for us today to realise just how important, until recently, interchange stations were.

These days we have an InterCity mentality. We want to go straight from A to B. Research shows that people do not like changing trains, a point which was emphasised in the Beeching Report.

But travellers had a different approach in the 19th and first half of the 20th centuries, when rail still had a virtual monopoly of overland public transport. Travellers then expected to have to change trains.

A typical journey would start at a local station (whether isolated village or city suburb), possibly on a branch line, from where one would travel to an interchange station, change to the mainline train, travel to the distant interchange station, change again, and take the 'local' to the final destination. The more prosperous travellers travelled with several items of luggage, usually far more than they could possibly handle themselves, and they relied absolutely on the presence of an army of porters at every station.

Most interchange stations were of course situated in big towns or cities, particularly those which had become railway centres, such as Derby or York. But up and down the country there were a number of special stations which were nowhere in particular, but important precisely because they were at junctions, where one changed from one line to another. Examples from the Midland Railway are Normanton, Hellifield, Ambergate, and Carnforth, though none of these was as important as Trent. This was because Trent was not a simple junction, but a complex, a 'ganglion' indeed, with lines converging from all directions.

Hellifield, another Midland Railway interchange station. Photograph by Judy Wheldon.

Carnforth Station in Lancashire was used as the location for the fictional "Milford Junction" in one of the most popular of 1940s films, *Brief Encounter*, with Trevor Howard and Celia Johnson. The story both starts and ends in the station's refreshment room, which was the place one went to while waiting for connections. City stations of course still have their refreshment rooms, but such facilities are rarely found these days at junction stations, even the few junction stations which still exist. Carnforth's facilities would long ago have been reduced to the "bus-stop" status of many surviving small stations if it had not been for the worldwide clamour of film buffs.

As an example of the importance of interchange stations, in the early years of the 20th century footballers selected for England teams due to play Scotland in Scotland were instructed to make their way, from all their different locations, to Hellifield where they could meet up and take the train north together.

In 1925 a young actor called Arnold Ridley (later best-known as Private Godfrey in the *Dad's Army* television series) found himself stuck on an interchange station in the West Country. He used that experience to write *The Ghost Train*, one of the most popular plays of the 20th century, which can still draw audiences today. Your author and his wife saw a performance at Nottingham's Theatre Royal in 2004.

The playbill for a 2004 performance of The Ghost Train at Nottingham's Theatre Royal. It is set in an interchange station remote from any village or town, but there the resemblance ends; it could not have been Trent, which was too busy and had staff on duty all night.

The play is set entirely in the waiting room of an interchange station on a cold winter's night in November 1925. A party of travellers have missed their connection, with no prospect of a train till morning. There is no hotel nearby, no taxi, and no choice but to stay in the waiting room. Needless to say, eventually there are ghostly apparitions, including a train which should not be there.

When your author has given talks to local societies about Trent Station, he has several times been asked whether Trent was the setting for *The Ghost Train*. The fact that at Trent, too, there was no settlement nearby, no hotel, and no taxi, and that countless travellers over the 105 years of the station's existence had had to overnight in the waiting room, must have given credence to that idea.

But *The Ghost Train* is clearly set in the West Country, and depends for the working out of its plot that no station staff were on duty during the night hours. Trent Station was much too busy a place for that, and always had a three-shift working pattern, with, usually, a foreman and two porters working the night shift.

For the first 13 years of its existence Trent offered a greater *convenience* (the word is used advisedly) for through travellers making their way north or south, even when they had no need to change. Every major northbound or southbound Midland express stopped at Trent, often for as much as half an hour. In the 1860s and 1870s there were no toilets on railway trains. So, just as long-distance coaches have to pull in somewhere during their road journey these days for a "comfort break" (on-board toilets have recently been introduced on buses but many people are still wary of them), so in the mid-Victorian era train passengers had to be given the occasional opportunity to de-train at a location where suitable facilities were available.

This is why Trent Station, isolated in fields and with no local population to serve, was built on such a generous scale.

Those early trains were singularly lacking in comfort and amenities. Not only were there no toilets, there was no food and there was no heating. Trent was there to remedy these defects too.

Many travellers, then as now, could arrange their own food supplies, whether carried in a hamper at one end of the social scale, or wrapped in newspaper at the other. But replenishment, especially in liquids, was always welcome. We know that it was possible to telegraph ahead from London St Pancras to Trent Station to order luncheon baskets to take to eat on the train. In the 19th century Trent Station's refreshment rooms had an excellent reputation. So much so, it is said, that people made the journey out to Trent from Nottingham just to eat there.

In an 1872 passenger timetable the following note is given:

> "Time is allowed at Trent Station for Refreshments by the principal through trains from London to the North (the North to London)."

When Trent was first built it had both first class and third class refreshment rooms, but this was found not to be practicable, the third class refreshment room was abolished in 1880 and after that there was just one refreshment room for all travellers.

Heating was another problem but the Victorians found a partial answer – footwarmers. A footwarmer was a metal or ceramic cylinder filled with very hot water which was placed on the floor of otherwise unheated coaches. There were also more sophisticated versions using acetate of soda, or baryta, which held heat longer.

On December 2, 1873, the Midland Railway Way and Works Committee "ordered that tenders be obtained for supplying Feet Warmer Boiler accommodation at Trent".

Footwarmers continued to be important for another 25 years. In 1895 we find the same committee allocating £140 for alterations to footwarmer boilers at a number of its stations, including Trent, and also consideration being given for a new boiler capable of holding 80 footwarmers to be erected at St Pancras.

Eventually, however, improvements in railway coach design would provide for toilets, food and heating on board trains.

The Midland Railway was a pioneer in this.

On June 1, 1874 the Midland Railway put on a special express between St Pancras and Bradford, via Trent Junction. The train was composed of five vehicles imported from the United States of America. Two coaches had been created by a leading American designer of railway coaches, one George M. Pullman, whose name was to become synonymous with luxury travel. The other coaches were what the Americans called day coaches. It was the first train in the country through which one could pass from end to end, though apparently passengers were not encouraged to do so. It was also the first in which everybody, third class passengers included, had access to lavatories. Furthermore, it was the first to carry a whole-train heating system, though the inaugural run being made in mid-summer, this could not be properly tested.

By the 1890s widespread experiments with the steam heating of railway coaches were being conducted, and as coaches were replaced steam heating eventually became the norm, and the use of footwarmers declined and then disappeared.

A picture of Trent Station from the early years of the 20th century. The engine in front of the Clayton coaches, on the up platform, is a rebuilt Johnson bogie engine. Samuel Waite Johnson was one of the most famous of locomotive designers, and was in charge of the Derby Loco Works from 1873 (succeeding the even more famous Matthew Kirtley) until his retirement in 1903. Also in the picture, taken from the southern end of the station can be seen a platform starting signal (in front of the gable on the left-hand side of the picture). Also in the picture are two of the lamp standards carrying the gas lamps used at Trent Station until the very end, and a handsome line of railings which were cut down and removed (in common with many of the country's iron railings) during the second world war when scrap metal was desperately needed. Photograph reproduced by permission of Stations UK.

Trent must have been a truly bustling place in those first 14 years, 1862-1876. Services from London to Lancashire, Yorkshire and Nottingham ran combined to Trent, where they were separated, seven minutes being allowed to do four separations – one to Lancashire, one to Yorkshire, and one each to and from Nottingham.

The problem was that Trent was becoming too successful.

In the late 1860s there had been a very strong growth in Midland Railway traffic generally. The directors were therefore anxious to use this to promote a further growth in the network. But traffic through Trent Junction at the base of the Trent Triangle was reaching saturation point, and an alternative was needed.

In 1880 the Midland Railway, having built two new links, opened up a new through route.

Trains could now run from St Pancras to Kettering then via the Glendon link to Melton Mowbray and Nottingham, then via the Radford-Trowell link to the north.

Writing about the opening of this route the *Nottingham Evening Post* commented tartly on June 1, 1880: "There is every appearance that the new condition of things, when full matured, will ... imply the practical extinction of Trent Junction so far as concerns the main line passenger traffic of Nottingham, and as this is a consummation for many years devoutly wished, it may fairly be taken to be a matter of general congratulation".

In May 1876 a few trains had started to run on the direct Derby line without going via Trent, and its importance further declined when the above-mentioned route from Nottingham via Melton Mowbray was opened. Expresses started to run on that line between St Pancras and Leeds on June 1, 1880.

At the start of the 20th century the "last main line", the Great Central, created a new direct route from Sheffield to Nottingham, Leicester and London, so that Nottingham people now had three choices of directions to London.

Though the alternative routes did end the situation where nearly every train from the Midlands to London had to go through the rail junction at Trent, Trent Station itself was still becoming busier and busier, its loss of route monopoly being more than compensated by the overall increase in rail traffic.

The Midland Railway still regarded it as its key junction, and not only for passengers. In 1870 all the major railway companies were prevailed upon to announce where animals, particularly cattle, could be fed and watered when they were being transported by rail or ship. What had happened was that in the 1860s there had been a number of letters to the press, particularly to the *Times*, from persons concerned by this issue. One of these correspondents was the noted philanthropist Angela Burdett-Coutts, "the richest woman in England", who was so influential she was made a peer of the realm in her own right. Animal welfare was one of the causes close to her heart, and she was president of the Ladies' Committee of the RSPCA. Another of her charities provided drinking fountains for dogs.

Faced with this outcry the Government appointed a committee to look into the matter. Many of the people who traded in cattle were opposed to feeding and watering them when they were being transported, because of the extra costs and delays this would cause, but evidence was given that sometimes cattle and sheep trucks were shunted into sidings and the animals were without food or water for long periods. Drovers argued that cattle would not feed or drink while they were on the move. The committee spent a lot of time considering whether provision could be made in the cattle trucks themselves, and experiments were carried out on "Mr Reid's patent cattle truck" which had built-in hay racks and drinking troughs. It had been claimed that in the experiment the cattle did drink while his truck was on the move, but the committee was given some contrary evidence:

> "That whereas Mr Reid's brother declared that a large quantity of water was consumed by the animals during their transit, he was himself seen by railway officials, whose evidence was taken on the spot, and restated to us by the manager of the line, on no less than two occasions, viz. at Trent Junction and at Kentish Town Station, to turn the tap connected with the trough and let out the water on to the permanent way".

This was substantiated in the evidence from James Allport, General Manager of the Midland Railway, who told the committee:

> "The guard, who came as far as Leicester, says, that at the Trent Junction, about 120 miles from London, water was put into the troughs; but before the train started, an attendant put his arm through these doors, turned the plugs, and let the water out".

The troughs had been filled with water from the same hose that supplied the locomotives after it had been found that the normal cistern was too high.

The results of the deliberations were eventually laid before Parliament, as the "Report from the committee appointed by the Lord President of the Council to consider the powers entrusted to the Privy Council by sections 64 and 75 of the Contagious Diseases (Animals) Act 1869, and to suggest the best mode of carrying into effect the provisions of such sections relative to the transit of animals by sea and land; together with the minutes of evidence and appendix ... including seven plans illustrating layout of vehicles and stations to cope with transportation of animals, e.g. Trent Station cattle feeding arrangements".

A copy of this report is held in the Glasgow University Library, and the author is grateful to the library staff for their assistance in locating it and making it available for examination.

Although the committee did not make any specific recommendations in its report, it was obviously attracted by a middle way, whereby cattle could be fed and watered by racks and troughs temporarily attached to the outside of cattle trucks while the same trucks were in a siding at some point during their transit. The Midland Railway's chosen site was Trent Station's Girder Yard siding, and drawings are attached to the Government report with plans of the site. It was estimated that there would be room for 35 trucks. However, your author has not come across any evidence of Girder Yard being actually used for this purpose, though, admittedly, neither is there any evidence to the contrary.

It does however illustrate how Trent Station and its complex of lines had become, within a few years of their inauguration, the “junction for everywhere” in the minds of the Midland Railway authorities.

A recent picture of Girder Yard as it is today, with many of its rails removed. In the background is the embankment and bridge of the high level goods line. Before the building of that line the space available would have been even more extensive. Photograph by Barry Cope.

Chapter 6

Three cheers for Mr Gladstone

The biggest crowd ever seen at Trent Station was on June 17, 1886, and just because a train carrying Mr Gladstone was due to stop there for all of three minutes. There was an election campaign in progress, and political excitement in the country was running at a high pitch. When it became known that the Great Man would be passing through Trent on his way from London to Scotland, Liberal Associations throughout the Midlands decided to make personal presentations of support.

The train was timed to stop at 1.14 p.m., and depart at 1.17. During the morning train after train brought contingents of admirers into Trent. They came mainly by the scheduled services, but a large number of working men in Nottingham clubbed together to hire a special train for themselves. Those living within walking distance of the station, including 150 members of the Long Eaton Liberal Association, led by their president Joseph Orchard, marched to the station in procession.

By 1 p.m., it was estimated, no fewer than 4,000 people were present, and the long platforms were jam-packed. According to a newspaper report, "Every coign of vantage was occupied, the niches in the iron supports being filled by many enterprising juniors, who sat perched like sparrows". One enterprising Nonconformist minister, the Rev. F. Knowles, had brought his own step-ladder which he used as his perch.

The train came round the bend on time, to a tremendous cheer from the jostling mass. When it was ascertained where the Great Man was seated a rush was made to the spot. But there was only time for one address to be handed in, from the Primitive Methodist conference at Derby. Mr Gladstone, it was reported, "briefly replied". A bouquet was thrown into the carriage, "and was graciously received by Mrs Gladstone". And then the train was on its way again to further loud cheering and much waving of hats.

Victorian prime minister William Gladstone, who attracted the biggest crowd ever seen in Trent Station's history.

Apart from Mr Gladstone, the visitors for which Trent Station was best remembered were the entertainers, usually on their way to perform at Nottingham's Theatre Royal. Theatres started their new programmes on a Monday, and star-struck children, and some adults, would regularly go to Trent to see who was coming through on a Sunday. Often the stars and the supporting company had to change trains at Trent. Dramatic actor Henry Irving and variety artiste Little Tich before the first world war, comic singer George Formby before the second world war, Jane of the *Daily Mirror* cartoon fame and Lancashire comedian Frank Randle during and after the second world war, American blues singer Ella Fitzgerald and top comic Norman Wisdom in the 1950s and 1960s, and many others, were all seen at Trent.

Frank Barber, a former porter at Trent Station, recalls that when they heard that Frank Randle was going to change trains there, the porters arranged as a joke to put a red carpet down for him, which caused him great hilarity. When, in the early 1960s, Norman Wisdom got off the train with his manager, he had a great deal of luggage, and gave a 5s 0d tip (thought then to be extraordinarily generous) to lucky porter Ivan Brown.

One of the best descriptions of Trent Station in its heyday came 20 years after Mr Gladstone's brief passage.

In 1906 the *Railway Magazine* published an article on Trent Station by its correspondent H. Wade, who seems to have been impressed by the facilities and by the efficiency of the staff:

"There is a spacious, well-furnished waiting room for first class passengers, a first class waiting room for ladies, with female attendant, and an exceptionally well-appointed refreshment room (first class) at which luncheon baskets may be obtained and where luncheon is also provided.

"An inspection of the station buildings shows a well-equipped station, for although Trent is not now used to the extent it formerly was by main line trains, it is still a busy junction for local trains, and everything is kept in first-rate order. The systematic manner in which the metal plates indicating the various waiting rooms, booking hall, refreshment rooms etc are polished, and windows regularly cleaned, might well be taken as a pattern to be followed, and the neat manner in which the notice boards are kept posted, is particularly noteworthy. The writer made a half-hearted attempt to count the company's own boards, but gave up. Including all the other railway companies' announcements, there is quite a picture gallery, owing to the numerous pictorial posters.

"The booking office is of fair dimensions, but presents a rather bleak appearance, as the floor is of stone flagging. The station is supplied with a manual fire engine, operated by the station staff. A porters' room, ticket collectors' room, inspector's office, and stationmaster's room, lamp room, and the usual lavatory conveniences comprise the rest of the building...

"Five arched openings in the buildings permit communication between the two platforms. The scheme of decoration of the interior of the roof is particularly pleasing, the paint being cream with a horizontal line of scarlet on each girder. The columns are painted chocolate half way up the base. There is a telegraph office for both railway and public messages on the platform, there being two or three operators constantly in attendance. Messrs W.H. Smith and Son have a bookstall on each platform.

"A water crane is available at each platform line, the water pumping engine and tank being situated within the angle at the point where the line from Trent to Leicester leaves the Trent to Derby line."

Incidentally the *Railway Magazine*, which started publication in 1897, making it one of the oldest railway journals in the world, is still going strong.

Figure 44 -- Another Edwardian postcard of Trent Station, dating approximately from the time of Mr Wade's visit.

Many daytime passengers waiting at Trent remember those "arched openings", not as an architectural feature, but because Trent always seemed a very draughty station and those arches only seemed to make the draughts worse.

The bleakness added to a sense of disorientation for many passengers who changed trains there. Often they had no idea where they were in relation to the geography of the Midlands. Looking out at the countryside they could only see trees and fields. Often, particularly at weekends, there was the constant noise of firing on the adjacent rifle range. This rifle range, which is still there, had been in use almost from when the station had been built. In the 1880s the Long Eaton detachment of the First Derby Rifle Volunteers, evidently an active body which met almost weekly, more often than not chose Trent Station as its assembly point. In the second world war the local Home Guard used to travel to and from Trent Station to use the rifle range, and on one occasion the platoon was sitting in the waiting room when one of the rifles, which someone had evidently forgotten to unload, went off accidentally and a bullet shot into the roof.

We have been unable to ascertain when the two bookstalls were reduced to one, on the up platform.

An oddity about Trent, mentioned by passengers from its earliest days to its last days, was that trains could be facing in different directions yet have the same destination. The disorientation was even more puzzling in the station's first 40 years since before that date there were near-identical lines of trees on either side. The building of the high-level goods line in 1901 meant the felling of the trees on the south-east (up) side.

An early comment, quoted in all subsequent publications, was attributed to Sir Edmund Beckett.

> "You arrive at Trent. Where that is I cannot tell. I suppose it is somewhere near the river Trent; but then the Trent is a very long river. You get out of the train to obtain refreshment, and having taken it, you endeavour to find your train and your carriage. But whether it is on this side or that, and whether it is going north or south, this way or that way, you cannot tell. Bewildered, you frantically rush into your carriage; the train moves off round a curve, and then you are horrified to see some red lights glaring in front of you, and you are in immediate expectation of a collision, when your fellow passenger calms your fears by telling you that they are only the tail lamps of your own train!"

Another more recent comment, was in a catalogue for a 1969 exhibition about local railways. "No account of railways in the Nottingham area would be complete without reference to that curiosity of the Midlands, Trent Station, from where it was possible to travel, either south to London, or north to Manchester or Leeds, setting off in either direction and from either of the two sides of its single island platform".

Even towards the end of the station's existence there would be on a Sunday two trains for London leaving from opposite platforms, facing opposite directions. The 3.40 p.m. Nottingham to St Pancras train would be there at the same time as a Derby to St Pancras express from Derby.

To clarify matters the Midland Railway provided a set of Platform Destination indicators, with slotted indicator arms.

If a train was to depart for, say, Attenborough, Beeston and Nottingham, the appropriate arm, like an old-fashioned signpost arm, would be fitted into the slot, and would point from the platform to the railway line. Next to the slotted arm was a clock, topped by the statement: "The next train will depart at". It was the duty of station staff, once they had slotted the arm into place, to adjust the clock to the departure time. Facing in the other direction (i.e. the platform on the other side of the station) would be another slotted arm indicating the next train from that other platform. When the passenger went to the other platform, he would find a similar departure indicator with the reverse information.

General view of the platform indicator. Photograph reproduced by permission of Malcolm Cross and Wild Swan Publications Limited.

Station foreman putting in a new board.

The 1861 census return shows that six people, refreshment room staff, actually lived on site at the station, in the first floor accommodation. They were Eliza Ward, manageress, aged 29; Ellen Lyddon, barmaid, aged 29; Rebecca Sutton, housemaid, 19; Sarah Gadney, barmaid, 22; Elizabeth Yates, cook, 26; and John E. Thomas, waiter, 20.

The upper storey, which was given over to the accommodation, can be seen on the front views of Trent Station elsewhere in this book.

On September 13, 1886 the refreshment room chimney was struck by lightning, and the "considerable damage" had to be repaired at a cost of £50.

In 1884 the Midland Railway, in a move in which they claimed to be supporting the temperance movement, reduced prices in certain refreshment rooms, including that at Trent, for employees for tea, coffee, soup, bread and butter.

H. Wade saw the refreshment rooms at Trent Station at the height of their fame, not only because of the excellence of their provisions, but also because of their reigning queen. For many years the refreshment room was under the management of Miss Luscott, generally known as "Ma", who in her younger days had been the belle among the barmaids of Derby. When Ma Luscott (described as 'chief bar attendant') lived in the rooms at Trent Station at the end of the 19th century, other rooms were occupied by persons described as bar attendant, housemaid, page, and waiter.

A coffee pot and a cup from the Trent Station refreshment room, both part of the Roy Burrows collection. Photographs Judy Wheldon.

The refreshment rooms continued in operation to just a year or two before the station closed, and David Archer, a temporary porter at Trent in the 1960s, recalls their Lyons fruit pies.

The crockery, pictured here, from the collection of Roy Burrows, was of the Midland Railway's standard pattern. Much of the silverware was collected up, and stored for a long time by BTH Hotels, before being sold off in Travellers' Fairs at St Pancras station.

Porter David Shaw was able to save the pewter measuring mugs, ranging from ½ gill to two pints.

Apart from Ma Luscott we know comparatively little of the early personnel of Trent Station. A tombstone in Long Eaton churchyard records the death of Mary Cathrick. On her tombstone little attention is paid to Mary. Her claim to fame, apparently, was that she was the wife of John Raine Cathrick (his name is printed in much larger letters, even though he was not the one who had died), foreman at Trent Station. The date is 1864, only two years after the station was opened.

John Raine Cathrick, a foreman at Trent Station in its earliest days, is commemorated here on his wife's tombstone. Photograph Barry Cope.

One of the best-known stationmasters (his "reign" was from 1880 to 1888) was "Taylor of Trent" (W. Taylor) who always carried a carriage key around with him.

A stationmaster in those days was a figure of considerable importance. Kelly's Directories, which gave details of the trading circumstances of each town (e.g. early closing day, leading citizens etc.) give the name of the stationmaster as a matter of course. Another stationmaster whose name has come down to us is Mr W. Foster, who was there at least 1893-1908. A Mr F.H. Pugh was there in 1909-1910.

Among the most familiar of Trent Station's customers in the 1890s was Ernest Terah Hooley. Hooley was a local man who at this time rose to the height of his fame as an international businessman. In the years 1896-1897 he made profits of £7 million, an unimaginable figure in those days, from his wheeling and dealing, involving major companies such as Singer, Raleigh, Schweppes and Dunlop. He became one of the best-known figures in Europe, friendly with titled heads, and was received everywhere.

He made good use of Trent, which he regarded somewhat as his local station. He would turn up without warning, and ask for a special train to be made up to take him down to London. According to one report the cost of commissioning a special train at around this time was £40. The author has not found any documentary evidence about the local hiring of private trains, but generally the practice more or less disappeared during the first world war.

Ernest Hooley's downfall came in 1898, when some of his more grandiose schemes collapsed, and he was made bankrupt. He actually lived on for another 50 years, but his glory days were over, and never again would he arrive at Trent Station and demand that a special train be made up to take him to London.

Staff at Trent Station, year unknown, possibly around 1900; though a poor photograph, this is one of the rare side views of the platforms. The curved arches below the platform give light to the extensive cellars.

An analysis of the 1912 timetable for Trent Station shows that something like 150 trains a day were calling there, ranging from local services, which called at every village station, to the Scotch Expresses. This meant, particularly during the busiest times of the day, that a train stopped at Trent every few minutes. The amount of activity going on must have been tremendous. Timetables throughout most of Trent's existence showed separate arrival and departure times, as they normally do only for mainline stations, because some trains waited at Trent for connections. Trent was usually mentioned in timetable headings, e.g.:

NOTTINGHAM, TRENT and DERBY

DERBY, CASTLE DONINGTON and TRENT

and its times were in bigger type than that for intermediate stations.

Another undated picture, possibly around 1914. In front are the telegraph boys. The Trent Station telegraph office was an important local resource, and used for public as well as railway use. After the start of the first world war families dreaded seeing a telegraph boy coming to the house, for a telegram was the normal way the Army communicated the death of a soldier to his next of kin.

The principal function of Trent by this time was becoming clear: it was seen as the feeder and distributor of passengers and parcels from and to main line north/south expresses, and from and to small stations on its local routes (Nottingham / Derby, Erewash Valley and Castle Donington lines).

In 1912 Nottingham / Derby trains through Trent were very frequent on weekdays, running approximately every 15 minutes at peak times and never more than 45 minutes apart during the day. There were also trains at something like two-hour intervals throughout the night, calling at Beeston and Trent.

A picture of a down goods, headed by an unidentified class 8F 2-8-0 locomotive, approaching Trent after emerging from Red Hill tunnel. Photograph reproduced by permission of Glynn Waite.

On the Castle Donington line, these days used only for freight (except in emergencies), there was in 1912 a passenger service approximating to one train an hour between Nottingham and Derby, calling at all intermediate stations.

Erewash Valley stopping trains between Sheffield and Nottingham were again at the rate of about one an hour.

Sometimes 'through' coaches or sections of trains were detached at Trent and attached to the appropriate 'through' train.

There was also extensive goods traffic passing through or by the station. Mineral traffic in very large quantities came out of the Toton marshalling yard, a couple of miles north of Trent, while a large number of mixed goods workings came from Nottingham.

One of the smaller stations served by connections from Trent. A rare picture of the station buildings at Sawley Station, sometimes known as Old Sawley to distinguish it from Sawley Junction. This station, remote from Sawley village, closed for regular traffic in 1930. The house on the right was the home of the stationmaster. Photograph, from the Rokeby Collection, reproduced by permission of the National Monuments Record Centre.

Chapter 7

Platform tickets and station signs

How did people get to Trent Station?

By far the great majority of visitors, of course, arrived by train, and knew Trent only as an interchange, never being quite sure of its exact geographical location.

Local people could catch trains from local stations such as Sawley Junction or Long Eaton, or could walk to it along the footpath from Long Eaton town centre, or make their way by vehicle along the access road, made originally from used cinders from locomotives. There was no bus service. Nor was there a car park, or anywhere to leave a car. If you were brought in a friend's car, you would get out at the entrance to the underpass. Once through the underpass you came up the steps (two flights) to the end of the station.

There were signs in Long Eaton indicating the way to Trent Station. It is known that before the second world war there was a sign in Long Eaton Market Place pointing to Long Eaton and Trent stations. A later sign (illustrated below), probably from the late 1940s or early 1950s (it was made in press alloy, which was not available earlier), was originally on a pole fixing but was later riveted and may have been fixed to a wall. There is a trace of yellow paint. The sign later came into the possession of collector Tony Laughton, but neither he nor the author have yet been able to identify where exactly it was positioned.

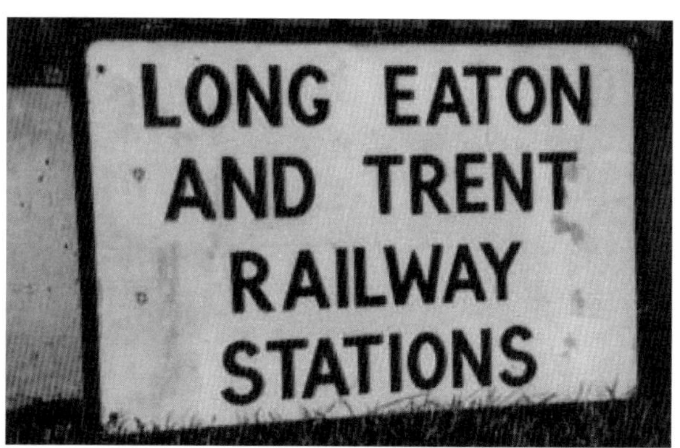

A sign, now in the collection of Tony Laughton, which may have stood in Long Eaton Market Place. Photograph Judy Wheldon.

If you came up the footpath (known locally as "Black Pad") from Long Eaton, and crossed the line by the unprotected passageway, you arrived at the platform ramp, at the top of which was the ticket collector's box. If you had come though the underpass, you emerged by the steps at the same place, by the sentry-box type construction where the ticket collector took his stand.

The subway was always likely to flood in wet weather, and duckboards were kept ready to make a crude raised wooden walkway for passengers.

In later years a cycle stand was positioned close to the steps.

The concept of closed stations, meaning that one had to be in possession of a ticket to gain access or egress, began at Burton-on-Trent on October 1, 1899, and spread to other stations, including Trent. This meant platform tickets.

The ticket collector would issue you with a platform ticket, or a white ticket if you said you were going to buy a travel ticket at the booking office.

Trent was one of the first stations to have platform tickets, issued from about the 1890s. The geography of the station meant that access to the booking hall could only be obtained by going on to the station itself, as distinct from the more usual pattern of railway station where the booking hall is a sort of anteroom or vestibule to the station proper. But no-one could be allowed on the station without a ticket, so the ticket collector, who controlled the only two approaches (through the underpass and along the footpath) was authorised to sell a platform ticket, for many years costing 1d (one old penny), but later 2d. Travellers who went on to buy a ticket for a destination had that 1d or 2d refunded, but those who had gone to the station to meet travellers had to hold on to their platform ticket, because it had to be surrendered when they left the station. No-one was allowed to leave the station without a ticket.

The pasteboard ticket which was used throughout the railway system until recent times (you can still get one at the Midland Railway Centre at Butterley) was invented in 1839 by Thomas Edmondson, and they are today called Edmondsons. They are collectables. Edmondson was a station clerk on the Newcastle & Carlisle Railway. He then set up his own factory in Manchester to manufacture ticket printing machines, issuing cabinets and other ticketing equipment. The Midland Counties Railway had adopted his system by August 1841, and it was also taken up by the two other companies which became part of the Midland Railway, the Birmingham & Derby Junction and the North Midland. After the formation of the combined company ticket printing appears to have been concentrated at Derby.

Other tickets were also sold at Trent. Enthusiastic anglers who wanted to fish in the nearby borrowpit known as Forbes Hole had to buy a Fishing Ticket from Trent Station. A 'borrowpit' is where soil had been 'borrowed' to construct the many railway embankments in the area. These pits – there are several of them in the Trent Station area – quickly fill with water and, once stocked with fish, become popular with local anglers.

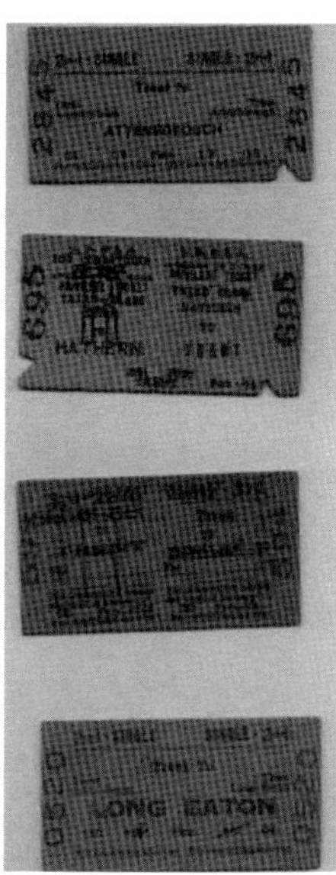

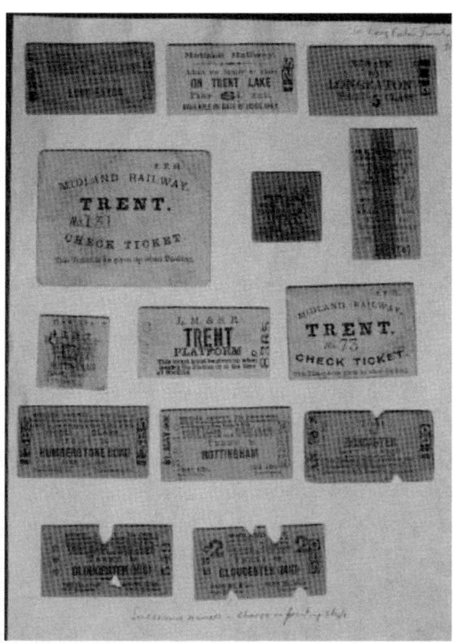

Various types of tickets issued at Trent Station, or with Trent as the destination, all from the Glynn Waite collection.

Unfortunately none of these Fishing Tickets appear to have survived, but Glynn Waite's collection includes a Skating Ticket for Trent Lake, which was a large (100 acres) expanse of water in Sawley, another borrowpit, and this ticket was probably sold at Trent. Glynn Waite, at the time of writing president of the Midland Railway Society, is one of the country's leading experts on railway tickets.

The extensive Trent Lake attracted sailing enthusiasts, and led to the formation, in 1887, of the Trent Valley Sailing Club. However, as the lake started to become shallower, with the tipping in of ash from locomotives, the club moved (in 1906) to the headquarters it still occupies, on part of a large island between the river Trent and the Cranfleet Canal, and close to the Trent Junction. Members of the club were drawn from a wide area, as it was one of very few clubs in the Midlands. It also had the advantage, from being near Trent Station, of being well served by train services. The members, who came from as far afield as Sheffield, Lincoln and Leicester, as well as more locally from Derby and Nottingham, travelled to Trent Station and were allowed, by special permission, to walk along the railway lines to the club. Even with the advent of the motor car some members still continued to come this way, right up to the time of the closure of the station. One discouragement to coming by car was that many car suspensions could not stand crossing the fields or the steep hump-backed bridge over the Cranfleet Cut.

The sailing club remembers its long association with Trent Station by proudly displaying at its entrance one of the station signs rescued when the station was demolished.

Trent Valley Sailing Club, proudly showing the old Trent Station sign at its entrance. Photograph Judy Wheldon.

The "lakes" round Trent Station were a source of revenue to the Midland Railway, leased out at one time to a Mr Bembridge, who in turn leased out fishing rights.

At one time a railway line ran alongside Trent Lake, between the lake and the canal, and was used by trains bringing ash and clinker waste from locomotive fireboxes. The wagon sides were let down and the ash shovelled out. There is a strongly-held belief in the district that on one occasion the whole train, engine and all, toppled over into the lake and was simply left there, it being too much trouble to lift it out again. The author has not yet found any documentary evidence of this. Perhaps at some time in the future archaeologists will take the matter up.

As more and more ash accumulated the water in the lake disappeared, and for some 50 years the area, known as the "Tip", was left waste. In the 1990s it was turned into a golf course.

But let us now return to gaining access to Trent Station.

Having obtained your platform ticket you could go along the platform. The first offices in the brick buildings were the men's toilets, then an archway. Then came the Signal and Telegraph Room. Then on the up platform there was the foremen's office, and with access from the down platform the booking hall, and adjoining it the booking office, with the booking window providing communication between the two. Then another archway, in which was the GPO letterbox.

Next came the parcels office, with its huge weighing scales, and then the telegraph office with a small lobby accessed from the down platform. Then came the refreshment rooms, then another archway.

Next was the ladies' waiting room, accessed from the archway, and the stationmaster's office, accessed from the down platform.

Then came the general waiting room, accessed from the fourth archway.

On the other side of this archway was the porters' room, followed by the old telegraph office, which was turned into a storeroom, and then the lamproom. After the fifth archway came the loco relief cabin.

The bookstall was on the up platform, outside the ladies' waiting room.

The parcels office at Trent Station handled parcels unloaded from the London train which were destined for addresses near stations on the Derby-Nottingham line. Also a van came from the Long Eaton Post Office (then in High-street - the building still stands though it has long since ceased to be a post office) with mailbags which had to be put on the appropriate trains.

The refreshment rooms had around 12 tables. After the second world war it no longer served meals, just drinks and some cakes, kept in a big glass showcase. The tea was made in a big urn.

We have already mentioned the first floor accommodation for the refreshment room staff.

The booking office was approximately 10 ft x 10 ft. Wages for all the station staff (including signalmen from the Trent North, Trent South, Sheet Stores Junction and Trent Junction boxes, these men being regarded very much as an integral part of Trent Station) were paid from the desk in this office.

In the 1930s, opposite the down platform, and also alongside the footpath to the station from Long Eaton, there were advertisement hoardings. These seem to have disappeared during the second world war, as did the railings at the end of the south end of the platform.

At rare intervals in Trent Station's history changes were made to the usage of some of the rooms, but change was not the norm; the station continued year after year with the same routines and the same layout.

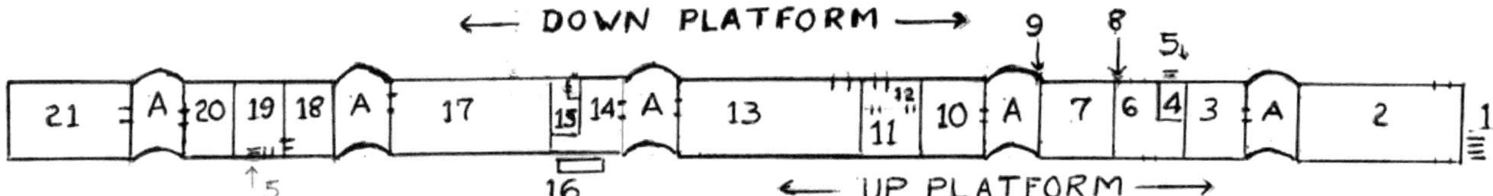

Figure 56 - Approximate sketch illustrating the use to which the ground-floor buildings at Trent Station were put to in later years, based on information from David Shaw. Working from right (the north or Nottingham-direction end of the platform) to left, the key is as follows:

1 – Steps from underpass. 2 – Men's toilets. A – Archway. 3 – Signal & Telegraph Office. 4 – Foreman's Office. 5 – Steps to cellar. 6 – Booking Hall. 7 – Booking Office. 8 – Public Telephone. 9 – Letter Box. 10 – Parcels Office. 11 – Telegraph Office. 12 – Lobby. 13 – Refreshment Room. 14 – Ladies' Waiting Room. 15 – Station Master's Office. 16 – Bookstall. 17 – General Waiting Room. 18 – Porters' Room. 19 – Old telegraph office, now used as store. 20 – Lamp Room. 21 – Loco Relief Cabin.

During the first world war railways had been subjected to a degree of centralised government control, and after that war it was clear that it no longer made sense to have what was in fact over 200 different railway companies. Accordingly the Government negotiated with the railway owners to produce, on January 1, 1923, what was called the Grouping. The companies were now merged into four big companies, the Great Western Railway (GWR), the London Midland and Scottish Railway (LMS), the London and North-Eastern Railway (LNER), and the Southern Railway (SR). The old Midland Railway formed the core of the LMS, and Trent became an LMS station.

In LMS days many signs were wooden. It is not thought that any Trent Station signs from this period survive.

Figure 58 - The date is June 29, 1945, and LMS Class 2P locomotive heads a short goods train past Trent Station. A solitary passenger, a businessman by his appearance, is half-hidden by one of the stanchions on the up platform. Photograph reproduced by permission of V.R. Webster / Kidderminster Railway Museum.

Figure 57 - There are comparatively few views of Trent Station from the 1930s. This 1936 picture is reproduced with the permission of Bernard Matthews.

When the four major railway companies were nationalised in 1948, British Railways formed six regions. The largest of these regions was London Midland, which was broadly the old LMS without Scotland. Trent Station obviously belonged to this region.

The other regions were Western, Scottish, Southern, Eastern, and North-Eastern.

One change which nationalisation brought about was standardisation in railway station signage.

On September 27, 1948, British Railways issued a document with the title, *Code of Instructions for Station Name and Direction Signs*. This gave detailed instructions on the manufacturing process, materials to be used, and precise layout. The lettering to be used was called Gill Sans. The signs were to be rigidly suspended from platform roofs near to station lamps so they could be easily read. Tens of thousands of signs of every description were made.

The standardised signs in vitreous enamel on a VE CR4 grade steel base replaced many of the old wooden boards or metal signs that were situated at the ends of the platforms and at various points on the station buildings.

Any station sign made to the new specification was called (for no good reason) a totem. Totems were produced in six regional colours, maroon for the London Midland region (very similar to the crimson lake which had been the livery colour of the Midland Railway), green for the southern region, tangerine for the north-eastern region, chocolate and cream for the western region, dark blue for the eastern region, and light blue for the Scottish region. The station name was picked out in white. About 3,000 stations had totems. Everything was created to the same pattern, so that door plates (Waiting Room, Refreshments, Ladies, etc) and direction signs were all to a consistent design.

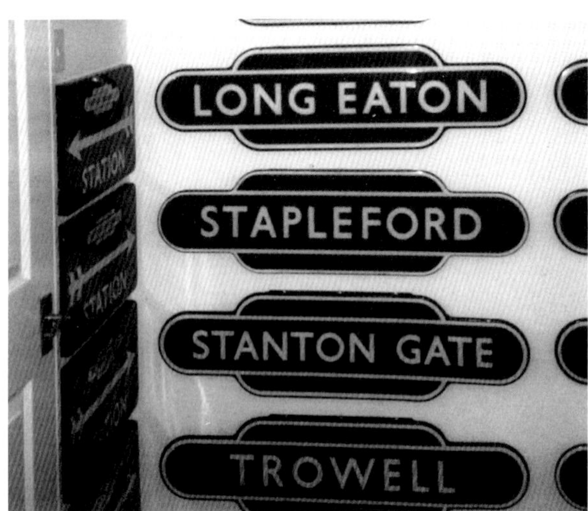

Examples of totem signs, from the Brian Amos collection.

The origin of the name may have been a mystery, but the history of totem signs has been well documented, culminating in the definitive book on the subject, *The Book of British Railways Station Totems*, by Dave Brennand and Richard Furness (from which much of our information is taken).

The policy of totem signs and the lozenge logo, however attractive, did not last long. The 1955 Railway Modernisation Plan, which started the move away from regional colours, and the 1965 Corporate Identity Programme, both looked forward to a more anonymous blander look. The 1965 programme prescribed black and white signs.

The actual implementation took some 20 years to complete and some of the signs were simply thrown away. Today every totem sign is a collector's piece, and when one does come on the market, at one of the regular major railwayana auctions or in a collectors' magazine, it is always a recorded event.

We do not know the date when vitreous enamel signs (there until the end of the station's life) were installed at Trent Station. The London Midland Region generally started re-signing with enamels in 1948.

Trent Station enamel sign, from the Brian Amos collection. Photograph Judy Wheldon.

But the enamel signs at Trent Station were an odd shape. They are specifically mentioned in the chapter on 'The Rare and Unusual' in the Brennand and Furness book.

> "Other curiosities in this [London Midland] region were the rectangular signs that hung on the station at Trent. We are unsure whether this was meant to be a totem derivative, but it is certainly enamel, certainly made for BR and station-used. Does this make it a totem? We think not....

As Brennand and Furness report, the Trent station signs were rectangular, the only station known to have that pattern. The probable explanation is that most totems were affixed beneath the electric lights which provided the station illumination. But Trent Station did not have electricity, and the gas lamps were much too high for any sign to be read. So Trent Station, unique in so many things, had this rectangular sign.

When the impact of the Beeching report began to increase the amount of redundant railway material available, one man, George Dow, public relations and publicity officer at British Railways Stoke-on-Trent, realised the heritage value of what was being lost, and organised the first auctions.

Auctions of railwayana are now big business, and anyone with an interest in railways ought to attend one such occasion to savour the excitement of it all. The biggest events of this kind are the Sheffield Railwayana auctions, held every three months (details on their website, www.sheffieldrailwayana.co.uk)

There may have been 14 (possibly more) of these signs on Trent Station, and they were carefully saved for sale. We even know the date when they were sold. The sale was held in the former British Railways research department offices in Calvert-street, Derby, on June 29, 1968. Offered for sale at the fixed price of 10s. 0d each were "Vitreous enamelled Station Lamp Totems in regional colours" for 37 stations, including Trent.

Station totems these days are valuable collectors' pieces.

It is thought that on Trent Station, in BR days, there were running-in boards (large-format signs) at each end of the station, and about 14 totems. Of these totems one is known to be owned by Trent College public school, one by the Trent Valley Sailing Club, and two by local collectors Brian Amos of Breaston and David Jones of Long Eaton. Five others have passed through auctions.

Brian Amos has in his collection a square enamel sign the same size as the well-known Trent Station squares but it is of a different colour and layout. It has a grey background with a maroon totem emblem in its centre with the name Trent in white within the totem shape. Although the fixing holes show signs of screws being applied it was probably never fitted at Trent. It may have been a design exercise that was never carried forward – perhaps a reader of this book may know the explanation of this mystery.

The 1955 Railway Modernisation Plan not only arranged for common signage, but also signalled the end of steam locomotion to be replaced largely by diesel.

The date is February 24, 1934, and Midland Compound 1017 in immaculate condition passes Trent North signal. It was probably on a test run from Derby, and had just come off the North Curve preparatory to returning to the works. Some of the hoardings which were displayed in different locations near Trent Station between the world wars are seen in this picture. Photograph by E.R. Morten, reproduced by permission of John Morten.

Chapter 8

Trent for Trent College

Trent College is a public school in Long Eaton, some three miles away from Trent Station. Either because of the similarity of the name, or because Trent Station was a main line station, it was Trent which was used as the disembarkation or embarkation point for all pupils of Trent College when they arrived or departed at the start or finish of each term. The station even at one time displayed the sign, "Trent, for Trent College".

The connection of Trent Station with Trent College almost certainly can be traced back to the founder of Trent College, Francis Wright.

As one of the college histories puts it:

> "Francis Wright was a substantial shareholder in the Midland Railway and his firm [the Butterley company] was already heavily committed in the construction of the Midland's London St Pancras terminal at the time he decided to go ahead with building Trent [College]. So that it is probable it was more than a coincidence that he decided upon his educational endowment suitably adjacent to the Midland Railway's Trent Junction Station; where in the breast of many generations of new Tridents [Trent College pupils] a multiplicity of hopes and fears were afterwards excited by the platform notice declaiming, parenthetically, that they had arrived at Trent (for Trent College)."

In fact Trent Station's connection with Trent College goes back to the very beginnings of the college. The four gentlemen, who travelled to Long Eaton to confirm the selection of the site, disembarked at the recently-opened Trent Station in the summer of 1866, and lunched there (presumably in the refreshment room) before walking to Long Eaton and to the fields where the college would later be built. The foundation stone for the college was laid by the Duke of Devonshire on December 3, 1866, and the school was opened in April 1868.

The official history of Trent College contains a recollection of classics master P.C. Matthews and how he arrived at Trent Station on a showery September day in 1914 and was driven to Trent College in a horse-drawn cab.

Peter Brack, who was a pupil at Trent College 1936-1940, remembers that when he and the others arrived at Trent, their luggage was taken from them and the pupils were conveyed even then by horse-drawn cabs to the school, at least for the first year or two he was at the College. Now in 1936 the sight of a horse-drawn cab was unusual, a quaint survival of a past age, and the sight of it filled the boys with hilarity. "It was like arriving at the end of the world", he says. He thinks that one of the reasons this form of transport persisted so late was the state of the lane which led to Trent, an unmade track which, wide at the station end, quickly narrowed, and was full of loose stones and mud. From about 1938 an old motor bus replaced the horse-drawn cabs, but the luggage continued as before being loaded on to a large horse-drawn dray, carried to the school and dumped on to the drive, from which the pupils had to recover their possessions.

It was during the second world war, when troops in particular were constantly travelling by train, usually going to and from leave, that Trent acquired its reputation as a cold, desolate place. Because the coming and going of trains had become disjointed, soldiers could be stranded at Trent for hours.

Stan Hough, a Royal Navy rating, put his war diary on the internet site:

http://forums.wildbillguarnere.com

In between hair-raising war adventures the diary records how he finally got the chance of home leave, but found himself stuck on Trent Station.

This is his laconic account of his passing:

> *December 2, 1943:*
>
> *"14 days' leave. Took Len Wheeler home with me. Bloody cold. We arrived on Trent Station in the middle of the night, and had to make our own fire in the waiting room. They were a few wooden notices short when we left."*

One earlier visitor, however, had found the station more welcoming. It was 1940, and trains were conveying to their home depots troops who had been rescued from the beaches of Dunkirk. While still on the beaches some of the troops had found a tomcat wandering forlorn and apparently lost. They brought it back to England with them, and when their train passed through Trent, presented it to the station, where it lived for a time.

A sadder occasion occurred in 1941. A soldier, Ernest Alfred Foulger, of Erdington in Birmingham, had been home on 48-hour leave. He said goodbye to his wife at Birmingham New Street station at 1.15 p.m. on February 4. Later that day a passenger waiting at Trent Station heard a shot and cries for help which came from the men's toilet. He ran to the spot and found Mr Foulger lying on his back with his rifle nearby. He told his helper, "I tripped over my rifle".

It was found that the bullet had passed through his body and struck the ceiling above where he was lying. Nine cartridges were found in the soldier's pocket, and one had been in the rifle. He was taken to the Nottingham General Hospital but died a few days later. The coroner said he felt that the soldier should not have had the ammunition in his possession.

During the second world war there were two women porters, but no photographs or details of them survive.

Frank Barber, who still lives in Long Eaton, worked at Trent Station just before and after the second world war. He had started in railway service as a telegraph boy on Nottingham Midland station, was promoted to Borrowash as a junior porter, before moving to Trent in the same role.

Frank clearly remembers an alarming incident during the second world war, the only occasion when Trent seems to have been fired on by the enemy.

Figure 62 - Glass was still missing from the platform canopies two years after the end of the war, as this picture of the down platform, taken on July 12, 1947, shows. In the right foreground is one of the old wooden Trent station signs which preceded the totems. Photograph reproduced by permission of H.C. Casserley, Berkhamsted.

Figure 63 - A view of the same platform, taken from the other end, the same day. The 9.40 express to Glasgow (from London St Pancras), double-headed but fronted by a Midland Compound locomotive 1077 calls at Trent. Photograph reproduced by permission of H.C. Casserley, Berkhamsted.

Figure 64 - Later the same day. Another Midland Compound locomotive, 556, waits with the 12.10 p.m. from Derby to Nottingham train. Photograph reproduced by permission of H.C. Casserley, Berkhamsted.

The same locomotive pulls away from the platform and, with the Nottingham direction signals giving a clear road, approaches the Trent North signalbox. Photograph reproduced by permission of H.C. Casserley, Berkhamsted.

"It was the 2 [p.m.] to 10 [p.m.] shift. I was with Teddy Gregory [ticket collector] at around 3.30 and we were mashing. We were just talking, when all of a sudden there was this roar. Old Teddy had just bent down to see to the fire when there was a [here Frank Barber whistled], just like that, and something shot by him. It just missed him. It embedded itself in the wood. 'You are the luckiest bloke alive', I told Teddy. All the glass was shattered on that side. We just got the sweeping brushes, big wide brushes, and swept up all the glass".

Frank Barber was in the Royal Air Force 1942-1946, but came back and worked as a Grade 2 porter again at Beeston, and at Breaston and Draycott, before being promoted to lamp-man, working at Spondon and Chaddesden sidings. He came back to Trent Station as a lamp man, working a length of track as far as Chaddesden. In the cold weather the job of climbing up signal gantries to top up the oil in the lamps was not an enviable one. He went on to finish his railway career as a leading porter, and relief van driver, at Long Eaton Station. He later went to work at the Chilwell Ordnance Depot.

A disadvantage of being a lamp man was the smell of paraffin which you took home with you, and which impregnated your uniform.

At night time, passengers disembarking from the midnight arrival train from London found they had to wait until 5 o'clock in the morning for the next train for stations to Derby. In Frank Barber's time the porters would make sure in winter there was a good fire in the waiting room, and sometimes, out of the goodness of their hearts (and with a good prospect of a tip), they would take cups of tea to the passengers faced with their long wait.

Frank Barber (back row right) with colleague Arthur Cooke and two unidentified trainspotters at Trent Station in 1948. Photograph reproduced by permission of Frank Barber.

Frank Barber remembers as a boy on an annual trip to Cleethorpes, walking down 'Black Pad' at three o'clock in the morning to be there by six o'clock. Black Pad was the name given by Long Eaton people to the tarmac footpath from the town to the station.

Pigeon racing kept the station staff busy. Trent Station was a regular point for pigeons to be released, this being the job of the Parcels Porter. He did this from the south end of the platform, and carefully noted the time of release.

Nottingham railway historian and retired librarian Stephen Best recalls an incident which, though embarrassing, illuminates a serious point. In his younger days he played for the Nottingham City Library Cricket Club and after a match at Sutton Bonington, and the usual post-match celebratory drinks, they had all gone to Kegworth station to catch a train to Nottingham. Their train was just about to pull out of Trent Station when one of his colleagues put his head out of the window and yelled to a porter: “Is this the right train for Carlisle?”. The porter rushed to him shouting “No” and pulled the door open. The porter was not best pleased when told it was all a joke.

But what impressed Stephen Best then, and impresses him more now, is the seriousness which a member of the station staff took in trying to serve the travelling public.

Porters, a species that has practically disappeared on today’s railways, had to be ready to turn their hands to any job around the station, from cleaning (a regular weekly job was polishing the letterbox in one of the archways, another to scrub the floors in the signal boxes) to handling newspapers, from releasing racing pigeons to helping with Post Office sacks. Actually carrying passengers’ luggage, the task most people thought they were there for, occupied hardly any of their time in later years. But, as the Stephen Best anecdote clearly shows, they were also expected to be sources of information, and at Trent, because of the multiplicity of lines and trains, their knowledge was often sorely tested.

The date is June 28, 1952, and an ex-LMS 0-4-4T locomotive, heading a Stephenson Locomotive Society special tour, is starting to tackle the North Curve. The line in the foreground is the ‘Up’ side of the North Curve. In the background a goods train trundles past the up platform. Photograph reproduced by permission of V.R. Webster / *Kidderminster Railway Museum. The train is watched by teenagers, two with bicycles, from the Trent Station footpath. This section of the footpath was a well-known vantage point for trainspotters, and Phil Burton remembers when there would a crowd of them all along the path. Although boys were in close proximity to the trains, especially at the end of the path where there was an unfenced crossing to Trent Station, there were never any problems. Common sense, rather than Health & Safety regulations, were then the norm.*

The diagram illustrated below is a page (now in the possession of Glynn Waite, chairman of the Midland Railway Society) from a railwayman's notebook and shows a hand-drawn map – so accurate it must have been copied from an official diagram – of the lines round Trent which the porter probably kept as an aide-memoire.

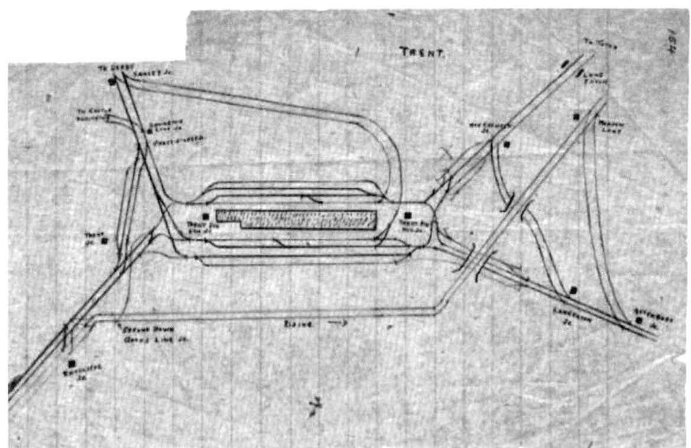

Hand-sketched plan kept by a Trent Station porter in his pocket as an aide-mémoire. From the Glynn Waite collection.

No-one has mentioned to the author the garden at the south end of the platform, but it was colourful with bushes and flowers, especially lupins. Unfortunately we have only black and white photographs to remember it by.

The garden at the south end of Trent Station. This was 1947. Photograph reproduced by permission of H.C. Casserley, Berkhamsted.

David Panter, who now lives in Beeston, left school in 1955. It was his godfather who himself worked on the railways who persuaded him to join the service. Accordingly he went to a training school at Derby, and worked on clerical jobs, and then as a booking clerk, before coming to Trent Station as booking clerk in 1957.

He was there for 18 months, until he was called up for National Service.

A booking clerk worked one of two shifts, 6.30 a.m. to 1.30 p.m., or 1.30 p.m. to 8.30 p.m. By the end of Trent Station's existence the clerk would expect to sell only a dozen or so tickets for the morning trains, and perhaps 40 to 50 tickets in a day. He had to balance his books at the end of each shift, and on the slate under the ticket-rack chalk down the number of tickets left. There were two racks with 50 lots of tickets in each. Some tickets, not used, to places no-one ever went to, were getting old and faded. Seaside tickets, however, went fairly well.

A midsummer (July 12, 1947) picture from Trent Station looking south showing (left) the garden, and (centre) one of the gas lamp standards, and the Trent South signal box, with its gantries, with the main lines to Derby curving off to the right. Some of the crossovers can be seen. Photograph reproduced p.m. by permission of H.C. Casserley, Berkhamsted.

One unusually busy period was before the 2.30 p.m. departure to Bradford, particularly with soldiers from Chilwell Depot, and also the southbound Thames-Clyde Express, between 4.30 and 4.45 p.m. The northbound Thames-Clyde express, for some reason, went straight through Trent without stopping. However, generally speaking, the work of a booking clerk was light. There was, however, one exception. One weekend David Panter arrived at 6.30 a.m. as usual, to find a queue already stretching down the platform – there was a bus strike!

The most important train of the day, the Thames-Clyde Express, coming off the Erewash Valley line to enter Trent Station on a sunny afternoon in August 1960. The locomotive is Black 5 4-6-0 number 44984. Photograph reproduced by permission of V.R. Webster / Kidderminster Railway Museum.

The booking hall had a big desk, and two ticket racks, with rows of pre-printed tickets. Wages were also paid out in the booking office. The money came from Derby in a large cash bag.

David Panter remembers that at that time the ticket collectors were called Albert Cade and Reg Richardson. He remembered, too, the foremen, Arthur Talbot, Rex Steele and Reg Titmuss.

Rex Steele, who had started as a ticket collector at Trent, was a noted local singer. He was sometimes known as the Railway Robeson because of his deeply rich bass voice and his liking for singing Negro spirituals. A favourite of his was the folk song *The Driver of the 8.15*, about engine drivers. During the war he had appeared at 198 troop concerts. He was a founder member of the Toton LMS Male Voice Choir, a vice-president of the Nottingham LMS Male Voice Choir, and a member of three other choirs, as well as appearing in a solo spot or as compère in local concert parties. He won a number of trophies for singing in local festivals.

Judith Dakin of Long Eaton recalls that her father, Ernest Dakin, had been a paper boy working from the W.H. Smith bookstall on Trent Station. After he left school, he worked on the bookstall for a while.

Ernest Dakin undertook various paper rounds. One was round Trent Lock. He also delivered newspapers in Attenborough. He was put on a certain train at Trent for the journey to Attenborough, had to deliver papers around the village and get back to the station to catch the train back to Trent. On visits to Attenborough more than 60 years later, he could recall the names of the people who lived in the various properties, and what newspapers and magazines they took.

W.H. Smith seemed to have made good use of the railway; Ernest Dakin did deliveries to Stanton Hall, probably by going to Stanton Gate station, and was always rewarded with a drink and a slice of cake by the cook. He spoke of selling papers from the platform to passengers on the London-bound trains which had stopped at Trent, and of making up bundles of papers which were dropped off, or thrown from trains, for distribution in outlying areas. He told of being sent to Thrumpton Hall with a newspaper account for a Lord Byron who was staying there at the time.

The date is now August 1960. This train is a London St Pancras to Bradford express, and requires two Black 5 4-6-0s to haul it. Photograph reproduced by permission of V.R. Webster / Kidderminster Railway Museum.

This picture and the next were taken on H.C. Casserley's visit to Trent Station June 9, 1956. The garden, which ten years before was one of the glories of Trent, is now looking distinctly untended. Here 40931 is leaving Trent's up platform. Photograph reproduced by permission of H.C. Casserley, Berkhamsted.

40504 entering the down platform with the 11.15 Leicester to Nottingham local train.

Three Sawley boys had differing experiences of Trent Station.

Keith Breakwell remembers as a boy engine-numbering there. The stationmaster in those days (Jack Hardy) was an irascible but unpredictable man with a very red face. The boys knew him as "Strawberry Face". He usually disliked boys collecting engine numbers on his station, but occasionally, if boys were well-behaved, he took a different attitude and let them stay on the platform. Keith remembers the W.H. Smith newspaper stand on the south side, with its roller shutter.

The inside bend was so sharp that on one occasion Keith travelled on a London to Derby train from Trent just for the experience. And an extraordinary experience it was to see the train curving round sharply behind one, a sight which could probably not be replicated anywhere else in the country.

Roy Talbot recalls the incredibly strong tea which the staff had from their mash cans. He was also fascinated by the entries in registers in fine copperplate writing.

Keith Reedman remembers coming home when he was in the Royal Navy, and finding no connection from Trent, walking home along the north curve tripping over the sleepers.

Even in the 1950s and 1960s Trent remained a busy station. In the mid-1950s Trent had 63 staff (of which 24 were signalmen) dealing with 64 local trains and nine expresses a day.

So far we have not considered the problems of signalling at Trent. The signalboxes were Trent North, Trent South and Sheet Stores Junction. The signalmen felt themselves very much part of the Trent Station team. The signalboxes all worked a 24-hour shift system, all working the same shift pattern. The Trent North signalman, for example, was pivotal in the regulation of Toton trains heading for the Castle Donington branch. The box's frame had 75 levers. As Alan Bowler comments: "Due to the sheer volume of freight, traffic staff were often under considerable pressure to shift as many trains as possible. So despite the apparently solitary nature of the job, movement of trains across the area was very much a team effort, not merely passing trains on. The objective was to get a loose-coupled freight train moving and to keep it going.

A fine view of the up platform, the best picture we have of one of the arches. Photograph reproduced by permission of the National Railway Museum.

Two trainspotters on the Trent footpath, next to the boarded crossing, watch a Peak Class diesel locomotive running light (i.e. without a train) passing the Trent North signal box and the signal gantry, leaving Trent, probably en route for Toton. The signals are set for the Erewash Valley main line. Photograph reproduced by permission of Colin Garratt Milepost 9 ½ Publications.

Snappy signalling would ensure that train crews saw clear signals sufficiently far ahead to enable them to take a run at the grade from Trent South to Sheet Stores. If everyone played the game there would be no more satisfying sight than the plume of smoke from a wide open Class 8 heading for 'Castle Don'. A missed distant would generate a heated exchange over the omnibus phone circuits that linked the boxes! The bulk of the men were not train enthusiasts (if you were then you were open to some 'stick') but they were enthusiasts for their job – even if most of them wouldn't admit it.

Signal box signal status indicators, from the Roy Burrows Collection. Photograph by Judy Wheldon.

Operating a busy manual signalbox required a considerable degree of fitness. Until the late 1950s only a minority of signalmen had cars and many of them cycled or walked to work. Due to the shortage of staff in the signalling grades some men stayed on long after the official retirement age of 65. George Fox, a signalman at Long Eaton Station, was at least 70 when he retired. One relief signalman, George (Twink) Burrows, was passed (qualified) for every box on the Erewash Valley line from Pye Bridge southwards, plus the boxes in the Trent area. He either used trains or cycled, relying for protection from the elements on his BR-issue mackintosh, and was working until well into his 60s.

Traffic from Nottingham to the West Midlands was often routed via Trent Junction and through then on to the Castle Donington line via Stenson Junction and Burton-on-Trent. The freight trains would often be kept in a siding at Meadow Lane in Nottingham until there was a sufficient gap in the timetables for them to be worked through Trent, crossing the busy Loughborough-Derby line, to reach the Castle Donington line at Sheet Stores Junction. If delays were allowed to build up on the Loughborough-Derby services then this would impact on the Nottingham to Derby traffic and then on to the goods traffic. Goods trains coming up from the south were not so much of a problem. If they were headed towards Derby and the direct route was blocked, they could always be run through Trent Station and on to the North Curve, and kept there until a path became available.

Some of the local Nottingham to Derby trains in the late steam era were of interest to train spotters since many of them were worked by redundant main line locomotives which in an earlier existence had been pulling expresses. Earlier, in the 1930s, the once ubiquitous Midland Compound survived the introduction of later 2-6-4 tanks by working on many of the Midland secondary services. Even in the 1950s Derby shed had ten Compounds and Nottingham six Compounds.

A view from the Nottingham end of the station, showing the cycle shed and the down platform. Photograph reproduced by permission of Frank Nixon Collection / Derby Museums and Art Gallery.

George Hibbert, who now lives in Sawley, and often worked trains through Trent Station, had an extraordinary railway career, unusual in that he rose through all the grades, starting in 1937 as a cleaner, and moving up through fireman, foreman, inspector, train crew supervisor, and motive power supervisor. He has prepared his own 200-page memoir, *Up the line*, for which he is currently seeking a publisher.

Many goods train staff who worked out of the Toton marshalling yards would come by train into Trent Station. The distance to Toton was just over two miles, and the railway authorities allowed for 42 minutes "walking time" to drivers and firemen. Guards, however, were allowed 45 minutes, because of the bag (with signal flags and detonators) which they had to carry.

Trent was of course a favourite spot for trainspotters, and some of them have vivid memories of the place. John Shaw, now a well-known Nottinghamshire freelance journalist, remembers a particular day trainspotting at Trent in 1967. He was ten years old at the time and recalls his excitement – there seemed to be trains everywhere. John's father was a keen photographer, with a number of cameras, and had lent him a "proper" camera for the day. In his excitement, running across to the up platform he dropped the camera. At that age this seemed a huge drama, and he recalls sitting down, wanting the world to end. He took no pictures that day, and when he crawled home and confessed the disaster to his father, his father replied nonchalantly, "Oh it doesn't matter, it was only an old one".

Trainspotters, this time on the platform, watch a diesel-hauled passenger train approach the up platform. Photograph reproduced by permission of Transport Treasury.

By the time John Shaw was trainspotting there was no steam. The Peak Diesels were the stars of the day. Sometimes they would not call at Trent, but could be glimpsed in the distance on the direct line to Derby. It was often just possible to read their numbers. For some unknown reason that part of the Derby line bypassing Trent was known to generations of trainspotters as "Bunker", and earlier generations would be heard shouting "Namer on Bunker" (a "namer" was a locomotive which carried a name – *Camperdown*, perhaps, or *Jellicoe* – as well as a number).

In those earlier steam days the great majority of boys became involved in train spotting at one time or another. Certainly all the boys in the author's street gang did, and Trent Station was a favourite location. We did not call it train spotting; to us it was 'engine numbering'. Books published by Ian Allan listed all the locomotives by class and number, and name if applicable, and you underlined in the book those you had spotted. But more impressive even than the namers were the mighty LMS 2-6-6-2 Garratts which were regularly seen passing Trent hauling coal trains. Though most coal trains through Trent were worked by Midland 0-6-0 locos of different types, until the Stanier Black 8 became available after the second world war.

Trent Station was always popular with trainspotters and one of their big thrills was to see one of the powerful Garratt locomotives; here Garratt 47979 has come off the Castle Donington line and is passing Trent Station with an empty coal train of 90 wagons. Photograph reproduced by permission of Transport Treasury.

Steamclass 4F 4-6-0 locomotive 43953 hauling an enthusiasts' excursion in 1966, a rare treat for trainspotters in Trent's later days. Photograph reproduced by permission of Brian Amos.

Another hobby, popular then as now among its own habitués, was model railways, and Trent Station played a part in this. In 1954 Hornby brought out a new model station, and called it Trent. It was an island station, but otherwise bore no physical resemblance to its namesake.

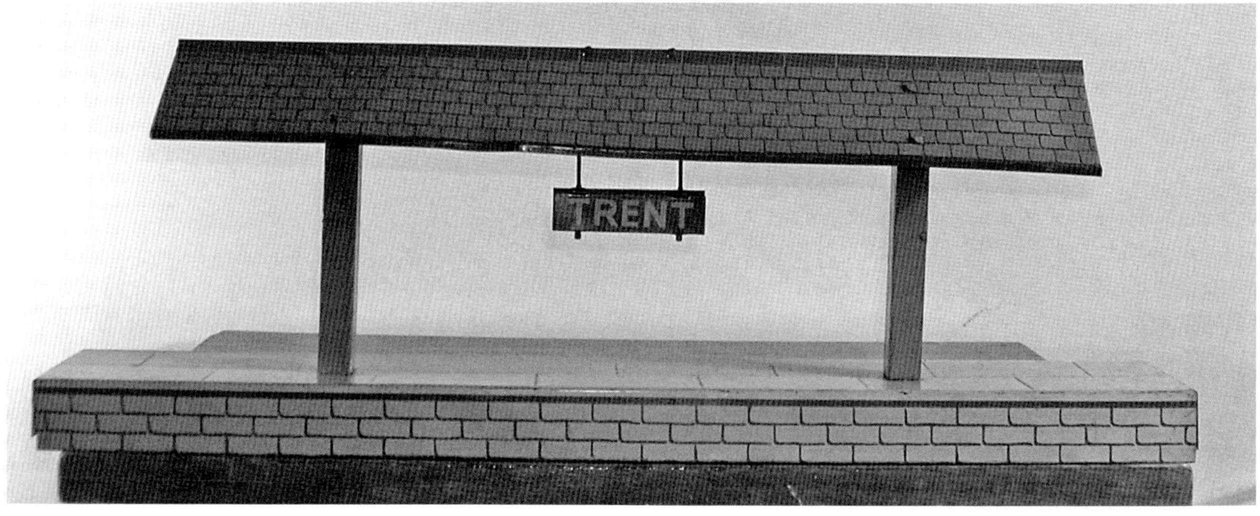

The Hornby model in the author's possession. It is an island station, and Hornby have given it the name Trent.

Occasionally one of these models is advertised on e-bay, the internet's sales and exchange site, and the author was able to purchase one through these means. It was not a pristine model, and lacked its end ramps, and was otherwise intact.

I am indebted to Chris Graebe, archive officer of the Hornby Railway Collectors' Association (which has 3,000 members), who kindly researched the history of the model for me, for the following information. The research was not easy, as after trawling through 10,000 or so factory documents, he was no nearer finding out why Trent was chosen, except that it was well-known as an island station.

The model station started life in 1926 as Windsor, then after 1936 it was successively Wembley, Ripon, Bristol, Reading and Margate. In 1954 it was changed to Trent. There are three known versions: white columns with green roof 1954-1955, a briefly-made intermediate version with orange columns and a green roof (this is the version which your author purchased), and finally, 1955-1957, orange columns with an orange roof. Production of the item ceased in 1957.

Chris Graebe found that 3,500 boxes were printed for the 1954 version, and 3,000 for the 1955 version. From experience with other Hornby items, he thinks that most of these (probably 60%) have survived, so there are probably quite a few more out there.

The significance of the model, of course, is that it is a demonstration of just how well known Trent Station was in the mid-20th century to those who used the railways.

Chapter 9

Memories of Trent Station

When it comes to memories of Trent Station, no-one can match David Shaw. David Shaw's father had worked at Toton. David himself started work at Trent Station as a junior porter at 6 o'clock one Monday morning in 1948, when Jack Hardy was the stationmaster. Jack Hardy, who came from Sileby, eventually took up residence in the stationmaster's house. Later in his career David Shaw worked at Nottingham, Mansfield and Sawley Junction, before returning to Trent, where he remained until the station finally closed. After closure he was assigned to a position in the Trent North signalbox, and from there he took the remarkable series of photographs which are featured in Chapter 11.

One of David Shaw's jobs was to work in the Telegraph Office, which was open round the clock. This office catered for an area 25 miles around (just as the present-day Trent power signal box does). The work entailed train movement reporting, taking messages, and reporting these messages to the signal boxes. Standards were high in those days. Going through a red light, which is now, if we are to believe the newspapers, a not infrequent occurrence, was then "a sacking job".

David Shaw remembers when poachers would take the 11.55 p.m. from Nottingham to Trent, go out after rabbits, bring them back to the waiting room where they worked at gutting them, and then take 3.15 a.m. train (the "late mail") back into Nottingham. The same 11.55 Nottingham to Derby train was also a favourite with the mods and rockers from Leicester in the 1950s/1960s. They would take the train to Trent, and then wait for the 1.15 a.m. London-bound train to take them back to Leicester.

In David Shaw's day the station was busy with main line trains from 6.20 in the morning till the 8.20 p.m. London to Nottingham train (train number 153). There was a parcel train at 8.40 p.m. The porters all used four-wheel barrows.

A regular early morning chore was to go through the station and down the footpath to Long Eaton pulling the string on each lamp standard in order to put out the gas lights.

For a stationmaster, Trent ranked as a top grade. It was an ambition to end one's career at Trent.

In the 1950s, when he was 19 years old, David Archer got a summer job as a porter at Trent. He too recalls the four-wheeled trolleys they used to transport goods around the station. The station was generously manned at that time, with three foremen – one for each shift, six porters – two for each shift, plus a booking clerk and a ticket collector. There was, he recalls, very little to do, especially on the night shift. On this 10 p.m. to 6 a.m. shift there were two trains up to midnight. From 12 to 1 there would be a general cleaning, of the toilets etc. On that shift, perhaps between 2 and 3 in the morning, the porters might have a short sleep, but at 3 o'clock there was a strict duty, that of taking the wide brush and sweeping the platforms from end to end. And there was no short cut in sweeping the rubbish on to the tracks – it had to be collected up in a pan and properly disposed of.

One of the more alarming duties he was given was to check the detonators at Ratcliffe-on-Soar, which meant walking along the railway lines, over the bridge and through the Red Hill tunnel. He was told that if a train came he had to take refuge in one of the many cubby holes, but to his relief none did.

David Archer today, but still wearing the porter's cap he has retained from the days when he worked at Trent Station.

Earlier one of the porters, Paddy Cassidy, on a similar expedition, did have an alarming experience. With a train approaching he backed into one of the cubby holes, only to be encircled by a pair of arms. A railway guard taking a short cut through the tunnel was already in the refuge, and put his arms round Reg as a precaution, presumably to stop him starting out again.

Latter days at Trent Station. The signal gantry is already denuded. A British Rail type 4 diesel locomotive, Peak Class (later class 45) no. D150, with the 'up' Thames-Clyde Express. Photo by Brian Amos.

But this one did not stop. British Rail's crack train of the 1960s, the 3.30 p.m. Nottingham to London St Pancras Midland Pullman, thunders by on the passing line. Photograph by Brian Amos.

The stationmaster at the time David Archer was there was a Mr Warren Smith. A keen railwayman and observer, Warren Smith wrote a detailed article for *Trains Illustrated* about the problems of traffic movements and signalling at Trent.

In 1961, during each period of 24 hours, nearly 100 passenger and parcels trains called at Trent Station. There was a frequent service from Derby to Leicester, calling at Trent with a connection from Lincoln and Nottingham. The time allowed for the connection was normally in the range three minutes to ten minutes. The big problem was whether to hold the Derby to Leicester service if the service from Nottingham was running late. Experience quickly indicated that it was not wise to hold the ongoing service for more than five minutes.

Another problem was the important 8.15 departure from St Pancras to Nottingham which did not stop at Trent but was scheduled to pass through at 10.59. Its timing practically coincided with the 10.47 departure from Derby to Nottingham which was a stopping train. Both these trains used the same piece of track. If the express was a few minutes late the decision had to be made whether to hold the stopping train back from entering the Trent Station section, or let it through. If the express was only three or four minutes late the local could obviously be held back. If the express was more than 12 minutes late, the local was allowed to proceed since it would arrive in Nottingham before the express. But if the delay was between four and 12 minutes the decision had to be made by the signalman at Trent South signalbox. A further complication was that the Derby to Nottingham local had a connection with the Nottingham to Leicester.

The up Thames-Clyde express coming down from the Erewash Valley line had two connections, one to Nottingham and Lincoln, and the other a slow train to Leicester and Birmingham. As the train to Leicester used the same track as the express, here again there were decisions to be made by the signalman if there was late running. In this case, however, the Thames-Clyde express was considered so important that the Leicester slow could be held back by as much as 17 minutes.

Actually at this time all trains, including goods trains, were classed in order of priority: A, B, C, D, E, F, G, H, J and K (the letter I was not used to avoid confusion with the number 1). Signalmen and station staff generally had to take these priorities into consideration when making decisions as to which trains to let through and which trains to hold when there was late running.

Fortunately for the Trent signalmen a large proportion of freight services passing through their sector had just started their journey, either at the Toton marshalling yards or at the Beeston freightliner depot, and usually were running at or near their pre-booked time. However trains coming the other way, especially those with empty wagons, were often very late indeed.

As reported in the previous chapter, the biggest traffic flows resulted from the coal trains from Toton to Castle Donington or Willington power stations, both on the Castle Donington branch, running at half-hour intervals and cutting across the path of passenger services at Sheet Stores junction. The signalman at Trent North had the difficult job of regulating the passage. There had to be a spirit of teamwork between the signalmen in Trent North and Trent South. A long goods train, extending back from a stop signal, could 'foul' both up and down lines. A further complication was a gently rising gradient from North Erewash Junction to Sheet Stores so it was to everyone's advantage to keep heavy freight trains moving.

Another conundrum was the Toton to Chaddesden (near Derby) goods train which was due to pass through Trent every day at 8.56. The signalmen had to try to enable it to weave its way through the various junctions without getting in the way of very busy morning passenger traffic, two expresses and a Derby to Nottingham parcels train. This was one freight train which tended to be given priority by signalmen because of the cascade of complications failure to run to time could cause. If there were any delay the goods train would be on the Derby line in the way of the Nottingham to Liverpool express, due out of Trent at 9.17. The timekeeping of parcels trains was also considered important, and the 6.35 p.m. Lincoln to Crewe parcels train calling at Trent was ranked as class A.

After Trent Station closed the signal boxes were replaced by a power signal box at Trent which controlled all lines for about 25 miles around.

The head signalman at Trent in the 1920s was Fred Smythen, maternal grandfather of Alan F. Smith, Derby Road, Long Eaton. Fred Smythen was a devout Christian, and his beliefs would not let him join a union. In the 1926 General Strike he continued to work, and had to be escorted to and from the signal box by police. He retired in 1932.

A presentation being made to Arthur Talbot, long-serving foreman at Trent Station. Those who have been identified are: Ted Thompson (ticket inspector), Reg Titmuss (station foreman), ? (station master), ? (divisional manager), Albert Jones (signalman, Trent North), Douglas Lawson (signalman, Sheet Stores Junction), Ted Whitfield (relief signalman), ?, Douglas Fisher (parcels porter), ?, Albert Cade (ticket inspector), Arthur Talbot, Arthur Cooke (parcels porter), ? (refreshment room), ? (refreshment room), Paddy Cassidy (porter), , ?, Picture by courtesy of Roy Talbot.

A picture of staff at Trent Station in the latter days. The ladies are from the refreshment room. Picture by courtesy of Roy Talbot.

A later signalman was Charlie Pearson, who was there for 47 years, and finished in 1959, and died in 1960 aged 60. His daughter-in-law Vera Pearson lives in Sawley. On Sunday mornings, as a young woman, Vera Pearson used to visit him and have breakfast with him in the signal box. One of his expressions was "The paint's out", meaning that the whole of the platform at Trent had been painted white: this was done when the Train was stationed on North Curve.

In August 1940 King George VI and Queen Elizabeth, en route from London to Derby, had their sleeping coach shunted on to the North Curve. The local Home Guard provided the guard for the night, and saluted when the train moved off at 9 a.m. the next morning.

In June 1949 Nottingham celebrated its quincentenary, and was visited by the then Princess Elizabeth and the Duke of Edinburgh. The Royal Train spent the night on the North Curve at Trent. Another royal occasion was July 4-5, 1955 when Queen Elizabeth II, as she had now become, and the Duke of Edinburgh were attending the Royal Show at Wollaton Hall.

In the collection of Lawrence Knighton, a stalwart of the Midland Railway Society, who has an interesting array of railwayana, are the detailed instructions for a visit by the Royal Train in 1958. It was all highly secret, and given the codename *Deepdene*. Timings of the train are given to the minute. It left St Pancras at 11.30 p.m. on Thursday, November 20, and passed through Sheet Stores Junction at 1.58 a.m. From there it went into Sawley Junction at 2.02 a.m., and there paused, for a change of engine. The instructions now become even more precise.

"On arrival at Sawley Junction the Special Train must be brought to a stand with the centre of the Engine cab opposite to a point at which a Hand Signalman will be stationed to indicate the place at which the train must stop. After the Special Train has come to a stand the automatic brake must be entirely destroyed and the brake held on the train. The Class 5 MT engine from Derby Motive Power Depot arriving Sawley Junction at 1.30 a.m., and already standing on the North Curve Up line at Sawley Junction, will then be attached to the rear of the Special Train.

A front view of Trent Station, unusual in that the photographer had to have permission to stand on the lines. Were the bushes a decorative feature for a royal visit? Photograph reproduced by permission of the National Railway Museum.

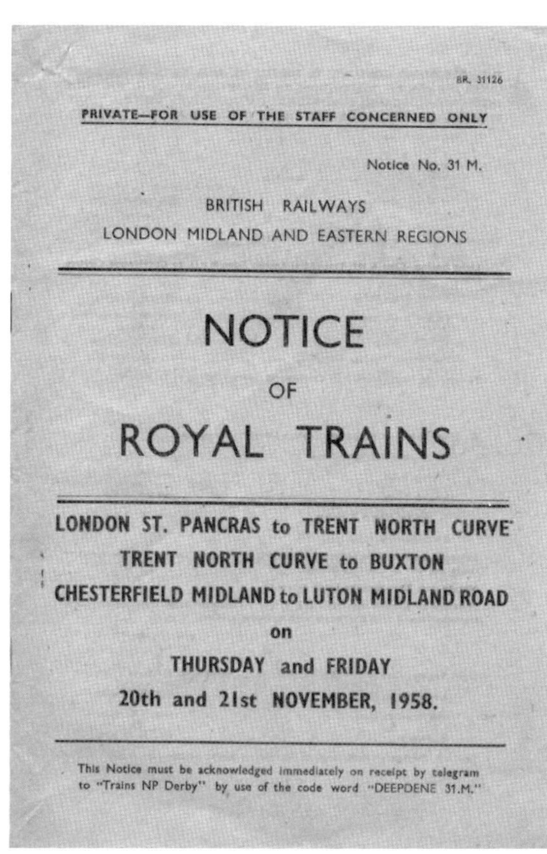

BR. 31126

PRIVATE—FOR USE OF THE STAFF CONCERNED ONLY

Notice No. 31 M.

BRITISH RAILWAYS
LONDON MIDLAND AND EASTERN REGIONS

NOTICE
OF
ROYAL TRAINS

LONDON ST. PANCRAS to TRENT NORTH CURVE
TRENT NORTH CURVE to BUXTON
CHESTERFIELD MIDLAND to LUTON MIDLAND ROAD
on
THURSDAY and FRIDAY
20th and 21st NOVEMBER, 1958.

This Notice must be acknowledged immediately on receipt by telegram to "Trains NP Derby" by use of the code word "DEEPDENE 31.M."

The cover of the Royal Trains notice. From the Laurence Knighton collection.

"After this engine has been attached to the Special Train the train engine will be detached and must remain stationary until the Special Train has left and the Driver receives instructions to run light to Derby Motive Power Depot. The Special Train will then be drawn back on to Trent North Curve Down Line and must be brought to a stand with the centre of the engine cab opposite to a point at which a Hand Signalman will be stationed to indicate the place at which the train must stop. After the Special Train has come to a stand the automatic brake must be entirely destroyed and the brake held on the train.

"During the time the Special Train is standing on the Down Line at Trent North Curve the points at both Trent Station North Junction and Sawley Junction must be set for the alternative route and padlocked in that position until the Special Train is ready to leave for Buxton at 8.35 a.m., except during the time movements are being made with the engines concerned in working the Special Train. No train or engine must be allowed to travel between Trent Station North Junction and Sawley Junction via Trent North Curve in either direction from one hour before the Special Train arrives until after the Special Train has left at 8.35 a.m."

When the Royal Train was parked on the North Bend, it was the job of the Trent stationmaster to deliver the newspapers in the morning. A less fortunate railway employee, Jackie Tideswell, had to clean out the buckets from the toilets.

It is recalled that the GPO (General Post Office), which in those days ran the telephone service, would put up telegraph poles before the Royal Train arrived and take them down after it had left, to ensure overnight telephone communication.

Trent was quintessentially a Midland Railway / LMS station, and locomotives in LNER livery were rarely seen there. But the date is now September 10, 1966, and the railway heritage movement has started. So even the Flying Scotsman, pride of the LNER, could be received at Trent. It was fronting the "Farnborough Flyer", a charter train for the Farnborough Air Display. Photographs (above and on the following page) reproduced by permission of Brian Amos.

The "Farnborough Flyer" draws into Trent Station.

Having taken on water the Flying Scotsman waits for the "Right Away".

In 1967, the last full year of operation of Trent Station, railway collector and photographer Brian Amos chartered a light aircraft to record for posterity the layouts around Trent Station and the Toton marshalling yards, as a way of paying tribute to his father, railwayman Walter Amos.

Trent Station itself is towards the bottom left of the picture, with the North Curve above it clearly showing the tightness of the bend into the station. Forbes Hole is to the right of the bend. Photographs reproduced by permission of Brian Amos.

Next page - The pattern of lines north of Trent Station. The North Curve is the sharply curving lines towards the bottom left of the picture. The next curve above that is the Erewash Valley line. Between the North Curve and the Erewash Valley line is the Forbes Hole fishing lake. The course of the section of original Nottingham-Derby line taken out in 1862 when Trent Station was built, was the straight alignment to the left of Forbes Hole and continuing, past the site of Platts Crossing, on the other side of the Erewash Valley line. The line to Nottingham is in the centre of the picture making a slight curve to the right; the curve linking the Erewash Valley and Nottingham lines is seen towards the top of the picture. The high level goods line is on the right-hand side of the picture, before curving left to pass over the Nottingham line then the Erewash Valley line on its way to Toton. Between the high level goods line can be seen, top to bottom, the Trent Cottages, the Power Signal Box then under construction, and the stationmaster's house (white building). Photograph reproduced by permission of Brian Amos.

One of the first-ever pictures of a diesel-hauled passenger train. It is March 29, 1948, and, no. 10000, which had only entered regular service a few days before, has reached Sheet Stores Junction with the 2.15 p.m. London St Pancras to Manchester express. Photograph reproduced by permission of Transport Treasury.

Trainspotters on the north end of Trent Station look on as a DMU comes off the North Curve and into Trent Station's up platform. Photograph reproduced by permission of Brian Amos.

Chapter 10

"The economic facts have to be faced".

If one were to carry out a huge exercise in simplification, one could reduce the history of railways in Great Britain to seven headings: (1) Waggonways, (2) The impact of steam locomotion, (3) Railway Mania, (4) Consolidation, (5) Grouping, (6) Nationalisation, (7) End of Steam, (8) Beeching, (9) Privatisation.

Trent Station shared in developments 4 to 8.

Many people believe that railways suddenly happened, with the opening of the Stockton to Darlington Railway in 1827. The Stockton and Darlington Railway was the first public railway, which also used steam locomotives to pull the trains. But for over 200 years before that it had been known that the efficiency of traction (loads which could be pulled by horses or bullocks) was vastly increased if the carts or carriages could be run on rails. When the flanged wheel, which avoided slippage, came into existence, rail traction became even more advantageous. There were waggonways up and down the country, usually between an industrial site and a canal, where horses towed trains of trucks.

Once steam locomotion had been discovered and applied, and was combined with the advantages of railway tracks, railways quickly became the prime means of long-distance transport.

So clear was the advantage, and so profitable did the new railways appear to be, that the age of Railway Mania set in, and soon the country was being covered with railway lines, and more and more railway schemes, some of them wildly impracticable, were being proposed. After the initial bubble had burst, the period of consolidation set in, with lines linking up to form a national network, and larger companies, such as the Midland Railway, coming to prominence.

The building of Trent Station, as described in Chapter 3, was a result of the Consolidation phase. Trent was always very much a Midland Railway creation.

We have already described, in Chapter 7, what happened as a result of Group (1923) and Nationalisation (1948).

The Railway Modernisation Plan of 1955 was a key document of its time. We have already seen how it transformed and standardised railway signs. It also prepared the way for the end of steam locomotion, which was to be replaced largely by diesel. With hindsight, and with the experience of what other countries such as France and Japan were doing, the switch should have been directly from steam to electric traction, but there can be no crying over spilt milk. There is of course a certain romance about steam locomotives, but once alternative motive power units were available steam was doomed for general purpose railway operation.

In the 1960s economy was the order of the day on the railways. The biggest cost was staff, so ways were sought to streamline railway staffing. This led to the abolition of the position of stationmaster, a position which had enjoyed prestige and authority from the earliest days of passenger railways. The last Trent stationmaster to live in the stationmaster's house had been Mr E. Callard. Under the re-organisation there was no longer a stationmaster for each individual station; instead stations were grouped into 'areas' and controlled by an Area Manager.

And so we come to Beeching. There are several government reports a year, usually known after the name of the chairman of the inquiry committee, and some of them were for a time familiar to all newspaper readers – the Crowther Report, the Robbins Report, the Allen Report – but after a time they become forgotten.

But there is one report which, even 40 years after it was issued, is still familiar. The Beeching Report. Officially, as our picture (next page) of the cover of the report shows, the report's title was *The Reshaping of British Railways*, but it will forever be associated with Dr Richard Beeching.

In 1961 Government embarked on one of its periodical reorganisations of public transport, which resulted in a new British Railways Board. Dr Richard Beeching was appointed as chairman of this Board, and given a simple brief, which was essentially to make the railway network pay its way.

He decided that there was not enough information available, so he set about producing a comprehensive survey of the system, to find out which parts were profitable, and which parts were loss-making.

The 148-page report was published in 1963 by Her Majesty's Stationery Office, and immediately became one of its best-sellers.

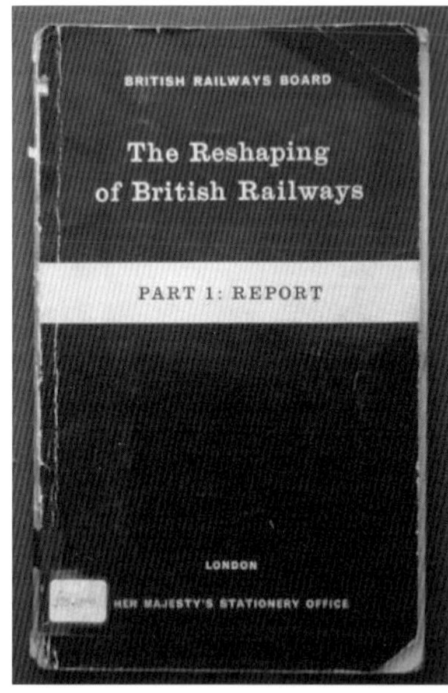

The cover of the Beeching report, which doomed Trent Station and many another railway line and station up and down the country.

The Beeching Report led to the most radical shake-up in the railway infrastructure in the whole of the 20th century, much more far-reaching in its effects than the railway company amalgamations of the 1920s, rail nationalisation in the 1940s, or the modernisation plan of the 1950s. It doomed many long-established railway stations, and even whole lines, to closure. And Trent Station was one of those scheduled for the Beeching axe.

In many quarters the Beeching Report was unpopular, and still is. The British people are attached to their railways. There is no other country in the world where there is greater nostalgia for steam locomotives. And the British people are instinctively conservative; they do not like change, particularly radical change.

But the Beeching Report is an impressive document. Its analysis of the transport infrastructure of 1960s Britain was thorough and wide-ranging. And far from being anti-railway (a common perception), it sought to free the railways from the shackles of an out-of-date set-up so they could be freed to do the jobs for which they were best suited.

The problem of course was the growth in vehicular transport on the roads – freight lorries, bus services and private car transport. Just as the stage coaches had virtually disappeared in the face of competition from the railways, so it was feared that the railways would disappear because they could not compete with the flexibility of road transport. Not so, said Beeching. There are still functions which the railways can do better than the roads. But to perform these functions efficiently they must throw out the deadweight ballast of the past.

The key analysis was stated in the foreword to the report.

> "Railways are distinguished by the provision and maintenance of a specialised route system for their own exclusive use. This gives rise to high fixed costs. On the other hand, the benefits which can be derived from possession of this high cost route system are very great.
>
> "Firstly, it permits the running of high capacity trains, which themselves have very low movement costs per unit carried. Secondly, it permits dense flows of traffic and, provided the flows are dense, the fixed costs per unit moved are also low. Thirdly, it permits safe, reliable, scheduled movements at high speed.
>
> "In a national system of transport we should, therefore, expect to find railways concentrating upon those parts of the traffic pattern which enable them to derive sufficient benefit from these three advantages to offset their unavoidable burden of high system cost. In other words, we should expect the provision of railways to be limited to routes over which it is possible to develop dense flows of traffic, of the kinds which lend themselves to movement in trainload quantities and which, in part at least, benefit from the speed and reliability which railways are achieving.

> "Moreover, we should expect that, having been concentrated upon traffics matched to the advantageous features of rail transport, the system would then be operated so as to develop those features to the full".

Beeching was anxious to get rid of uneconomic commitments which dated from when the railways had a virtual monopoly of all transport of over a few miles. In 1960, by and large, we still had a railway infrastructure where every large village had its own railway station, often with its own siding for goods wagons. British Rail was a "common carrier", committed to moving any piece of freight from a single passenger trunk (many people, especially at holiday times, used the 'unaccompanied luggage' service) to hundreds of tons of coal. Every train had a guard's van for conveying small parcels, bicycles and prams.

Much of the Beeching Report was concerned with freight traffic, which has always been much more important economically to the railways than passengers ("Without freight the main railway network could not exist"). It is something we tend to forget. You will hear many people speak of the railways as if they were concerned solely with the conveyance of passengers. In fact passengers are often rather a nuisance for a transport system; depending on the season they need to be kept warm or cool, they need to be nourished with food and liquid at regular intervals, and they need to be provided with toilet facilities. And their conveyance must be without unreasonable interruption – no shunting them into a siding for a day or two. And they are very price-conscious. In terms of space occupied and trouble caused they are nothing like as profitable as a bolt of cloth or a bale of newspapers, let alone a ton of mineral ore or a wagonload of iron girders.

In the area of freight "wagon-load general merchandise" and "sundries traffic" were the problems. But what was true for freight was also true for passenger traffic – "through movement of well-loaded trains" was what the railways should concentrate on. In the passenger field local stopping trains were by far the greatest loss-maker. The conclusion was that the railways should aim to concentrate on express inter-city passenger services and single-product (such as coal or minerals) trainload freight services.

The inexorable analytical eye of Dr Beeching then looked at the infrastructure – the route system (he devastatingly found that one third of the route mileage carried only one per cent of the total passenger miles) and at the stations. In April 1961 British Railways had about 7,000 stations open to traffic, equivalent to one station for every 2 ½ miles of route. Here again one third of the stations (including Trent) produced less than one per cent of the total passenger receipts, and one half of the stations produced only two per cent. At the other end of the scale 34 stations, less than one per cent of the total number of stations in the country, produced 26% of the passenger ticket revenue.

The harsh economic facts could not be avoided, the report went on. The revenue from the least used half of the total number of stations was £6.5 million per year, and the direct cost of running those same stations (not counting any contribution to general railway costs) was £9 million per year.

> "There can be no question, therefore, that the railways would be better off financially if a high proportion of the stations were closed, even if this resulted in a total loss of the traffic passing through them."

It was clear what this was leading to in terms of passenger services: get rid of as many of the local stations and local stopping trains as possible, and thereby save on all the costs of maintenance and staffing. The analysis of freight traffic pointed to the same conclusion:

> "Our railways were developed to their fullest extent at a time when the horse and cart were the only means of feeding to and distributing from them. Therefore, as the railways grew, because of the deficiencies of horse transport on poor roads, the main network of routes was extended by an even closer network of branches, with close spacing of stations over the whole system, in order to reduce road movement to a minimum"

Little local stations, so the argument runs, had no place in an age when road traffic could look after local passenger movements and small units of freight. Railways should "cease to do things for which they are ill suited". And so we came to the 15 conclusions, of which conclusion number three proposed: "Closure of a high proportion of the total number of small stations to passenger traffic".

A total of 2,363 stations was earmarked for closure, of which 235 of which had already been closed. The report also proposed that about half of the country's railway tracks (estimated at about 17,000 miles) should be closed.

Beeching had been appointed by a Conservative government. In 1964 a Labour Government came to power. But the policy did not change. The government continued to approve closures.

As we saw in Chapter 5, some had forecast that Trent's days were numbered when the Manton loop in 1880 made Nottingham a mainline station, and again in 1900 when the Great Central line opened, but even in 1961 Trent Station was still handling nearly a hundred passenger trains a day. There were also over 300 freight trains daily. By this time Trent Station was largely used by passengers who were changing from mainline expresses to local stopping services. Once those local stopping services had been scheduled for closure, Trent lost its *raison d'être*. It still had very little in the way of a local population, although, ironically, this was to change in the next few years when housing estates were opened up in the part of Long Eaton where Trent Station lay.

There was also a need to have more efficient line and signalling organisation. All coal trains to Castle Donington and Willington power stations had to use the junctions at Trent, and if a coal train was held because of a train coming through from Leicester, South Erewash junction could be blocked.

As a result of the Beeching Report all the remaining stations on the Erewash Valley line were closed: Long Eaton, Sandiacre & Stapleford, Stanton Gate, Trowell, Ilkeston Junction, Langley Mill & Eastwood, Codnor Park, Pye Bridge, Alfreton, Westhouses and Clay Cross. Trent Station had been the gateway to main line travel for passengers served by these stations. Then two stations on the line to Derby: Draycott & Breaston, and Borrowash, were closed, as were the intermediate stations, Kegworth and Hathern, between Trent and Loughborough . So the writing was on the wall.

There were some flaws in the Beeching calculations, which became clear later. For example, ticket sales were calculated from those made at the point of departure of the outward journey. So, many seaside stations were earmarked for closure since they showed little ticket revenue, when in fact their very existence, as favourite destinations, generated ticket sales, but such ticket sales took place at departure stations not destinations.

Tipton St. John's
Tisbury
Tiverton
Tiverton Junction
Todd Lane Junction
Toller
Tollerton
Topsham
Torrington
Tower Hill (Devon)
Trench Crossing
Trent
Trentham
Tresmeer
Trouble House Halt
Troutbeck
Trowell
Tumby Woodside
Tunbridge Wells West
Tunstall
Tyldesley
Uckfield
Uffington (Berks.)
Ulceby

The page of the Beeching Report which clearly shows Trent among the stations scheduled for closure.

Trent Station, obviously, could not show much in the way of passenger ticket sales, since it was essentially an interchange station. But even the interchange role was disappearing, particularly when more and more emphasis was being placed on through trains. There was no point in changing trains at Trent in order to catch a local stopping train to Breaston & Draycott or Borrowash if those stations were also going to disappear.

The killer fact (as far as Trent Station was concerned) was the analysis of routes. The local lines through Trent, which were the Derby to Nottingham stopping train service, the Erewash Valley line, and the stopping service between Trent and Leicester, were all shown as dotted lines on the Beeching map. Dotted lines indicated services which carried less than 10,000 passengers a week. And stopping services with less the 10,000 passengers a week lost money heavily, as the Beeching report went to great trouble to prove, with extensive use of tables and cost comparisons. Even when the same lines were used for inter-city trains the services needed to be discontinued, in order to save the costs of all the little stations.

What the Beeching Report failed to do was to predict the inevitable long-term consequence of the expansion of road traffic – road congestion. By the 1990s the tide had begun to turn, and new local railway lines and new tramway systems were being constructed in different parts of the country. Much too late, however, to save Trent Station.

The report also ignored – as all railway bosses like to do – the heritage value of railways. Because local railway services were thought to belong to the past, the concept of mothballing a station such as Trent against possible future requirements never occurred to anyone.

In the city of Nottingham the railway viaduct at Weekday Cross was demolished in the 1990s, and yet ten years later, at great expense, another viaduct almost in the same place was erected to take the new Nottingham tram system.

The tramway viaduct in Nottingham, built on the same alignment as the railway viaduct, which had been demolished only a few years previously.

If Trent Station had been preserved, it could have been re-opened as the station for the Nottingham East Midlands Airport.

Because another factor not foreseen by the report was that in the 40 years after 1963 there would be an exponential growth in provincial airports, and an accompanying demand for fast transit, i.e. rail, access to such airports. Successful airports these days all have their own railway station adjacent to the terminals – Birmingham, Manchester, Stansted.

The East Midlands airport at Castle Donington has no such access. So there are plans to create one, a complete new railway station. probably somewhere near Ratcliffe-on-Soar, which is six miles from the airport. Because it is so far from the airport, there will have to be a coach link. But Ratcliffe is the wrong side of the M1 motorway, and coaches will have to use the already congested A453 road, and then negotiate their way through the M1/A453 junction, one of the busiest motorway junctions in the country.

Ratcliffe is also only on one railway line, the old Midland Railway north-south line. If Trent Station were still in existence, it would serve not only that line but also the Erewash Valley line and the Nottingham-Derby line. But, more importantly, Trent was also placed at the junction for the Castle Donington line, now normally used only for freight. And that railway line runs past Castle Donington village, at a point (where Castle Donington station used to stand) only two miles from the airport, and on the airport side of the M1.

Incidentally that Castle Donington line, though supposed freight only these days, has many times proved to be an essential passenger link. During the 1960s many Manchester – Stoke – London expresses used the Castle Donington line while the West Coast line was being electrified, and it has also been used whenever there was a temporary closure of the Nottingham-Derby direct line.

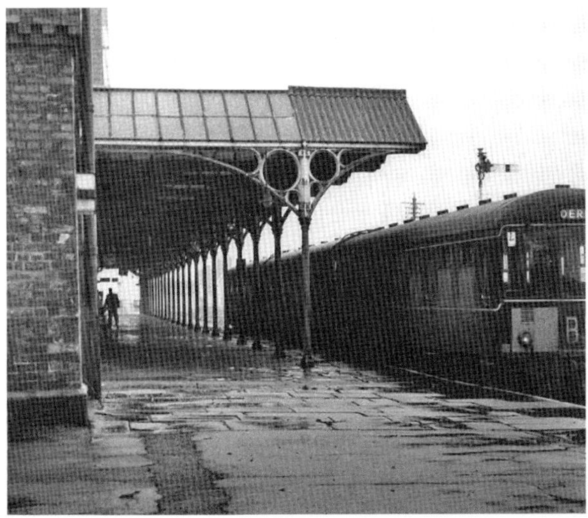

Trent Station as many people remember it. A rainy day, and a three-coach DMU has stopped at the up platform. A solitary figure, probably a passenger who has just alighted, makes his way off the platform. Photograph reproduced by permission of the Derby Evening Telegraph *and Derby Industrial Museum.*

One factor not mentioned in the Beeching Report, but which strongly influenced the decision to close Trent Station, was the desire to simplify route layouts in order to facilitate the introduction of more remote power signalling. As we have seen, signalling through Trent Station was a complex affair demanding constant instant decision-making by a small army of signalling staff helped by on-the-spot controllers.

So the decisions were made.

The start of the North Curve from Trent Station, inMarch 1967. Photograph reproduced by permission from Brian Amos.

A further view of the North Curve in this, its final period, here clearly illustrating the tight bend. Photograph reproduced by permission from Brian Amos.

First to go was the North Curve, over which trains ceased to run on March 6, 1967, and weeds started to grow over the track. For some years few trains had been routed round the curve, and its chief use was as a reserve place to 'park' goods trains from Derby or from the south temporarily until there was a gap when they could be fed through the system. But there were now fewer goods trains (the decline had started as long ago as 1955), and it was felt that the system could cope without it. The North Curve was taken out of service, and its railway lines were taken up in early 1968.

Before those lines were actually taken up, though after the points at each end had been taken out, as in the photograph below, the North Curve railway lines were used for one last time. Local resident John Blackburn, a railway employee himself, had a garden the end of which ran close to the railway line. He was interested in buying some of the slabs from Trent Station, and this was eventually agreed under what was oddly called a Firewood Order. He was then faced with the problem of how to get the slabs home. He was able to borrow a Permanent Way trolley on which he loaded the slabs, and push the trolley along the line to the point closest to his garden. He became very aware of the uphill gradient! So John can still proudly claim to be the last person to navigate the North Curve!

It is December 1967, and the North Curve junction has now been severed. Photograph by permission of Brian Amos.

In May 1967 the Nottingham to London line via Melton Mowbray was closed. It will be recalled (Chapters 2 and 5) that the opening of this line in 1880 reduced to some extent the importance of Trent Station, because for the first time all Midland Railway trains had an alternative to going through Trent Junction. Once again direct Nottingham to London services had to be re-routed through Trent Junction, but the running down of intermediate stations meant that it was no longer thought necessary to have the trains stop at Trent. At the same time the Midland Region timetable was completely revised. Trains to the north often only went as far as Sheffield, and there were now no through trains going up the Erewash Valley. Trains from St Pancras ran hourly, either to Derby or Nottingham, and Leicester took over Trent Station's role as the interchange.

On August 30, 1967, all stopping passenger services between the North Erewash Junction and Trent Station North Junction, and between Trowell Junction and Long Eaton Junction, were withdrawn.

In the months immediately before the scheduled closure some people were at last alerted to the loss which the disappearance of Trent Station would cause, and there was a flurry of letters to Trevor Park, MP for the South-east Derbyshire constituency, which covered Trent.

Trevor Park fought hard against the closure. He wrote to the Minister of Transport, Barbara Castle, asking what investigation of the possibility of economic operation "within the terms of her recently announced transport policies" had been made before she had consented to the closure of Trent Station. He received a letter back from John Morris, Parliamentary Secretary at the Ministry of Transport. John Morris's letter made it clear that the decision to close the station would stand. The decision, he wrote, had been taken "only after a very detailed study of the use being made [of the station] and of the trains and alternative services available". After careful consideration, wrote Mr Morris, there was no prospect that passenger services at Trent Station could be economic. "This was a statutory decision and because it cannot be reversed was only taken after the most careful consideration."

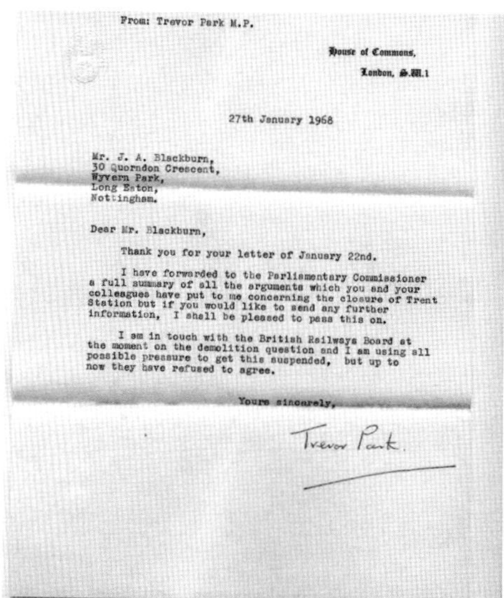

From: Trevor Park M.P.

House of Commons,
London, S.W.1

27th January 1968

Mr. J. A. Blackburn,
30 Quorndon Crescent,
Wyvern Park,
Long Eaton,
Nottingham.

Dear Mr. Blackburn,

Thank you for your letter of January 22nd.

I have forwarded to the Parliamentary Commissioner a full summary of all the arguments which you and your colleagues have put to me concerning the closure of Trent Station but if you would like to send any further information, I shall be pleased to pass this on.

I am in touch with the British Railways Board at the moment on the demolition question and I am using all possible pressure to get this suspended, but up to now they have refused to agree.

Yours sincerely,

Trevor Park.

One of the letters exchanged between Trevor Park MP and Mr John Blackburn. Courtesy of John Blackburn.

It is a carefully-worded letter which repays some study, as it does detail Government strategic thinking of the time, yet is aware of local circumstances:

> "As the Minister has asked me to take a special responsibility for railway matters I am replying to your letter of 30th November with which you enclosed these letters about the closure of Trent Station.
>
> "Before reaching her decision to allow the Railways Board to close Trent Station the Minister examined the Transport Users' Consultative Committee's report on hardship and all the other social and economic aspects involved. It was only after a very detailed study of the use being made of the trains and the alternative services available that the Minister concluded she would not be justified in asking the Railways Board to keep this station open to passenger services. This was a statutory decision and because it cannot be reversed, it was only taken after the most careful consideration.
>
> "The main function of Trent Station over the years has been to provide interchange facilities between various train services but, as the result of recent changes in the pattern of train services, its use for this purpose has declined. The Minister was satisfied that Attenborough Station would meet such need as remained for this facility. Other users of the station come, as evidenced by the bulk of the letters you have forwarded, from the nearby housing development, the centre of which is about half a mile from the station. They have found the rail services more convenient than the frequent bus services available rather more than a mile away at Long Eaton Green. The Minister was satisfied however that the revised bus services which have been recently introduced from the centre of the housing development would meet the needs of the relatively small number of passengers originating at Trent Station who travel to and from work and those who make shopping and other casual journeys. In view of the very small use made of the trains and the wide choice of buses available at Long Eaton Green, the Minister did not feel justified in asking the Railways Board to provide additional buses to the centre of the housing development for casual evening use. If, however, experience following closure indicated that the essential needs of former rail users were not being met, the Minister would be willing to consider whether improvements were necessary. We should, of course, need evidence of the number of people affected and the particular journeys where they were experiencing difficulty.

"The Minister knows that the decision to close Trent Station must be a disappointment to those people who have found the trains convenient for particular journeys, but the economic facts have to be faced. The Government are now meeting the total railway deficit which is currently costing the taxpayer many millions of pounds a year; we should be failing in our duty if we did not try to reduce this burden. The provision of a halt in place of Trent Station would, of course, defeat the object of closing the station. Where the Minister is satisfied that alternative services will cater for rail users she must, subject to detailed consideration of all the probable consequences, allow the Railways Board to discontinue passenger services which do not pay their way. But financial considerations are certainly not allowed to outweigh the many social factors that are taken into account when local transport needs are examined. The consent given to the closure of Trent and certain other stations on the Birmingham – Leicester – Nottingham line provided that closure should not take place until certain additional bus services were available for use. The Board are not yet ready to close all the stations concerned but they need to close Trent Station on 1st January 1968 to avoid abortive expenditure in relation to an expensive resignalling scheme in the area. As none of the additional bus services was required to meet the needs of users of Trent Station the Minister has decided to vary the conditions attached to her consent to exclude Trent Station from this particular requirement. I attach a copy of a letter sent to the Railways Board notifying them of this decision."

A view of Trent Station down platform in its later days. Track lifting has evidently already begun. Photograph reproduced by permission of Frank Nixon Collection / Derby Museums & Art Gallery.

Chapter 11

Turning out the lights

The decision to close Trent Station was final. But the local MP, Trevor Park, did take the somewhat unusual step of tabling a House of Commons motion regretting the decision to close the station.

The closure notice is posted at Trent Station. Photograph reproduced by permission of Brian Amos.

The sun setting at Trent Station. A picture (also used on our inside front cover) taken two days before closure. Photograph reproduced by permission of Brian Amos.

The motion recognised "the hardship and inconvenience which will be caused to the travelling public and the residents of Long Eaton in particular, it notes the objections from the Long Eaton Urban District Council as well as of substantial number of constituents; it regrets the decision by British Railways to close the station, and states that the Minister of Transport should have withheld her consent to the closure".

About two weeks before the actual closure date Trevor Park expressed his disappointment in an interview with the lobby correspondent of the *Derby Evening Telegraph*. He had, he said, made every effort to secure a postponement of the closure pending a full investigation of the objections which have been made. "It seems, however, that once a closure procedure is under way it acquires a momentum of its own", he added. "Once a minister has decided to approve a closure it is impossible for it to be reversed, no matter how strong the representation may be. The lesson to be learned was that if a public campaign was to be effective it had to go into action from the first moment that the intention of closing a station was announced. It must reach its peak before the final inquiry into objections is held, otherwise, as happened in this case, it would be too late to affect the issue".

One of the last trains to stop at Trent Station. The hut towards the left of the picture will be used the following week by the demolition workers

Trevor Park still did not give up. He referred the matter to the 'Ombudsman' (Sir Edmund Compton, the Parliamentary Commissioner for Administration), and that august official duly produced a five-page report. Basically this found that all the proper procedures had been complied with.

"I find that...the Ministry fully considered each aspect of hardship which was identified..

"I find that the Ministry gave detailed consideration to the travelling requirements of passengers...

"I find that the then Minister satisfied herself that the existing bus services...would meet the needs of the displaced rail passengers...

"I am satisfied, therefore, that the Ministry did not fail to take into account the possibility of greater future need for the station...."

In dealing this last point, of future potential, the Commissioner could not help making a snide remark about the very few passengers who bought tickets at Trent Station, totally ignoring the fact that its very role was as an interchange, not as a starting point for journeys:

"The complainant refers to the traffic potential of Trent Station and to the track layout and signalling methods. The assessment of traffic potential, the provision of services to meet that potential and all aspects of the physical operation of services are the sole responsibility of the British Railways Board and, as I have said in paragraph 10, the Railways Board is not an authority within my jurisdiction. I accept that the Ministry, in considering the proposal for the closure of Trent Station, could only concern themselves with the use of the rail services then being provided and I note that, in fact, the total number of trains which were daily available at that station before the closure (about 60) was only slightly less than the average number of passengers buying tickets there."

The last full day of operation of Trent Station was December 31, 1967. Normal operations continued throughout the day, and station staff were still on duty as the two station clocks ticked round till midnight, and the New Year. It was estimated that fewer than 20 people had boarded the last train at Nottingham Midland station. There were 22 people (including the author and his wife) waiting at Trent.

Last official ticket issued from Trent. 31 Dec. 67.

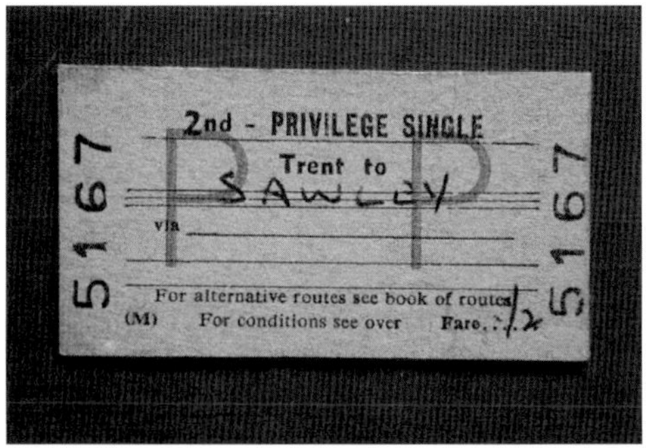

After the death of the author's father-in-law this envelope and ticket were found in his effects.

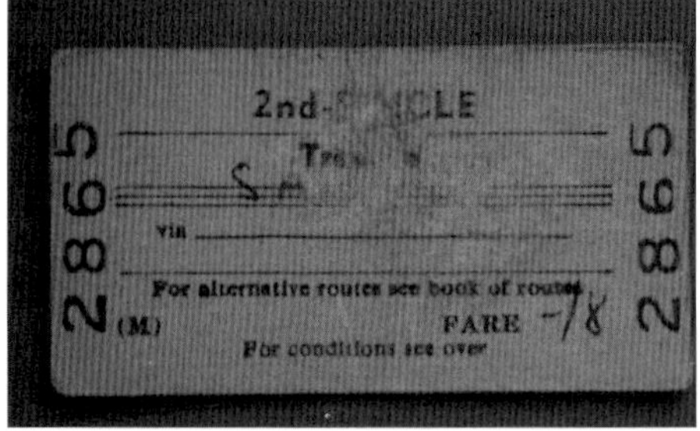

But the booking clerk had been persuaded to date-stamp the author's own ticket as Jan 1, 1968 even though the ticket had been purchased a few minutes before midnight (the last train left at three minutes past midnight).

Among those at the station was George Hornbuckle, assistant station manager for the Long Eaton area. He was not actually on duty, but had turned up in case anything unforeseen should arise. As he explains, "I did not want to get to work on Monday morning and find a problem on my desk". The particular area for which George Hornbuckle was responsible went (inclusively) as far as Draycott on the line to Derby, Attenborough on the line to Nottingham, Kegworth on the Leicester and London line (plus Hathern signal box), and Lock Lane signal box on the Stenson Junction line. The boundaries were the down distant signals on each line. Trent Station was very much part of his responsibility.

George Hornbuckle today.

It was a standard three-coach diesel unit which was destined to be the Last Train from Trent Station. It arrived at a minute past midnight, the driver looking somewhat bemused at the sudden barrage of camera flashes as everyone tried to picture the moment.

But there was no time for sentimentality, no streamers or singing of *Auld Lang Syne*. British Railways were determined to play down the moment. The passengers were urged on board and at three minutes past midnight, exactly at its scheduled departure time, the diesel unit pulled away from the platform.

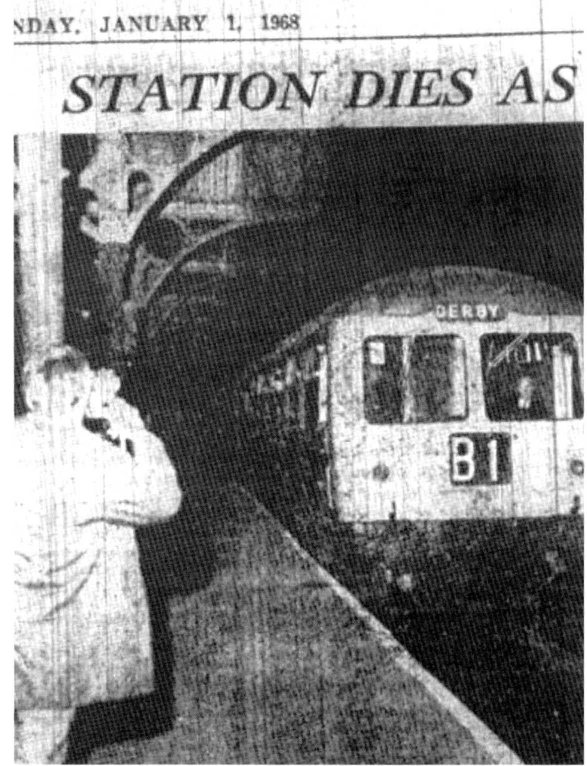

NDAY, JANUARY 1, 1968

STATION DIES AS

A somewhat bemused driver of the last train to leave Trent Station pulls away as people try to take a photograph. This was the Nottingham Evening Post report. We have not been able to trace the original photographs of this or the next picture, which are not included in the Evening Post archives, and therefore are thought to be by an independent photographer. The cuttings were provided by Roy Talbot.

It was then left to station foreman Arthur Talbot, who had been connected with the station for 22 years, to turn out one by one the gas lamps along the platform, plunging the station into its final darkness.

The indefatigable Trevor Park was still refusing to admit that the matter was lost, and on January 15, 1968, he called for an immediate halt in any demolition work until the Parliamentary Ombudsman could announce his findings. But the demolition proceeded inexorably. Only four days later, on January 19, the glass awnings were being removed, and by the beginning of February a start was made on the demolition of the main station buildings.

Station foreman and Trent Station veteran Arthur Talbot turns out the final gas lamp at Trent Station, plunging the station into its final darkness.

David Shaw was moved to work in the Trent North Signalbox, and there he was able to watch as the station was knocked down piece by piece. His pictures appear at the end of this section.

The signals could have been valuable, some of them being rare examples of Midland Railway lower quadrants with wooden arms on wooden posts.

Some track lifting had actually started in May 1965, ready for the radical redesigning of the whole layout round Trent. After the complete demolition of the station a high speed layout, much simplified from the previous eight tracks, was brought into service in July 1968. It was altered again in 1984 and now only three tracks pass through what was the old station site.

The Power Signal Box (which entered service on September 28, 1969) overlooks what had been the site of Trent Station. The power signal box is itself now scheduled for replacement. Photograph by Barry Cope.

The name *Trent* was perpetuated on the new power signal box, close to the station site. The signal box entered service on September 28, 1969. This new power box at Trent, the largest in the London Midland region, controlled 209 miles of track including 74 route-miles, dealing with about 250 passenger trains a day and considerably more coal and freight trains. There is also a Network Rail depot close to the site.

The following pages show the demolition of Trent Station, in a remarkable series of pictures taken by David Shaw. Reproduced by permission of David Shaw.

Compare the last of David Shaw's demolition pictures, above, with the first in the series. In a few short weeks Trent Station has disappeared completely. All that is left is the demolition workers' hut.

H.C. Casserley took this photograph of the site of Trent Station from a passing train on April 27, 1974. Photograph reproduced by permission of R.M. Casserley, Berkhamsted.

Chapter 12

Relics and revivals

John Betjeman, later Britain's Poet Laureate, was one of those who regretted the demolition of Trent Station, and he produced a limited edition medallion to mark its passing.

The Betjeman medallion, from Roy Talbot's collection.

British Railways made sure that Trent Station was demolished to the last brick. Everything was removed, including the splendid York stone slabs from the platform surfaces. As soon as the station buildings and platforms had been removed, the tracks were re-aligned. There is nothing at the site to show that a major railway station ever stood there.

The North Curve embankment was taken away, but it was found that it had acted as a flood embankment, and after its removal special drainage arrangements had to be made for the area it previously protected.

However, a visit to the Forbes Hole nature reserve, maintained by the Erewash Borough Council, will reveal some clues. The parking area for Forbes Hole can be found at Fields Farm Road, Long Eaton, Ordnance Survey grid reference SK 495324. As already explained, Forbes Hole was one of the many borrowpits found in the area around Trent Station. Incidentally many local people in the Long Eaton area prefer the term "ballast hole" for borrowpit.

If you enter the reserve, and walk along the left-hand side of the pond, roughly in a north-easterly direction, you are walking along the site of the original Midland Counties Railway line of 1839, the section discontinued when the curves were put in leading to Trent Station. At the end of this path you will see, the other side of the fence, the Erewash Valley line of 1847, still in operation.

Track at Forbes Hole, Long Eaton, on the site of the former North Curve of Trent Station. Photograph by Judy Wheldon.

If you then retrace your steps to the car park you can look back along Fields Farm Road, which approximately follows the old North Curve.

In front you will see a five-barred gate, leading to a track. This track is on the site of the tightest part of the old curve, and by following it you will come to another gate, separating you from the Derby to Nottingham railway line. In front of you now is the site of where Trent Station used to be (SK49633).

To see the site from the other side of the tracks you have to go a long way round, travelling along Fields Farm Road towards Long Eaton town centre, and turning right at the major roundabout near the Tapper's Harker public house. Tapper's Harker is a good railway name although the public house is modern. Here you cross the Erewash Valley railway line by a level crossing. To continue to Trent Station, after going over the level crossing, take the road, Meadow-lane, to the right, passing under the bridge carrying the high level goods line, and over another level crossing, which was the site of the original 1839 Long Eaton Junction station. The immediate right turn here is the old access road to Trent Station. Go along this road for some 450 yards, and you will find, on the right, a bridge taking you under the high level goods line, leading to Trent Cottages, the Trent Power Signal Box, and the old stationmaster's house.

One of Brian Amos's pictures of the demolished station (right of picture) also shows, on the left of the picture, the top of the underpass seen from the top.

Retracing your steps to the lane, a little further on is the lodge to the Trent Shooting Range which is opposite where the station used to be. Here you will find, now part of the embankment, a construction in blue bricks where the underpass entrance used to be. And that is all there is to see on site.

The site of the underpass seen today, from below. The parapet is still there but the underpass itself has been filled in. Photograph by Judy Wheldon.

Some of the station memorabilia, however, were preserved.

The two clocks from Trent Station, one for each platform, were originally bought by Rowland Hoggard, of Thurgarton, in Nottinghamshire. Mr Hoggard, a lifelong railwayman, as had been his father before him, had worked at Trent as a junior porter from 1934-1936. He later became a railway guard, but in the 1960s developed a hobby of collecting old station clocks to save them from the scrap heap. He also bought the clocks from Nottingham Midland when that station went over to digital clocks. However, Mr Hoggard sold the clocks on to a Mr Lloyd, of Nuthall in Nottinghamshire. Mr Lloyd, apparently, had the amibition to build a replica of the station platform on his smallholding at Nuthall. He also obtained a few flagstones, and some oddments, which were transported back to the smallholding. Sadly the items were dispersed when Mr Lloyd died, and we have not been able to track any of these down.

We have already recounted (Chapter 10) how John Blackburn obtained some of the paving, and this now surrounds the pond at his home. A Mr Frost of Attenborough also has some Trent Station paving built into his rockery.

We have also mentioned (Chapter 7) the cast iron sign which may have stood in Long Eaton Market Place. Another footpath sign, in the collection of David Jones of Long Eaton, probably stood in New Tythe Street.

Trent Station sign with arrow, from the David Jones collection. Photograph by Judy Wheldon.

Windows went to various railwaymen for use as cold frames.

Blocks with the Midland Railway logo were incorporated at various places in the brickwork (one can be seen in some photographs under a gable) and two of these, one in stone and one in terracotta, were saved when the buildings were demolished and are now in the Burrows Collection.

Stone block with MR logo

Terracotta block with MR logo

As mentioned earlier, the same Collection also has a coffee pot and a cup and saucer from the refreshment rooms. The Roy Burrows Collection, made up of more than 20,000 artefacts, documents and photographs relating to the Midland Railway, was moved in 2004 from Roy Burrows's private house to new accommodation, part in a Midland Railway Study Centre at the Derby Museum of Industry and History in Derby, and part at the Midland Railway Trust at Swanwick Junction, where it will be on public display.

The assembling of the collection was started in the 1950s by Roy Burrows, who is an expert on the Midland Railway. The collection passed from Roy Burrows' private ownership to a registered charity, the Roy F Burrows Midland Collection Trust, in 2000.

Interest in all Midland Railway activities is maintained by the Midland Railway Society, website www.derby.org/midland.

When the station closed the refreshment room equipment was dispersed. Some of the crockery went to a voluntary organisation in Sutton Bonington, Nottinghamshire. David Shaw himself has still got the refreshment room measuring mugs, from a gill to a quart, which were used in the bar.

The Chasewater Light Railway Society acquired the double beer engine of Gaskell and Chambers manufacture from the refreshment rooms. This beer engine was restored in the early 1970s and put on display. Later it was put into store and the Society has not been able to locate it. It is thought ice-cream trays from refreshment room also went to Chasewater as did some drinking glasses but they have not been traced. Cups and saucers at Trent were apparently “there for the taking” but the Chasewater people left these behind. But what did go to Chasewater was a large quantity of delivery notes from Warwick & Richardson's brewery at Newark, who evidently supplied beer to the refreshment rooms, and the society used to sell these.

As already noted, there were probably about 14 of the not-quite-a-totem square signs on the station, and the whereabouts of five of these are known. One is in the possession of the Trent Valley Sailing Club, one is in the possession of Trent College, one is owned by the Chasewater Light Railway.

Two are are owned by local private collectors Brian Amos and David Jones, and five more are believed to be owned by collectors.

The collection of railway memorabilia is a passion shared by many who remember the glory days of the railways. "Railways are part of the British psyche", explained the greatest expert on railway memorabilia, Ian Wright, former owner and auctioneer of Sheffield Railwayana auctions, in an interview with the author.

The first collectors emerged in the 1930s, when the first items started being made redundant. Serious collecting began in the early 1960s when people were realising that steam locomotion was going to be coming to an end. Many collectors had collected engine numbers as boys (it is very much a male preoccupation). Many started to specialise – totems, nameplates, posters, clocks, postcards.

Ian Wright had started collecting engine nameplates, and then began to go to some of the early auctions. He was at that time deputy head at Myers Grove, a 2500-pupil comprehensive school in Sheffield. He looked at ideas for raising money for the school, and decided to try a postcard fair. It was a huge success, and soon became a regular event. Later, in January 1987, he started auctions for railway memorabilia in general, and by 1990 these were so well established, the work associated with them was absorbing every spare moment. He therefore resigned his position and turned to running the auctions as a full-time job. There are four auctions a year, and details of the lots to be sold can be found on the website:

www.sheffieldrailwayana.co.uk.

Brian Amos, one of those who have made a considerable contribution to this book, is a knowledgeable collector. Brian was born in 1942 in Long Eaton. His father spent 50 years on the railway, mostly at Toton, first as a guard, then in the Traffic Office, then as a yard inspector until he retired in 1963. As a child was taken round the sheds and so was interested in railways from the age of five. Later he went into engine numbering, then in the 1960s started in railway photography. When railways were disposing of signage in 1967-1968 they had sales of old signs in a warehouse.

Brian Amos bought some totems, four in one day (Codnor Park, Pye Bridge, Stanton gate and Westhouses & Blackwell from the Erewash Valley line) and eventually acquired an example of a totem from every Erewash Valley station. He also has the track layout plan, hand-drawn on linen, from the Trent North signal box.

Brian Amos (left) with the author in the garden of his home at Breaston in Derbyshire. Photograph by Judy Wheldon.

In this country there are thought to be about 500 serious totem collectors and probably another 500 less serious.

When Dr Richard Beeching produced that famous report over 40 years ago, it looked as if the railway tide was distinctly ebbing. Yet here we are in the 21st century, and it looks as if the tide is coming in again. Heritage railway systems have never been more popular. Within a 15 mile radius of the site of Trent Station we have the growing Midland Railway Centre at Butterley, the emerging Nottinghamshire Heritage Railway Centre at Ruddington, and the thriving Great Central Railway at Loughborough.

Nottingham and Sheffield are two of several cities in Great Britain which have reintroduced tramway systems, in some cases using old railway lines.

As a result of the Beeching cuts Mansfield, the second largest town in Nottinghamshire, came to share with Gosport in Hampshire the melancholy distinction of being the largest town in England not to have direct access to a passenger rail service. In 1964 booking clerk John Meade sold the last ticket at Mansfield station before it closed. However, on February 2, 2001, John Meade was brought out of retirement for one day, to sell the first ticket from a newly refurbished Mansfield station, now reconnected with Nottingham through the Robin Hood line.

There were two other stations on the Midland Railway system which, like Trent Station, were mainly built as interchanges, Hellifield in Yorkshire, and Carnforth in Lancashire. Hellifield was scheduled for closure in the Beeching Report, and Carnforth was destined to be reduced to a very minor status, almost a bus stop. The buildings at Hellifield were saved, just in time.

But a visit to Hellifield is a reminder of the grandeur of Midland Railway architecture, for the station buildings are intact, Grade II listed status having been obtained. Like Trent Station Hellifield station is approached along a narrow lane, and the island platform has to be accessed by an underpass. Another resemblance is the glorious expanse of glass canopy over the platforms. Unfortunately the ordinary rail passenger or member of the public has no access to the main station buildings, which have been rented out as private offices, and the greater part of the station is fenced off. The public is now confined to one end of the platform.

Carnforth has fared better, since it was the setting for one of the best-known and best-loved films of all time, *Brief Encounter*. At one time it was threatened with large-scale demolition, but this elicited so much protest that the opposite has happened, and part of the station has been restored as it was at the time of the film (1944-45). This includes the refreshment room in which a number of key scenes in the film take place. A visit to the refreshment room at Carnforth Station can illustrate to some extent what the refreshment room at Trent Station may have looked like.

It is unfortunate that Trent Station did not manage to survive long enough to get Grade II listed status for its Midland Gothic architecture and its curiosity value. It can only live on in the memories of an older generation who worked there or who used it as passengers, in a few mementoes, in the pages of this book, and on the author's website (www.geoffreykingscott.co.uk). This website will be used to report on any new information or photographs which may come to light as a result of the publication of this book.

Trent Station in its last autumn, photographed by Brian Amos in September 1967.

Works consulted

Amos, Brian: *Toton marshalling yards and locomotive sheds*, in *Railway Collectors' Journal*, no.139, 2004, ISSN 1476-9611.

Amos, Brian: *Trent Station – an overview*, in *Railway Collectors' Journal*, no.140, 2005, ISSN 1476-9611.

Beeching Report: *see British Railways Board – The Reshaping of British Railways.*

Brennand, Dave and Richard Furness: *The Book of British Railways Station Totems*, published by Sutton Publishing Limited, Stroud, 2002. ISBN 0 7509 2997 9.

British Railways Board: *The Reshaping of British Railways*, published by Her Majesty' Stationery Office, 1963.

Cross, Malcolm: *Departure indicator at Trent*, in *Midland Record*, no. 5, 1996, ISSN 1357-6399.

Ellis, Hamilton: *The Midland Railway*, published 1953 by Ian Allan Ltd.

Guise, Richard: *Lead us not into Trent Station*, published 2003 by Richard Guise.

Heath, John, ed.: *A brief history of Long Eaton and Sawley, from 1750 to 1914*, 1967.

Higginson, Mark (compiler): *The Midland Counties Railway, 1839-1989, A Pictorial Survey*, published by the Midland Railway Trust, Ripley, 1989.

Nottingham Evening Post, May 30, 1939, Centenary of opening Nottingham's first railway.

Henton, J.F.: *London Midland, Steam in the East Midlands*, published by D. Bradford Barton Limited, Truro, 1975. ISBN 0 85153 207 1.

Midland Railway: *Midland Railway scenery, industries, history*, an illustrated volume placed in Midland Railway carriages for the use of the travelling public, published by Bemrose & Sons Ltd, Derby, 1902.

Orton, David and others: *Trent Valley Sailing Club, The First Hundred Years*, limited edition publication.

Reedman, Keith: *The Book of Long Eaton*, published 1979 by Barracuda Books Ltd.

Sanderson, *Sanderson's Map, 20 miles round Mansfield, 1835*, reprinted by Nottinghamshire County Council, 2001.

Simmons, Jack: *The Victorian railway*, published 1991 by Thames and Hudson, ISBN 0-500-27840-7.

Smith, Warren: *The problems of train regulation – a study of operation at Trent*, published in *Trains Illustrated*, March 1961.

Tarver, M.A.J., *Trent College 1868-1927, a rough sketch*, published by G. Bell and Sons Ltd, London, 1929.

Vanns, Michael A.: *Rail Centres: Nottingham*, published by Ian Allan Ltd 1993.

Wade, H.: *A famous railway junction of forty years ago: Trent Station, Midland Railway*, in *Railway Magazine*, 1906, pp 418-423.

Williams, F.S.: *The Midland Railway, its rise and progress*, 1876.

Williams, Roy: *The Midland Railway – a new history*, published 1988 by David & Charles, Newton Abbot.

Web sites

Hornby Railway Collectors' Association: www.hrca.net

Midland Railway Society: www.midlandrailwaysociety.org.uk.

Sheffield Railwayana: www.sheffieldrailwayana.co.uk

Trent Station: see www.geoffreykingscott.co.uk

Trent Station - The Junction for Everywhere

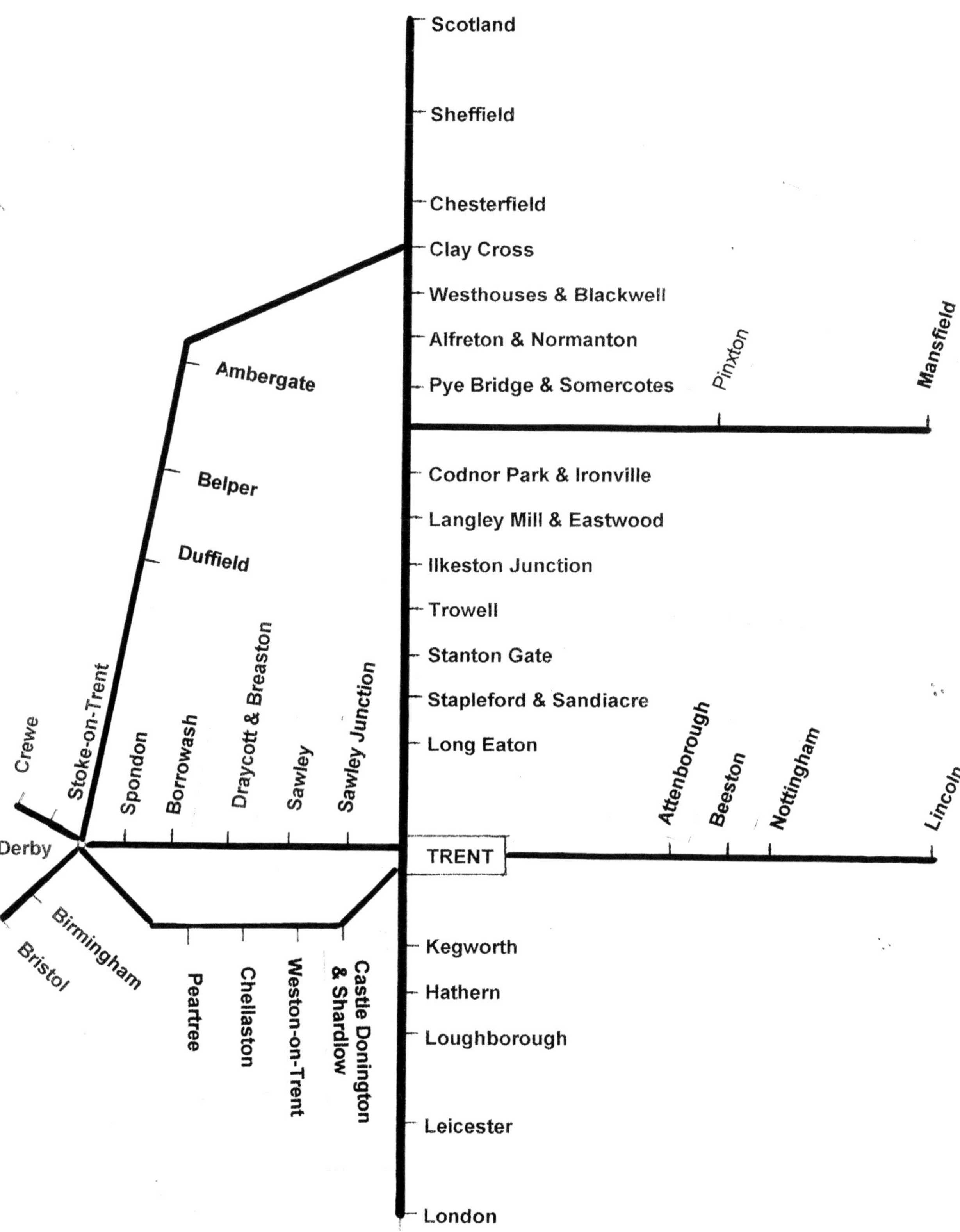

An attempt at a diagrammatic representation (as with a London Underground map) of the lines converging on Trent Station.

The DEATH and RESURRECTION of St HELEN'S, ESTON and the OLD CHURCHES of CLEVELAND

Together with an appendix detailing their remarkable

CROSS SLABS

Peter F Ryder

Published by Broomlee Publications

ISBN 978-0-9559093-2-0

Printed by Tees Archaeology/Hartlepool Borough Council

http://www.teesarchaeology.com/

Contents

Pre-Script

1.	Introduction	1
2.	Cleveland	3
3.	St Helen's Church, Eston: Background and History	6
4.	The Old St Helen's; the church as it last stood at Eston	11
5.	The Deconstruction: A Treasure House of Evidence	15
6.	St Helen's Today	19
7.	A Cautionary Tale	22

8. The Old Churches of Cleveland: A Gazetteer 23

Acklam, Bilsdale, Brotton, Crathorne, Danby, *Easington, Egton, Faceby,* Great Ayton, Guisborough, Hilton, *Hinderwell, Ingleby Arncliffe,* Ingleby Greenhow, *Kildale, Kirkleatham,* Kirklevington, Kirkby-in-Cleveland, Liverton, Lythe, Marske-by-the-Sea, Marton, *Middlesbrough,* Newton-under-Roseberry, Ormesby, Osmotherley, Roxby, Rudby, *Seamer,* Skelton, Stainton, Stokesley, Upleatham, *Westerdale* Whitby, Whorlton, Wilton, Yarm

(italics indicate rebuilt church on medieval site, but with significant non-structural earlier remains)

9. Cleveland Churches, Norman to Churchwarden – a unique regional character 62

Post script 67

Appendix: The Cross Slabs of Cleveland. 69

Acknowledgements

A lot of people need to be thanked. My wife Elaine for tolerating this project, the latter stages of which were conducted at our own expense, my daughter Megan for proof-reading, Cleveland friends who provided hospitality during the recent fieldwork – Gaynor and Alan, and Avril, and all the Cleveland church folk, incumbents and churchwardens, who opened their buildings and encouraged the fieldworker. To Robin Daniels and Tees Archaeology for support, and a generous grant towards publication costs, and of course, to the North of England Open Air Museum, who rehomed what would have been a lost church. And finally, and in particular, this book is dedicated to

Jim Rees

On whom the mantle of Nehemiah, the restorer of broken walls, fell, and without whose drive and enthusiasm St Helen's Church would by now have been a footnote in history. He has done a Good Thing.

Peter Ryder March 2016

Pre-Script

From a wrecked cemetery chapel to a museum showpiece visited by thousands - In which the writer briefly relates how he first visited St Helen's Church, and the happy circumstances which led to the rescue of the building – and also to his writing this book

---

It was the 1st April (perhaps an appropriate date) 1991 that I first visited St Helen's Church at Eston. Being raised in Darlington, not too far away, and having a lifelong interest in old churches, it is perhaps surprising that I had not been there before – but St Helen's was very much on the fringe of what would be regarded as an historic church. Some standard texts such as 'The Little Guide' volume for the North Riding did not even mention it; others gave it a line or two. Nikolaus Pevsner's 'Building of England' volume commented 'the chancel has medieval masonry', so I decided to check it out. What I found was frankly a bit disappointing - an abandoned and vandalised church in a cemetery, boarded up without any hope of entry. But I did find a couple of pieces of medieval grave slabs built into the walls, and make a few sketches in my notebook.

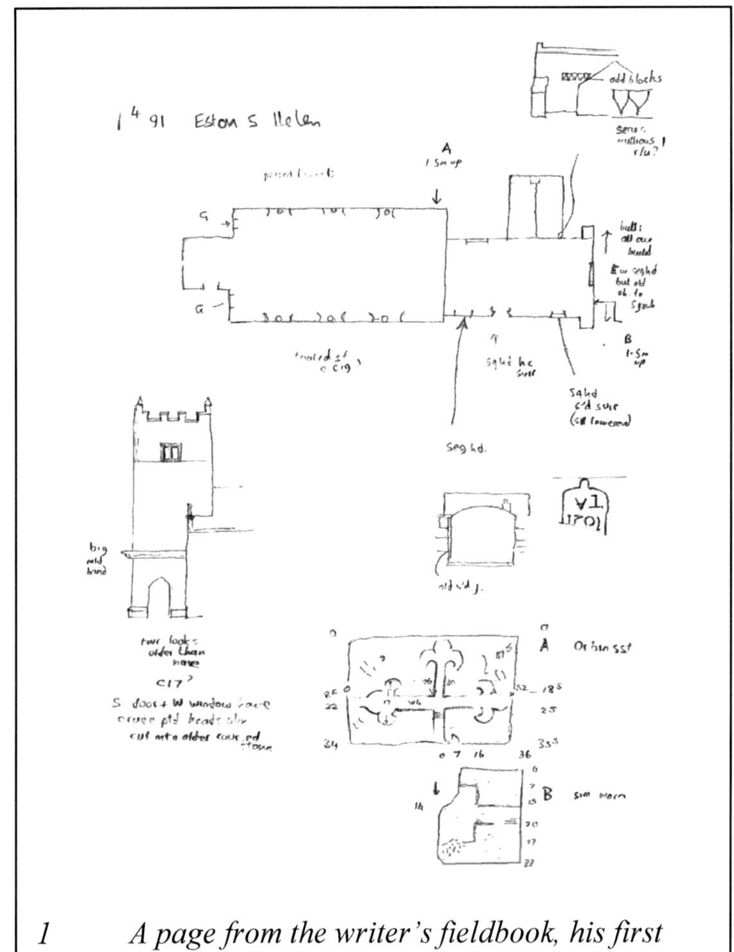

1 *A page from the writer's fieldbook, his first visit to Eston on 1st April 1991.*

Seven years later my mother sent me a press cutting, to the effect that St Helen's was to be demolished. The vandals had won; local authorities just could not keep them out, and the building had been completely wrecked, so, listing notwithstanding, with regret they were acquiescing to the inevitable…. That was awfully sad news – for a medieval church, however minor, to be pulled down, the oldest building in a parish to be erased from its landscape, just seems a defeat. I made a couple of phone calls, the first to Jim Rees at Beamish (the North of England Open Air Museum near Stanley, County Durham). Jim was interested; Beamish were looking to create a Georgian village, and the nave at least of St Helen's was a very typical late Georgian piece; Eston, being south of the Tees, was outside of the museum's 'catchment area' and he would not otherwise have heard of it. I also rang the chief planning officer for Redcar and Cleveland Council (who had reluctantly given permission for the impending demolition) and he turned out to be Alan Adams, an old friend from the days we both worked in South Yorkshire. So connections were made.

One thing led to another until in September and October 1998 a team descended on the wrecked church, now only a gutted shell, and systematically took it to pieces, numbering up the stones for future reassembly – and I ended up as archaeologist to the project. It turned out to be a fascinating few weeks.

At the end of it all St Helen's was reduced to an expanse of numbered stones stacked on wooden pallets sitting in a field at Beamish. No actual date for its reconstruction was scheduled – and, for a frustratingly long time, that is how things remained. Jim moved away to work in York and no-one else it seemed was interested – until, a decade or so on, he returned to become Assistant Director of Development at the Museum, and threw all his energies into rebuilding St Helen's, a man of Quaker sympathies resurrecting a steeple house…[1] And so it came to pass that in November 2015 the finished building, complete with appropriate fittings and furnishings brought in from all over the country, was reopened by the Bishop of Durham. Many people are already saying that it is their favourite building on the museum site. St Helen's lives on and what it is to become now, and how the building might be used, has perhaps yet to be seen; this is not the end of its story, but certainly a point at which that story is worth telling…

2 St Helen's Church, Eston. South east view in the early 20th century (reproduced by permission of Normanby Local History Group).

[1] A term of abuse used by early Nonconformists, who did not like church buildings; radical Quakers used to burst into Anglican services and shout 'come down hireling!' at the clergyman in the pulpit.

1. Introduction

In which the aims and intentions of this book are set out – the strange story of St Helen's, Eston – the three levels of looking at an old building - the old churches of Cleveland, a remarkable group

---

St Helen's Church was hardly an architectural gem; it made a Grade II listing, no more. Even a Victorian building has to be pretty average if it does not make it that far, these days. Other than a little masonry in the chancel and west wall nothing remained of the original medieval building at Eston, the ancient nave of which had been reconstructed in 1822 in the 'churchwarden' style so typical of the area, whilst the west tower was of 17th-century date. The careful dismantling of the structure however released a treasure trove of finds and information; much of the decorative stonework of the Norman nave had been pragmatically recycled in the core of the 1822 walls, along with lots of pieces of medieval monuments. Many of these stones have been re-set in the recreated church, where they can be inspected by visitors.

It has been said that that there are broadly three levels at which one can investigate an old building. Level one is the 'guidebook writer' approach – a brief glimpse at the obvious architectural features and a date, often incorrect, ascribed. A level two involves a careful look at fabric and features, along with readily available documents and old maps. It often produces more questions than answers, and usually shows the building to be much more complicated than you first thought. And, just occasionally, there comes along an opportunity for a level three analysis, when you actually get the chance to literally take the building to bits. A good example is the ruined parish church at Wharram Percy on the Yorkshire Wolds, in a deserted medieval village which saw many seasons of detailed archaeological work; the investigation of the church alone spawned a substantial tome of a report. Eston was almost in the same class, except here the below-ground archaeology has been left undisturbed for another generation; it was the standing fabric that really was taken to bits, and every piece of information retrieved that the available resources allowed.

For the writer, who acted as archaeologist on this deconstruction project, getting to know St Helen's so well prompted a look around for comparative material in the other old churches of Cleveland. As a group, Cleveland churches have a near-unique character. Many – away from the industrial fringe of Teesside that had engulfed Eston - are set in beautiful rural landscapes, and built in the richly-coloured yellow, orange and brown sandstones provided by the local Jurassic strata. Churches of a region often share a common history linked to regional economic fortunes, and Cleveland is a classic case. Right on the East Coast, this was an area of Viking settlement, evidence for which survives both in place names, and also in carved stones. The earliest standing buildings come from soon after the Norman Conquest, when the new landowners build a scatter of castles and many stone churches; most are small but there are some architectural gems such as the stunning chancel arch at Liverton. The later medieval period was quiet – unlike in the Pennines further west, where money from the emergent textile industry allowed churches to be rebuilt and enlarged. After the Reformation came remodellings in what was termed the 'churchwarden' style, a term used in a derisory manner by the Victorians who saw an idealised Gothic as the only acceptable style for Christian churches, and despised its humble nature. Yet for reasons discussed later, the region escaped the excesses of Victorian restoration, which resulted in its churches preserving 17th and 18th-century features which today are viewed with more appreciative eyes. If restoration came it often came late, and at the hands of architects who were inclined to treat all phases of the building with respect, as Temple Moore so memorably did at Danby.

So the aim of this book is first to tell the story of St Helen's Church, Eston, and then in its second part to look more briefly at twenty-five other Cleveland churches which remain as standing, fully or in part, medieval buildings, and also thirteen others where the medieval fabric has gone but significant features or monuments have been retained. Its third part is a little different, although linked to both others. Eston and many other Cleveland churches have collections of medieval cross slab grave covers, the commonest form of medieval monument to survive but one which has received relatively little attention. It has been the writer's pleasure to visit all of the old churches in the area, over the last thirty years or so, and make scale drawings of these fascinating slabs – so this book provides an opportunity to publish these, not in the form of an academic treatise but because they are attractive and most interesting stones and deserve a wider audience.

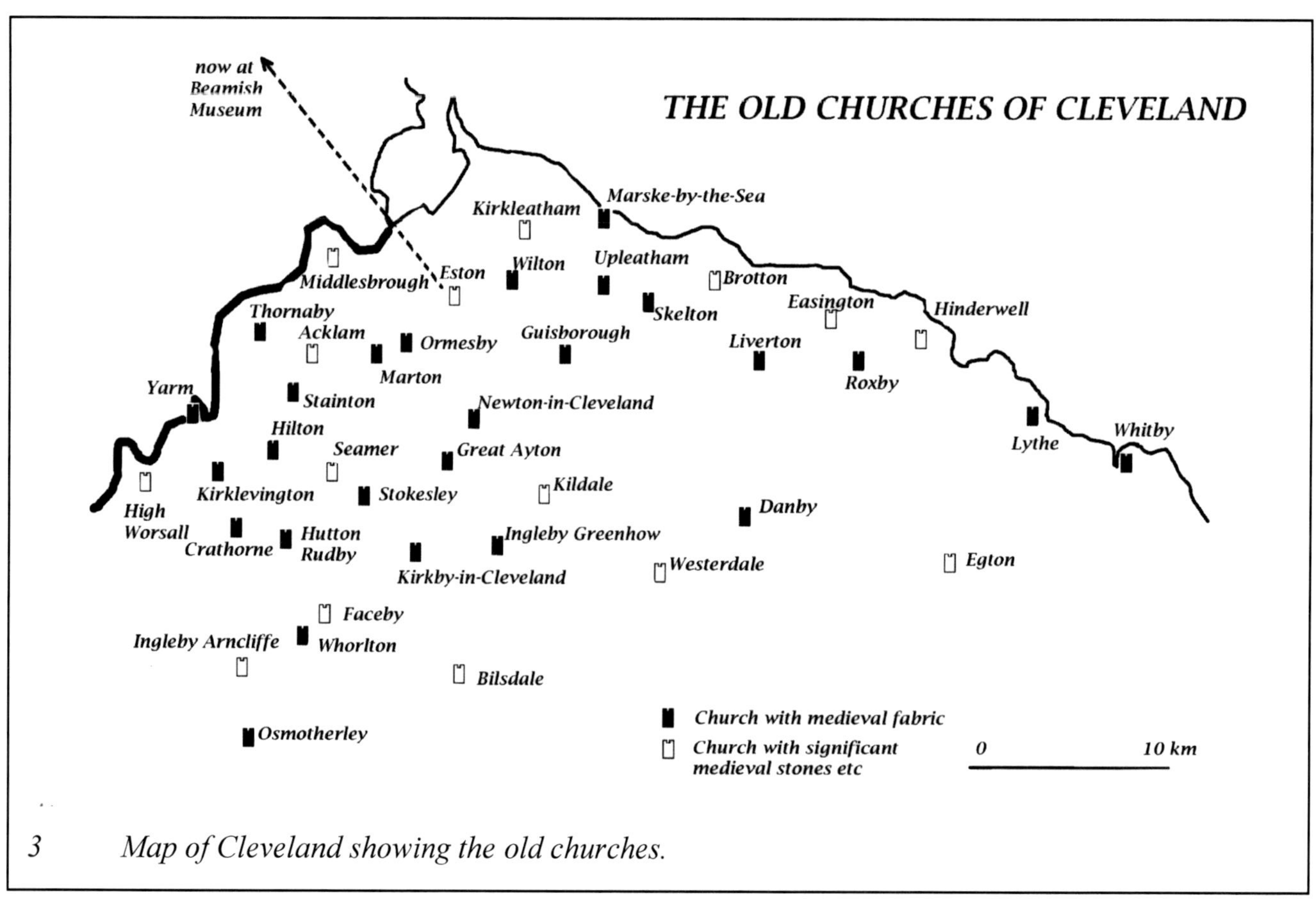

3 *Map of Cleveland showing the old churches.*

2. Cleveland

What is Cleveland? – putative boundaries - the Wapentake of Langbaurgh - a short-lived modern county - the landscape and geology – the real 'Jurassic Coast' – the history – Prehistory – Anglo Saxons and Vikings - the Norman Conquest and the Great Transition – the oldest buildings

---

The name 'Cleveland' is an ancient one, as ancient as the Danes who coined it. 'Cliff-land' could refer either to the great cliffs of the coast between Whitby and Saltburn, or the continuing thousand-foot escarpment bounding the North York Moors. Omnipresent on the southern horizon of the Teesside conurbation, this wooded rampart curves round towards Osmotherley then marches on southwards as the east flank of the Vale of York. The southern boundary of the area is formed by the valley of the Esk,[2] bisecting the moors from west to east and flowing out to the sea at Whitby.

Anciently the name 'Cleveland' was applied to the Anglo-Saxon land division of the Wapentake[3] of Langbaurgh (taking its name from what is now a hamlet to the north of Great Ayton).[4] However in the last half century it has been applied to a number of different areas. The area covered by this book was anciently a small part of the great North Riding of Yorkshire. Its northern part was included in the short-lived County of Cleveland created in 1974, which also purloined part of the historic County Durham, the industrialised lowlands on the north of the Tees, as far as Hartlepool. The county was abolished in 1996, but the 'Cleveland' name lives on in an Archdeaconry of the Church of England (covering a much wider area), the non-metropolitan district of Redcar and Cleveland, and the name of the local police force. The long-established Cleveland Hunt ranges over very much the same area of land as here chosen.

The Landscape

The bedrock of all landscape is of course geology, and the geology of the North York Moors is Jurassic, predominantly marine strata – shales and sandstones – laid down approximately 200 – 150 million years ago; the coastal cliffs are famous for their wealth of fossils. Alum has been mined, mainly along the coast, from the beginning of the 17th century; later on the mining of jet became popular in the 19th century - following Queen Victoria's predilection for jet jewellery - and more recently still ironstone mining was a mainstay of the urban growth of Teesside, peaking in the 1880s to finally stutter to a halt another eighty years later as heavy chemical industries took over its role. Today potash is mined at Boulby; at the time of writing a deep tunnel is planned to take the mined material far beneath the National Park and deliver it to the industry of Teesside.

At the mouth of the Tees this industrial conurbation sprawls east across the base of Eston Nab, but behind this a belt of farmland and affluent commuter villages running south-west develops in between the

---

[2] Not always thought of as Cleveland, although Canon Atkinson's 1891 classic, 'Forty years in a Moorland Parish' quotes 'Danby-in-Cleveland' in its subtitle.

[3] Yorkshire was divided into its three Ridings (original 'Thridings', i.e. thirds) and these were further divided into 'wapentakes', thought to derive from 'weapons touch' which would centre on an assembly point, where a vote could be taken by a show of weapons. Politics is done a bit differently now, but the wapentakes only slipped out of the administrative system at the end of the 19th century.

[4] Of the churches covered by this book, only Osmotherley and Bilsdale are outside the original Wapentake (from which Whitby Liberty was separated early in the post-Conquest period). Appleton Wiske, out in the lowlands at the head of the Vale of York, is in the Wapentake but not included here.

escarpment and the urban agglomeration to the north. Guisborough, the largest old town in the area, lies in a fold of the hills 8 miles south-east of Middlesbrough; beyond it is the best-known physical feature of Cleveland, the acute little cone of Roseberry Topping, a miniature Matterhorn which draws the eye in much the same way as Croagh Patrick does in north-west Ireland. Not far west is the market town of Stokesley, from which the road south to Helmsley scales the escarpment east of Hasty Bank, first of a series of four prominent hills rising to around 400 m, making up the south-eastern skyline familiar over much of County Durham. Then, beyond the mouth of Scugdale at Swainby, guarded by the Whorl Hill topped by Whorlton Castle, the wooded scarp of Arncliffe Wood curves south with the A19 trunk road, linking Teesside to York, at its foot, to Osmotherley, here taken as the south-west corner of the area covered by this book. The land behind the escarpment is less dramatic, rolling heathery moorland rising to a high point of Urra Moor at 454 m and bisected by valleys, in the east tributaries of the Esk, in the west feeders of the Rye draining south to Helmsley and the Vale of Pickering.

South-east of the mouth of the Tees, Cleveland provides one of England's most characterful stretches of coastline. The lowland around the estuary ends abruptly at Saltburn, beyond which the red Huntcliff is the first of an almost continuous wall of cliffs cut in fossil-rich Jurassic strata[5] which extend beyond Whitby, and are interrupted only by occasional narrow valleys still clearing themselves of glacial boulder clay. Boulby Cliff is the highest point, rising to over 200 m, between the industrialised port of Skinningrove and the traditional fishing village of Staithes; the modern potash mine contrasts with the older works for alum, jet and ironstone, the remains of which dot the area.

The Esk valley, here taken as the southern boundary of Cleveland, deserves special mention. Its mouth at Whitby is eroded on the line of a geological fault throwing the Estuarine sandstones of the West Cliff against the earlier Lias beds of the taller East Cliff, site of a Saxon settlement and the town's famous Abbey. Inland the Esk has many tributary valleys, especially on the south, including Eller Beck, Glaisdale and the wonderfully-named Great Fryup Dale. Above Castleton Eskdale divides into Commondale, Glaisdale and other headwaters. Villages, mostly small, all nestle in the valleys with broad and bleak moors omnipresent between, dotted with prehistoric burial mounds, and the occasional later wayside cross.

History

Whilst evidence has been found of Mesolithic hunter gatherers, the earliest really significant sign of human presence in the Cleveland landscape comes in the Bronze Age, with the hundreds of cairns and round barrows often set on the rounded ridge tops. There was Iron Age settlement too – Eston Nab has a fine hill fort – when herding cattle became the prime economic activity. The Romans seem to have kept a relatively low profile hereabouts, except for establishing a chain of signal stations on the high points of the coast, including Huntcliff and Goldsborough (near Kettleness); further down the line an excavated example can be seen at Scarborough Castle. Then came the Anglo-Saxon and Viking settlements, which provide the earliest of the artefacts seen in the region's old churches. Hilda's monastery at Whitby was established in 657; there were other early monasteries at Hackness, 25 km south of Whitby, and Hartlepool just north of the mouth of the Tees. Apart from excavated evidence at Whitby itself, nothing is known of any Pre-Norman church building in Cleveland, although pieces of stone sculpture of this period, and especially those relating to the incoming and rapidly Christianised Vikings, are found in many places; there is a notable collection of early stones at Loftus.

[5] Every much as classic a section of 'Jurassic Coast' as that of the South West, which has heinously hijacked this title.

The earliest standing church buildings date from the years after the Norman Conquest, when other monasteries sprang up to join the Benedictine Whitby. The Augustinian Priory of Gisborough and the Carthusian Charterhouse of Mount Grace on the western edge of Cleveland have left substantial remains but the smaller priories at Grosmont, Baysdale and Handale barely any traces. The new Norman landowners – the de Brus family predominant - built their own castles as well; dramatic ruins survive at Kilton and Mulgrave, both perched on steep-sided ridges in valleys close to the coast, and further west at Whorlton. There are also earthworks at Castleton, Easby and Castle Levington as well as extensive ruins of a later courtyard castle or fortified manor house at Danby. But the majority of surviving medieval buildings are churches, twenty five within the area here covered, along with thirteen more which have been rebuilt but retain significant features from their predecessors – often carved stones, either Pre-Conquest pieces or, like Eston, collections of medieval cross slabs. This great transition period in the landscape, and the locations chosen for churches, have been ably discussed in a paper by Robin Daniels which is essential reading for anyone really interested in the history of the area.[6]

The Middle Ages came to a traumatic end in the religious and political storms of the 16th century, the Reformation bringing a major shift in emphasis within Christian worship from the Sacrament to the Word. The old churches remained in use (unlike in Scotland) but were adapted for new purposes - by the 18th century spacious 'preaching box' naves had become the norm and the pulpit rather than the altar became the liturgical focus. Only occasionally were churches actually rebuilt, for example at Kirkleatham where the Turner family built a splendid family mausoleum, and soon after a new church to go with it. More commonly the old churches were retained but windows were enlarged, with sashes replacing decaying medieval tracery, and galleries were inserted to increase seating capacity as developing industries – alum, iron and then jet mining – prompted population growth. The same industries saw the explosive urban growth of the 19th century when Middlesbrough mushroomed from the single farmhouse that had succeeded its small medieval priory into the sprawling conurbation of modern Teesside.

And now the world has moved on again. Ironstone production peaked in 1883, then declined; the last mine, North Skelton, closed in 1964; the painful and slow death of the steel industry took another half century. The only extractive industry is the new one of deep potash mining. The old churches have by and large survived, although for Eston, as these pages relate, that has meant a move away from its native Cleveland.

6 Robin Daniels (1996). Ruralia I, Památky archeologické – Supplementum , Praha , available online at http://www.ruralia.cz/sites/default/files/doc/pdf/102-114.pdf.

3. St Helen's Church, Eston: Background and History

Origins shrouded in mystery - a Roman garrison chapel? A Sacred Well? Written History begins – the Domesday Book – a few documentary references – the first antiquarian records- the Churchwarden Era - 1822 reconstruction of the nave – the 19th century – replaced by a new parish church, not once but twice – the sad years of decline – last minute rescue the church reconstructed at Beamish

---

Beginnings

As with the great majority of our old churches, the actual beginnings of Eston church remain shrouded in mystery. There is plentiful evidence in the form of carved stones – lapidary material to be technical - that there was a chapel here in the 12th century, but before that - only surmise.

It is quite likely that there was a Saxon church here, although no actual hard-and-fast evidence of this has yet been found. Several Saxon carved stones are re-used in the walls of the parish church of St Cuthbert in Ormesby village, and its dedication suggests a link with the wanderings of the Cuthbert Community after they had fled the Viking onslaughts on Holy Island, in the 9th century. At Eston, originally a chapel of Ormesby, the dedication to St Helen is interesting, and could imply a still-earlier date. Helen or Helena (c250-330) was the mother of the Emperor Constantine. She was claimed as a Briton in popular tradition, and was said to have travelled to Jerusalem, where the ghost of Judas is said to have led her to the burial place of the True Cross, thousands of claimed fragments of which found their way as relics across Europe – so it could be that one was brought here. There was in fact some possible evidence, of the most tentative kind, for this, which we will consider later.

So the dedication just might imply a Roman origin, although the suggestion of Canon Stevenson, vicar 1937-1946, that this implies that the church was originally a 'garrison chapel of the Roman legions'[7] seems fanciful to the extreme. There is another explanation of St Helen dedications; holy wells are often dedicated to her, but it has been claimed that this is because they were originally shrines to a Celtic water deity called Elen, and they were later Christianised by only a slight change of name… Was there a well here?[8] Cross Beck flows along the south and then east sides of the churchyard, and near the corner there is a substantial drain cover; does this

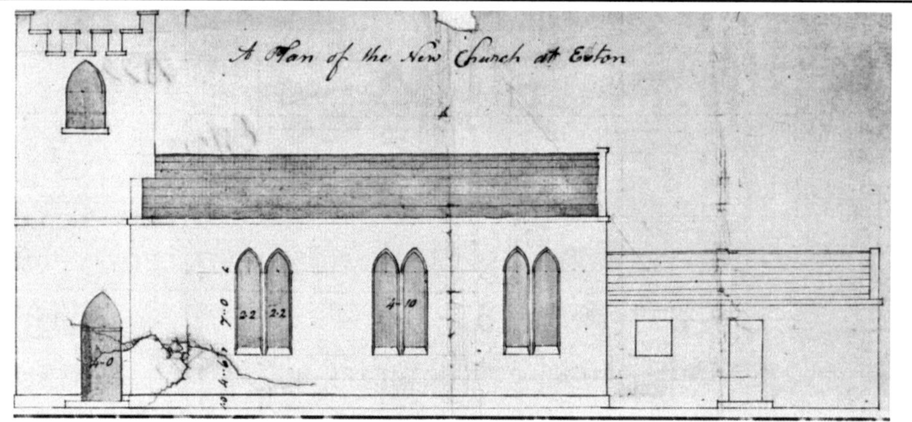

4 1822 faculty drawing, showing the nave as it was rebuilt, but a new tower as well, which was never constructed (reproduced by permission of the North of England Open Air Museum, Beamish).

---

[7] Quoted in Wilson, Maurice E, The Story of Eston (1972) 13-14.

[8] Beamish have created an 'Elen's Well' at the foot of the churchyard wall, but this is a product of optimistic antiquarianism I am afraid, not fact.

conceal a spring?

Eston enters Recorded History

It is only at the time of the Norman Conquest that written history kicks in; in the Domesday Book we are told that a Saxon called Waltef had held a manor here, which by 1086 was included in the many possessions of Robert, Count of Mortain (c1031-1090), half brother to William the Conqueror and second Earl of Cornwall. The earliest written mentions of the church itself come a little later – in 1253 the advowson of the 'Chapel of Eston'- the right to nominate a priest – occasioned a dispute between Stephen de Menyl and the Prior of Guisborough,[9] although the earliest reference to a priest actually being appointed comes as late as 1545. As often, there are early complaints of the building not being properly maintained; in 1575 the chancel was not 'in sufficient reparation' and in 1595 it was 'in great decay'; in 1663 two men were summoned for 'not repairing their chapel'.

The Medieval Church

Our first account of the actual building comes in John Graves' 'History of Cleveland' (1808, 447). 'The chapel is a small but ancient edifice, consisting of a nave and chancel, with a strong square tower; which, as well as the body of the chancel, appears to be of a more modern construction than the body of the chapel. The chancel is separated by a circular arch; and the entrance by the door on the south is partly walled up, and the upper part converted into a small window; the zigzag mouldings of the arch, which is circular, rising from a capital, and round pillars, discover this part of the building to be of great antiquity'.

The Churchwarden Era

In 1822 the old Norman nave was taken down and rebuilt in what has locally been termed the 'Churchwarden' style. Many churches in the area had their naves remodelled in the later 18th and early 19th centuries; it was the era of the 'Preaching Box', when in theological terms the Word had the dominance over the Sacrament, and the function of the church nave was to allow as many worshippers to hear the preacher as possible. The earlier remodellings or rebuildings were in a simple Classical style – e.g. Whitby in 1764 and Stokesley in 1771, but by the early 19th century a simplified version of the Gothic was coming into vogue, such as was used at Eston. The faculty for the 1822 works thankfully survives;[10] unfortunately the only drawings are for the proposed new building; later faculties often containing drawings of the church as it stood before works began. The 1822 drawings from Eston are signed by a William Lockwood and, as often, are somewhat at variance with the actual end product. The faculty gives permission 'to take away and cause to be removed the whole of the present chapel' (except the chancel); the new nave was to be of the same dimensions as its predecessor but to be two feet higher, with a 'loft or gallery' spanning the west end; a new vestry was to be built on the north of the chancel, and it was intended to erect a new tower, although the old one was in fact retained. The new parts of the building were to 'be built of stone and lime and Foreign Fir timber and covered with the best Westmorland Slates'.

---

[9] Yorkshire Archaeological Society Record Series, XVII p.74.

[10] In the Borthwick Institute at York, ref Fac 1822/36.

5 *The church decorated for a Harvest Festival, probably in the 1930s; note that the Georgian box pews have already gone (reproduced by permission of the North of England Open Air Museum, Beamish).*

Industrialisation and Urban Growth

With the mid-19th century expansion of ironstone mining in the area, Eston, previously little more than a rural hamlet, was changed forever. The transformation is illustrated by comparing the 1st edition of the Ordnance Survey map of c. 1860 and the second of c. 1890. The first shows some of the early mines and a few miners' cottages; by the second there are street after street of terraced houses in South Eston and California, and St Helen's stands in what has now become 'Eston and Normanby cemetery'. The old churchyard had been extended by three acres in 1861, with a new mortuary chapel (for nonconformists, whose chapels were multiplying throughout the area) built to the west in 1863. There were major changes for the church itself; in 1868 it passed from being a chapel of Ormesby into being a parish church in its own right, and c1870 a new east window was installed 'in place of a very poor plain barn-like' one.[11] It did not serve as a parish church for long; by 1884 this function had passed to the new Christ Church built on the main road nearer the new centre of population. Nevertheless, in 1899 the old building was renovated to serve as a cemetery chapel. The population still continued to grow, and in the early 1920s St Helen's had to be pressed into service as a parish church for a second time, this time to serve the growing settlement of 'Teesville' to the north and west, for around forty years until the new St George's Church was constructed. Although a service of 'Dedication of Rebuilding and Redecorating at St Helen's' was held on February 26th 1961,[12] the last parochial service in the church, a 6.30 evensong, came less than two years later, on December 30th 1962; the text for the sermon was Isaiah 41.8.

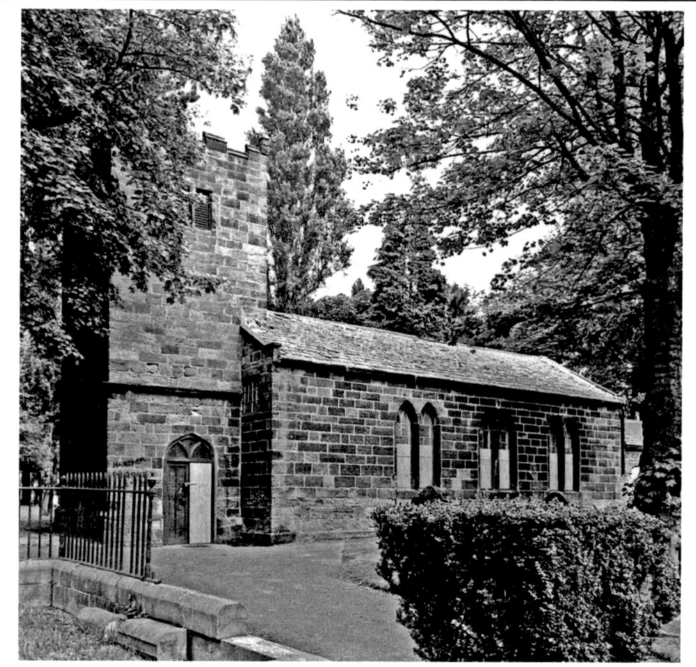

6 *St Helen's Church, Eston. South-west view in the 1980s, now derelict and sealed up (reproduced by permission of the North of England Open Air Museum, Beamish).*

Death

The next thirty years were sorry ones. St Helen's resumed its role as a cemetery chapel, now it would seem serving Anglicans and nonconformists alike; the separate chapel to

[11] Vestry Minutes 1870-2.

[12] Register of Services, Cleveland Archives, ref PRT/EST 55.

the west was in 'a very neglected state' by 1975[13] and was pulled down soon after. St Helen's itself suffered the continual attention of vandals; its last funeral was held in 1985 and by August 1987 it was 'in a critical state of disrepair'.[14] In December 1992 it was set on fire and the roof destroyed, after which the local authority sealed off the interior by bolting heavy metal plates across all openings. Listed building status did not help; vandals continued their attacks, to the extent that the 1822 vestry was removed stone-by-stone and the chancel arch and upper chancel walls were pulled down. Finally in early 1998 both the local authority and English Heritage reluctantly admitted defeat and gave permission for demolition.

Resurrection

Then, as already related, salvation came from an unexpected quarter; the North of England Open Air Museum (Beamish) stepped in and offered to 'deconstruct' the wrecked building, with the aim of reconstructing it as part of an early 19th-century village being recreated on the museum site.

7 St Helen's Church, Eston. Deconstruction 1998. The chancel looking east.

So every block of the external walls of the church was numbered, before the structure was carefully taken down in late September and early October 1998. The numbered stones were stored on pallets, and the rubble removed by skip. Archaeological recording was carried out as work proceeded; amazingly, over 200 carved and worked stones, mostly either architectural fragments or parts of medieval monuments, were retrieved, recorded and stored separately. Despite some harassment from locals – cars were broken into, cameras stolen, and the lead from the church tower roof vanished overnight – the project proved a memorable one for all concerned, several of the workmen offering their services unpaid for the reconstruction.

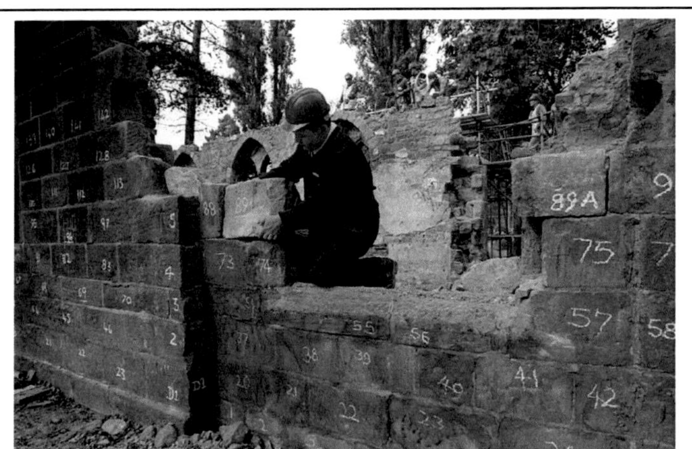

8 St Helen's Church, Eston. Deconstruction 1998. Jim Rees removes a block from the chancel wall, after numbering-up.

Then, as already recounted, came years of delay, until the project was rekindled in 2010. New drawings were prepared, and the task of reassembling the church began. St Helen's now sits on the hillside below Pockerley Manor, the one genuine medieval building already on the site before the museum began, and the 'new' Georgian village around it is already being called 'Pockerley St Helen's'. There was also the task of trawling the market to acquire ecclesiastical fittings and furnishings. Finally on Thursday 12th November 2015 the resurrected and candle-lit church was opened by the Bishop of Durham, seventeen years after its gutted shell was

[13] Singleton Church Survey 1975, which provides a useful architectural description of it.

[14] Letter from the Borough of Langbaurgh, dated August 1987, in the Council for the Care of Churches files.

removed from its original site, filled with suitably-uncomfortable box pews of 1829 that had been thankfully disposed of by a Somerset church (whose vicar was in attendance), with its recreated gallery filled by a children's choir from Eston. It was quite an occasion, especially for those who had followed the story of the building over the last seventeen years.

9 St Helen's Church, Eston. After deconstruction, the church is reduced to lots of numbered stones stacked on pallets in a field at Beamish, and a worrying few years ensued.

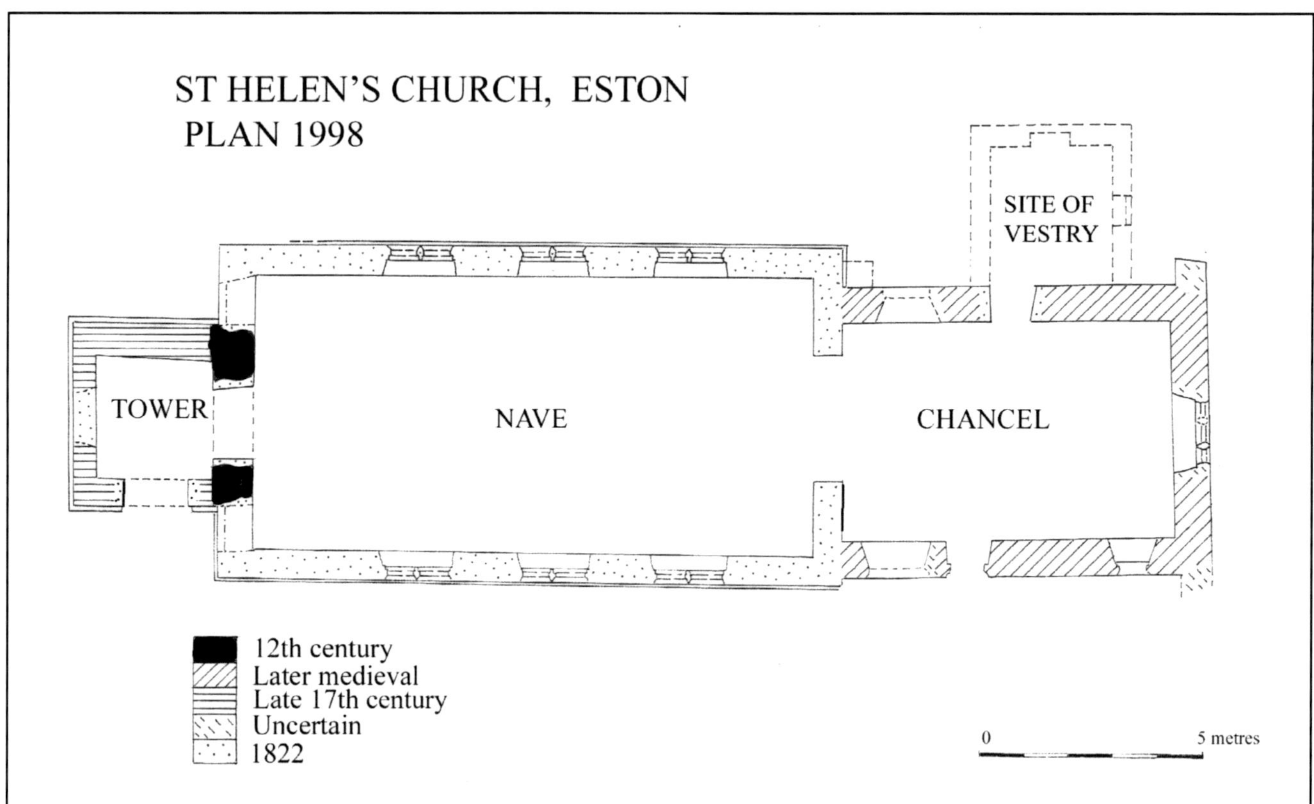

10 St Helen's Church, Eston. Ground plan in 1998. Vandals/opportunist rockery enhancers had removed the entire vestry stone-by-stone.

4. The Old St Helen's; the church as it last stood at Eston

'A small but very typical Cleveland church' – detailed descriptions – West Tower – Nave – Chancel – the Interior – Bells and Bell Frames – the Gallery – the Roof Structure

---

St Helen's is a small but very typical Cleveland parish church, consisting of a picturesque west tower, an aisleless nave with rudimentary Gothic features characteristic of what used to be termed, with an element of derision, the 'Churchwarden style' and a lower chancel with a north vestry.

The West Tower

The west tower, c. 4.2 m externally and c. 10.5 m high, was built of squared blocks of sandstone, roughly tooled in contrast to the distinctive diagonal 'diamond' tooling of the nave. There was a large chamfered plinth c. 0.70 m up, and bold moulded string course c. 3.5 m above the ground; on north and south the east end of this string had been trimmed back so as not to obstruct the gallery windows in the west wall of the nave.

The main entrance into the church was on the south side of the tower, and was a doorway with a roughly four-centred head crudely hacked into the coursed masonry, holding a pair of double doors with overlight above. It was probably an 1822 insertion replacing an older door on the west, evidenced only by straight joints breaking the plinth, and a patch of blocks with the characteristic early 19th-century diagonal tooling, below the west window which was again an insertion - it interrupted the string course and had a rough arched head like the south doorway, hacked into older walling. By the 1990s it had been walled up but old pictures show a 16-pane fixed window of 'Gothick' style, with the glazing bars intersecting in its arched head.

The belfry had simple two-light square-headed mullioned openings, in chamfered surrounds, and the tower was topped by a simple embattled parapet with a roll-moulded coping and small pyramidal finials, stepping out slightly beyond the wall-line, at each corner. The lead of the tower roof bore various incised and rouletted initials, including 'I H 1783' and 'C SMITH 1849'.

The Nave

The 1822 nave was a simple rectangle in plan, 14.2 m by 7.6 m externally; its north and south elevations had similar architectural features, but were quite dissimilar in fabric. The south wall – and south part of the west wall - were of large squared blocks of a fairly ferruginous sandstone, mostly quite elongate (but the odd squarer one) and bearing a distinctive diamond tooling; the angle quoins were no larger than the walling blocks. The north wall and north part of the west wall were of squared stone, the blocks of a variety of shapes and sizes, laid in smaller courses, with a wide range of tooling types; clearly much of this material had been re-used from the old church, and included part of a medieval cross slab (190) near the east end, 1.5 m above the ground.[15] There was a plain square ashlar plinth of shallow projection (partly buried on the north) and each side wall had three windows, each a pair of broad lancets, with chamfered surrounds; the dressings of the window heads were tooled-and-margined, except for the central block in the spandrel between the lights which was tooled but not margined. The windows themselves had been small-paned sashes, each light having a central glazing bar that divided Y-fashion at the head.

---

[15] Re-set in the same position in the rebuilt church.

The west wall had a pair of square-headed windows set high up so as to light the western gallery. At the north-east corner, set in the angle between the east wall of the nave and the north wall of the chancel, was a chimney stack, rising a metre above the eaves and having a corniced cap, serving a stove within the church. The roof was of a shallow typically Georgian pitch, and the gable ends had a flat slab coping.

The Chancel

The chancel, 8.3 m by 6.6 m externally, was considerably lower than the nave, and set markedly off-centre; it was built of coursed squared blocks, smaller than those in the nave, and lacking any distinctive tooling; all its stonework was quite badly weathered. There was no evidence of any plinth and there were short and rather primitive buttresses at the east ends of both side walls which were evidently secondary. Set a little west of the centre of the south wall was a square-headed priest's doorway, with a hollow-chamfered surround, rebated internally. West of the doorway was quite a broad window which had a shallow segmental-arched head cut from two blocks, the eastern of which was clearly a re-used piece (a lintel?) as it bore, inverted, an incised shield with the date '1621' and the initials 'T A' beneath. The west jamb of the window was chamfered, and the eastern square - evidence of alterations which became clearer when the wall was dismantled. The glazing was a simple grid of small panes, five wide and four high. Towards the east end of the wall was a single-light window with a chamfered surround, the sill of which had evidently been lowered at some time; its proportions were such that one might expect a mullion, but there was no sign of one; the lintel only bearing sockets for a pair of vertical iron bars. Close to the west end of the north wall was a plain square-headed window, holding a small-paned casement like that opposite, but in this case three panes high by four wide. Old photographs show the course above its head as having a splayed joint, perhaps one side of a 'keystone' or a keyed-supra-lintel (a practise, common in the 18th century, of relieving the weight upon a lintel by placing a wedge-shaped block in the course above). East of this was a square-headed doorway to the vestry, set rather skew to the wall. The low-pitched roof of the vestry cut through a course of around 20 triangular stones set alternately point up and point down; these were apparently sections of re-used roll-moulded coping similar to that on the tower. Below this course was a large patch of blocks with diagonal tooling, a repair to the wall made in c. 1990.

The east end of the chancel was of similar fabric to the side walls, and had a window under a shallow segmental head (like that of the western window in the south wall) but the inner ashlar frame, of three trefoil-headed lights, with trefoiled piercing in the spandrels, was clearly more recent (c1870). There were traces of a chamfer on the south jamb. Part of the stepped base of an incised cross slab (no.191), now quite faint, was built in c. 2 m above ground level to the south of the east window.

The 1822 vestry on the north of the chancel had a small window in its east wall, and a chimney stack capping its north gable.

The Interior

The principal entrance to the church was through the 1822 door on the south of the tower; a shallow recess in the west wall marked the position of an earlier doorway. It is not clear whether there was a stair in the tower (as there is in the reconstructed building); there were three floors, the lowest corresponding to the gallery in the nave, access above that may have been by ladders. In the belfry the bell frames had two parallel pits, set north-south, and were technically of the long-headed type, with king posts, braces from sill to head, and end posts.[16] The two bells are described by Stevenson;[17] one was thought to be of

[16] Pickford 1993 type 5L.

15th-century date and was inscribed 'Sancta Helena ora pro Nabis' (St Helen pray for us); it was sold and broken up in 1884, probably because it was cracked. The other, cast in 1725, is inscribed 'Jesus be our speed' and was transferred to Christ Church, where it is still in use.

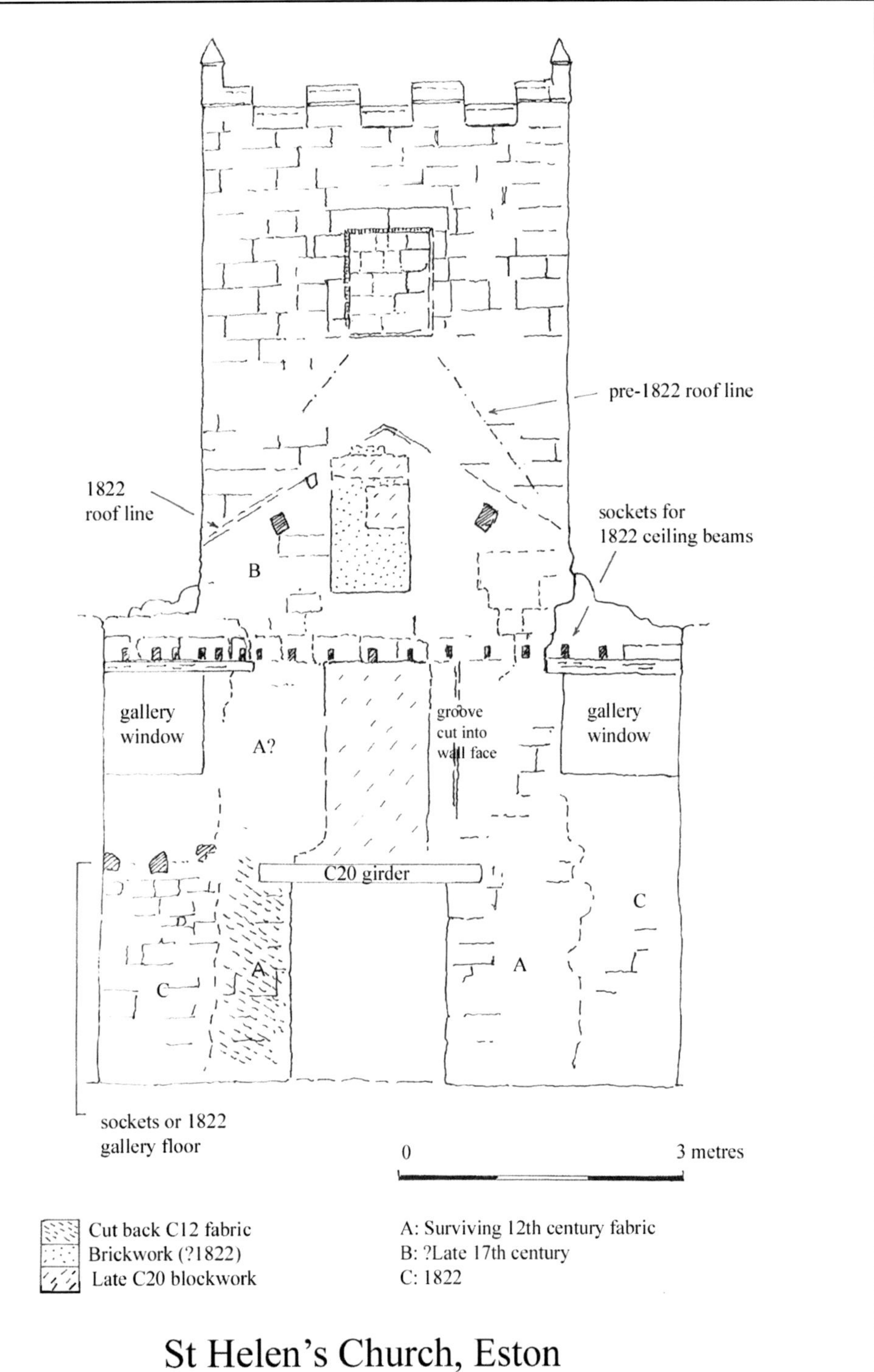

11 St Helen's Church, Eston. Drawing made during deconstruction of the west end of the nave and tower, showing multiple phases of fabric.

The internal walls of the nave were plastered; the windows in the side walls each had a single square-edged two-centred rear arch. The western gallery had completely disappeared by the time the ruined church was dismantled, but it can be reconstructed with the aid of old photographs. It appears to have had a level (rather than raked) floor, and had a front made up of two separate parts, a southern part with four fielded panels and a slightly-taller northern part with three taller panels, apparently surrounded by a beaded moulding, carried on a transverse beam which was supported by a pair of piers, perhaps cast-iron columns, with moulded capitals and pads above, flanking the central aisle of the nave. It is not clear how the gallery was originally accessed, whether by a stair in the tower (as in the reconstructed building) or by one within the body of the church. In the last phase of use of the building[18] a light stoothing partition was erected above

[17] 1948, 11.

[18] As shown on a 1983 photograph.

the front of the gallery, thus converting it into an enclosed room accessible from the tower.

The nave roof structure was of five bays, having low-pitched king-post trusses with raking struts springing from the jowelled base of the king-post; the principals were morticed and pegged into the tie-beam, but the king-post was secured by an iron bolt.

In the east wall of the nave the 1822 chancel arch was a totally plain opening with a two-centred arch of the simplest possible nature, rising from jambs of the same plain square section; all its stonework was plastered over.

The internal walls of the chancel were thoroughly plastered (over stoothing), and there was no evidence of any early ritual features such as piscinae or aumbries. There was a plain boarded dado and simple altar rails. The priest's door and the window to the east of it had large stone slabs (plastered over) as their internal lintels, but the east window had a series of old re-used timbers.

The floor of the chancel was of stone slabs, with a single step marking the sanctuary; towards the west end were more recent slabs, like those in the nave. The roof of the chancel was of three bays, with shallow-pitched collar-beam trusses; the collars were halved onto the west face of the principals, which carried two levels of staggered butt purlins and a ridge.

5. The Deconstruction: A Treasure House of Evidence

The wrecked building – the discovery of Norman walling – the complexities of the west wall – the tower compared to that at Upleatham – a Norman arcade disinterred (in pieces) – the later medieval chancel – post-medieval changes – the nave rebuilt in 1822 – the dubious Rev Moyle and his easy window

---

By the time of its deconstruction the church was a total wreck. All fittings and furnishings had gone, and charred timbers were all that remained of the roof structure and bell frames – all these were recorded to glean as much information from them as possible. The eastern corners of the nave were ruined down to more than half height, the chancel arch had been toppled (only a few weeks previously); parts of the side walls of the chancel were down, and the vestry had disappeared completely.[19]

The oldest part of the building turned out to be the central part of the west wall of the nave. The internal face of the west wall of the nave, no longer obscured by gallery and roof timbers, and having lost most of its plaster, proved an instructive piece of 'above-ground archaeology'. The broad opening into the tower, under a modern girder lintel, was of no great age, but on either side was much older masonry, roughly cut back in places, which appeared to represent an in-situ survival of part of the west end of the Norman nave; to north and south, ragged joints separated it from the outer parts of the wall rebuilt in 1822. A series of sockets marked the positions of the joists of the gallery floor, and above those were the two windows that lit the gallery, with older timbers re-used as their internal lintels and in the centre a doorway, sealed in recent blockwork, that gave access from gallery to tower; a vertical groove immediately to the north of this was probably made for a gas pipe. Then came a long series of sockets for the beams of the flat plaster ceiling of the 1822 nave, and above them an opening 1.2 m high and 0.8 m wide, blocked in old brick (with patches of recent blockwork); the manner in which the line of the shallow-pitched roof of the 1822 nave just about cuts this suggests that it is an older feature, a high-level doorway or hatch into the roof of the previous nave, the steep-pitched line of which remained clearly visible on the tower wall, its apex cut by the eastern belfry window, which had been walled up. This instructive elevation highlighted three major phases of the fabric, the 12th-century Norman nave – of which we were to learn much more from material re-used in the cores of the rebuilt nave walls – the 17th-century tower, and the 1822 rebuilding.

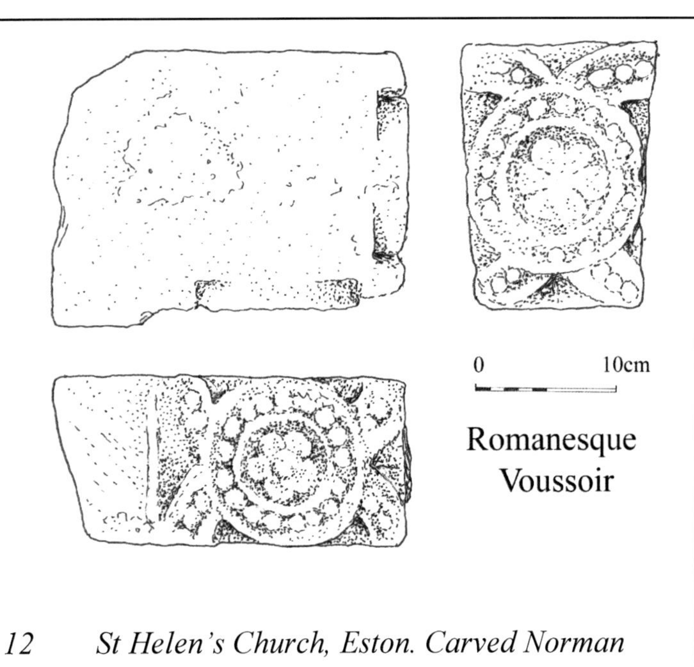

12 St Helen's Church, Eston. Carved Norman voussoir found during the deconstruction, and now re-set over the arch into the gallery in the rebuilt church.

[19] One envisaged nocturnal processions of local folk with wheel barrows gathering stone for their rockeries etc.

The precise date of the tower is not quite clear. It is obviously post-medieval – its string course is of distinctly 'Classical' section and the mullioned belfry openings are of simple vernacular type. However, another local church provides a close parallel – Upleatham has a very similar tower, although rather more slender, which offers close parallels to string course, belfry openings and parapet, and this one is helpfully provided with an inscription 'WILLIAM CROW/BVLDED STEPLE 1684'. On the strength of this it would seem reasonable to place the Eston tower in the late 17th century.

As already mentioned, it was the re-used material that allowed the Norman nave to be reconstructed, at least on paper. The 1822 faculty expressly stated that its successor was to be the same size, so we know its dimensions – the 1822 nave is 14.2 m by 7.5 m externally, although its walls at only 0.6 m thick are rather thinner than one would expect those of its predecessor to have been. Graves describes the old south door has having a round arch with zigzag ornament, and jamb shafts, and a 'round' chancel arch. Several stones were identified as coming from the chancel arch, which was tentatively reconstructed as being of at least two orders, with double-cone and billet ornament, carried on shafts, with capitals with interlace; most of these can be paralleled on the re-set chancel arch at Easington, where one capital has interlaced foliage issuing from the mouth of a grotesque, perhaps a 'Green Man'.

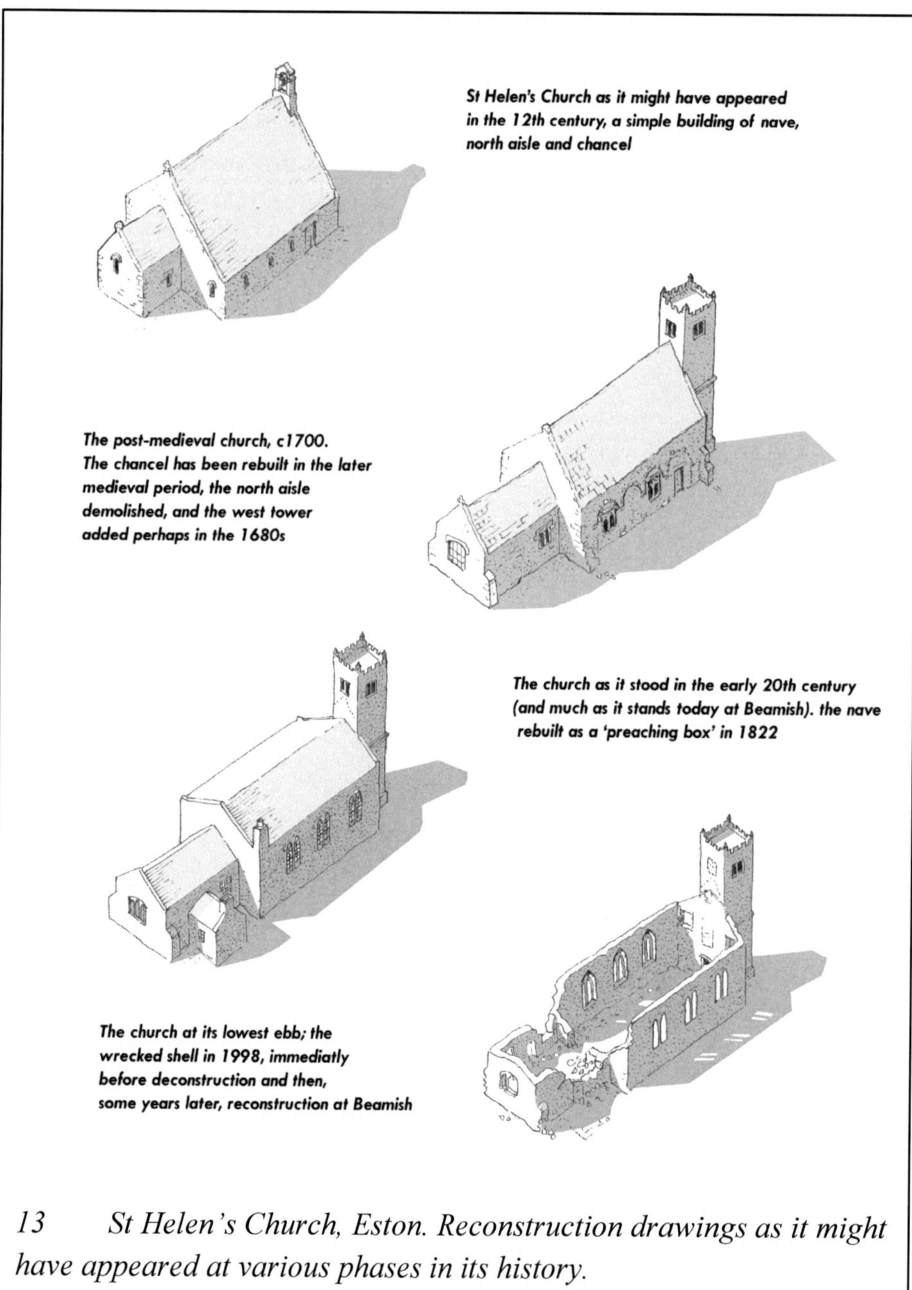

St Helen's Church as it might have appeared in the 12th century, a simple building of nave, north aisle and chancel
The post-medieval church, c1700. The chancel has been rebuilt in the later medieval period, the north aisle demolished, and the west tower added perhaps in the 1680s
The church as it stood in the early 20th century (and much as it stands today at Beamish). the nave rebuilt as a 'preaching box' in 1822
The church at its lowest ebb; the wrecked shell in 1998, immediatly before deconstruction and then, some years later, reconstruction at Beamish

13 St Helen's Church, Eston. Reconstruction drawings as it might have appeared at various phases in its history.

Most of the Romanesque architectural pieces retrieved at Eston come from one or more nave arcades, so the nave must once have been aisled. It is not uncommon for a church to lose an aisle or aisles – Egton, Upleatham and Whorlton are cases. But did Eston have one aisle or two? No less than 39 half-drums from Norman piers were found, along with 5 capitals, heavily recut from re-use in the heads of the 1822 nave windows. We know there were no aisles when Graves wrote, and that there was a Norman south door, which suggests that the south wall of the 12th-century nave survived, although the doorway might of course have been re-set when a south aisle was removed. A four-bay north arcade could just about accommodate all the material found; at Upleatham the 12th-century nave, only 10.6 m long (as against 12.7 m at Eston) had a four-bay arcade. The drums are from plain round piers, and the capitals are quite simple, too, with a roll mould at the neck and an octagonal abacus. The fact that no recognisable arcade voussoirs were found suggests that the arches were of one or two plain square orders. One Norman voussoir was found which bore elaborate carving, with medallions enclosing petalled rosettes, a high quality piece. Where is it from? It is difficult to place either in the south door (which Graves tells us had zigzag ornament)[20] or the chancel arch. Did Eston ever have a separate sanctuary beyond the chancel, such as Hilton had?

There is little evidence of the Norman chancel, although it is possible that some masonry from it survived in the north wall of its successor, which was thicker than the others. Sections of small rebated arches may come from piscinae or aumbries, and a whole series of interesting corbels may relate to features around the altar.

Apart from the early masonry in the west wall of the nave, only recognised during deconstruction, the only part of the church to retain standing medieval fabric was the chancel. As already mentioned, Norman fabric might have survived in the thicker north wall; the fact that the central axis of the chancel is offset to the south of that of the nave suggests a rebuilding, and slight enlargement, with the south and east walls being rebuilt just outside their original lines?[21] Also, a number of early (12th-century?) coped grave covers were discovered, which seem to have already been badly weathered before being cut up into blocks and re-used in the lower courses of the walls, all pointing to a later medieval date. Such original features as survive would tally with this; the square-headed priest's door on the south has a simple hollow-chamfered surround which could be of 15th or early 16th-century date. Both priest's door and the square-headed 'St Helen' window to the east had big tapering slabs as their internal lintels, which were probably re-used plain grave stones. The greater part of the head of a two-light 15th-century window was found re-used as a quoin at the south-west corner of the nave and has now been re-used again in the east window of the reconstructed church. When the south wall was taken down it became evident that the window near its west end had been widened on the east – as suggested by the fact that it only had an old chamfered jamb on the west – perhaps in the 18th century.

Quite a number of re-used blocks still carried remains of late medieval wall painting, with black-letter texts which would be characteristic of the 15th or early 16th century as well, and have survived to be re-used again in the present building at Beamish. The internal decoration of the medieval building would have been very different to its re-created Georgian phase; the walls would have been covered in paintings, garish to modern eyes, with a rood screen between nave and chancel carrying a carved Crucifixion group and perhaps figures of saints also. Another re-erected church, St Teilo's from Landeilo Tal-y-Bont, has been returned to its medieval form at the National Museum of Wales (St Fagans), and this is very different in feel to St Helen's as it stands today.

Further alterations are hard to date; at some stage the church lost its aisle or aisles, leaving the arcade or arcades walled up in the contracted nave. Such a loss could well have taken place in the medieval period, perhaps after the Black Death and other vicissitudes of the mid-14th century. At around the same time that the west tower was added (or rebuilt?) the chancel walls seem to have been heightened, to judge from the

---

[20] None of the re-used material correlates with such a door, which is interesting. Was the doorway removed, perhaps by someone with antiquarian tastes, to be re-used elsewhere?

[21] This might also explain the subsequent structural movements, which the two crude buttresses to the east wall were intended to counteract.

evidence of the high-quality lime mortar used in both. In the chancel, both the east window and the western window in the south wall seem to have originally had shallow segmental arches, like those of the 1741 nave windows at Ingleby Greenhow.

Then came the 1822 reconstruction, which replaced the Norman nave with a 'Churchwarden' preaching box, the pointed arches of its windows the first glimmerings of Gothic Revival. The faculty stipulates the renewal of all the furnishings in the nave; they have long gone but Ingleby Arncliffe preserves an almost exactly contemporary interior. After 1822 there was relatively little change; the erection of Christ Church in 1884 eased the need for restoration, although the box pews which were presumably introduced in 1822 were removed (an early 20th-century photograph shows the interior with chairs) whilst c1870 Gothic tracery was introduced into the 18th-century east window, given at the expense of the vicar, the Rev Vyvyan H. Moyle – or quite likely at someone else's expense because in 1873 the vicar, a wealthy and apparently popular man, was convicted of fraud and forgery, on quite a grand scale. He was imprisoned for seven years, but was later reinstated as a clergyman (in Reading) but in his seventies was jailed a second time, again for fraud, setting up fictitious companies. Not one of Eston's more virtuous sons.

(A more technical detailed account of the findings appears in 'St Helen's Church, Eston, Archaeological Recording and Analysis during Deconstruction, Autumn 1998', Peter F Ryder, published by (and still available from) Tees Archaeology. This includes scale drawings of all monuments and lapidary material.)

6. St Helen's Today

The church resurrected – a visit to the building as it stands today – a recreated Georgian village - the carved stones – the imported fittings and furnishings

---

14 St Helen's Church resurrected at Beamish, with the medieval Pockerley Farmhouse, aka Pockerley Manor, on the hilltop beyond.

Visiting St Helen's today is a surreal experience for those who knew it in its final sad days back in Cleveland; one disembarks from the vintage bus or tram that circumnavigates the sprawling museum site at Beamish, and enters a track beside a noticeboard welcoming one to 'The Georgian North';[22] walk over the crest of a gentle hill and the church appears, nestling below a slope capped by Pockerley Manor, the one genuine ancient building which actually belongs here. St Helen's sits very happily in its new landscape, with a hearse house under construction at the corner of its churchyard,[23] entered between gate piers with a handsome iron overthrow; capping the churchyard walls immediately to the left and right of the gates are a prehistoric cup-marked stone (actually from Northumberland, and probably the oldest thing on the museum site) and a medieval corbel from the church. The churchyard is as yet bare of any monuments, bar a venerable cross.[24] Further to the east is 'Elen's Well' in a recess at the foot of the wall, with another 12th-century corbel and a couple of other moulded stones set above it. A second entrance, from the north-east, is set between the remains of a whalebone arch, once a common feature around North Eastern Ports. The resurrected church has been returned to the appearance it would have had just after the 1822 nave was completed, the only evidence of its story being the white numbers still painted on some of its sandstone blocks to aid in the reconstruction; where possible every stone of its external envelope is back in its rightful position.

Walking around the outside of the building first, look at the south wall of the chancel. Part of the segmental head of the western window is a re-used slab bearing an incised shield with the initials 'TA' and date '1621'. Near the east end of the wall is part of the head of a good cross slab (5)[25] with an incised bracelet-derivative cross – it was actually found re-used in the adjacent buttress. Round the corner on the east wall, 1.5 m from the south end of the wall and 1.5 m up is a fainter piece of cross slab (17) with the stepped base of a cross and what may be a sword blade. The east window is a conscious piece of

---

[22] Between banks which in December 2015 were scattered with fake 'snow' and alongside an enclosure full of grazing reindeer: Father Christmas was resident in the nearby engine shed. It has to be said that the economic significance of reindeer in the Georgian North has largely gone unrecognised...

[23] Based on an original at Marrick Priory in Swaledale, North Yorkshire, the hearse from which is already at the Museum.

[24] Only the odd geologist will realise this is of granite, and from Devon or Cornwall.

[25] The cross slab numbers relate to the drawings in the Appendix.

Beamishian remedievalisation;[26] most of the head of the simple 15th-century window of two trefoil-headed lights was found recycled as a quoin at the south-west corner of the nave. The east window in 1998 was the Rev Moyle's very obviously Victorian one, and what was left of it now forms a pretty surround to a flower bed a few metres from the east end. Go round the north side of the chancel; above the re-created 1822 vestry a line of puzzling triangular stones are built in the wall, which seem to be pieces of a roll-moulded coping, like that of the tower battlements. In the angle between chancel and nave is a chimney stack serving the stove at the north-east corner of the nave. Just beyond, 1 m above the ground at the east end of the nave wall, is another re-used piece of a cross slab (18) showing a simple incised crosshead with fleur-de-lys terminals.

In the west side of the tower a rather vague patch in the masonry indicates the position of the pre-1822 main door; when the nave was rebuilt the doorway was moved to the south side of the tower. The base of the tower forms an entrance lobby to the church; in its north wall a little recess re-used the round-arched head of a small 12th-century window found at the deconstruction. The stair in the tower is a new creation in a 17th-century style; at its head a doorway opens onto the gallery, again a new creation but re-using part of a genuine one from a Methodist chapel. Above the door onto the balcony an arch has been formed from some rediscovered Norman stones, voussoirs from the original chancel arch with one more richly-carved specimen which is something of a mystery but may have come from a doorway.

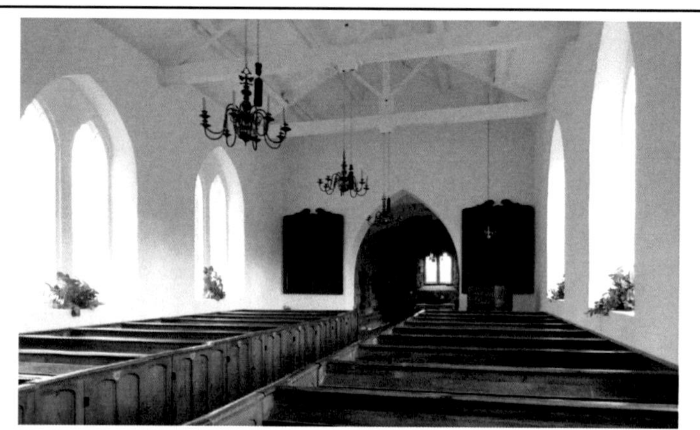

15 Inside the new St Helen's, the church fitted out as it would have looked in the 1820s soon after its nave was rebuilt.

The walls of the nave are plastered, and it is filled with near-contemporary (1829) box pews. Like the churchyard cross these are an import from the south-west, this time from Wiveliscombe in Somerset, a happy solution to a long battle between a church wishing to dispose of its excruciatingly uncomfortable seating and the planning authorities who demanded they retain it. In their new setting historical rectitude overrules discomfort. Historical rectitude is also served by the numbers and names on them; albeit newly painted, they were provided by an 1820s pew register. The present fittings are mostly imports from all over the country; the bowl of the font looks suspiciously like the decorated top of a medieval chimney shaft, but the shaft it sits on is made up of four medieval Eston corbels. Creed and Commandments boards, and the pulpit dated '1695' are more authentic imports. A recent acquisition is a barrel organ perhaps dating from the late 1820s, a remarkable combination of organ and music, with two drums, each with ten contemporary hymn tunes on it. Inside the chancel the masonry of the walls has been left exposed – which certainly would not have been the case in the Georgian church – so as to show off re-used medieval stonework. This includes a number of blocks in the north wall which, despite being re-used twice, have still managed to retain the remains of late medieval or early post-medieval painting, both decorative patterns and black-letter script, sadly now illegible. Two figurative corbels have been re-used in the walls, 'Fish Man' over the priests

[26] A museum speciality; in nearby Pockerley 'Manor' the south window of the mid-15th-century strong house, weathered to convincing authenticity, is totally spurious – a perjorative term, because it looks great, and is quite likely a correct reproduction of what was once there. When Beamish inherited the property there was a plain Victorian sash in this position...

door – a bizarre 12th-century head with a salmon in his mouth – and 'Toothache Man' over the south-western window. Two cross slab fragments with incised cross shafts and bases, (4) and (11), have been re-set in the sill of the same window and slab (15) with moulded edges and the beginning of an inscription in the sill of the window opposite, along with a stone with a lightly-incised inscription, maybe the name 'Aeniaus' which could be a piece of medieval graffiti. Two other small incised cross slabs, one with a sword (8) and one with a pair of shears (16) are now in the sanctuary floor on either side of thc altar, and another slab with a simple cross carved in high relief (10) behind the altar.

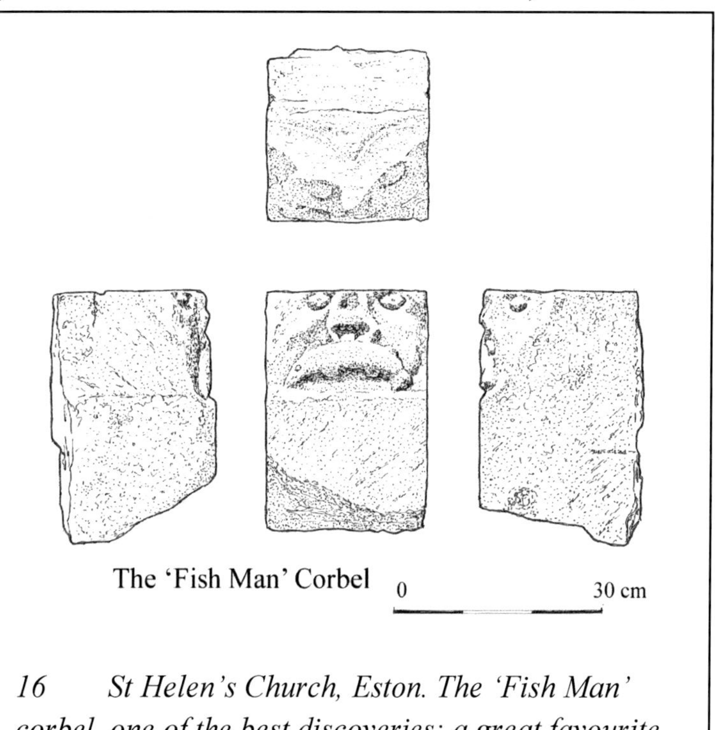

16 St Helen's Church, Eston. The 'Fish Man' corbel, one of the best discoveries: a great favourite with the deconstruction team, although his significance remains unclear.

One of the recent imports into the restored church is worthy of special mention and that is a barrel organ (now named the 'Swan Organ' after the collector from which it came). Barrel organs were a remarkable invention, a prototype of the CD player, as they possessed interchangeable wooden barrels each with a series of different tunes. Their introduction sadly signified the end of 'gallery bands' as mechanical contrivance replaced real musicians. This one has two barrels, each with 20 hymn tunes. No organist was necessary - it was simply operated by turning a handle. The first recorded barrel organ was installed in a Derbyshire church in 1700 and in 1967 there was only one left in ecclesiastical operation in the country. The Beamish organ - its original provenance is unknown - probably dates from the 1840s and was made by Henry Bryceson. It is still in full working order and the quality of its sound is really surprisingly good. Try and be there when one of the museum staff gives it a whirl.

St Helen's Church, with many of the features that came to light at its deconstruction now displayed, is now an infinitely more interesting building that it ever was when it stood where first built. And yet as an archetypical Cleveland church it is now thirty miles out of context; so many of its features – the diagonally-tooled brown sandstone, the simple 'churchwarden' post-medieval work and now the rich collection of earlier sculptural fragments and grave covers – are all resonant of its North Riding home. The church stands out as even more of a treasure when viewed in the context of the distinctive group of old churches found in and around the moorlands between the Tees and the Esk, and it is this group that we will move onto next.

7. A Cautionary Tale

A seemingly trivial discovery that may have had more significance than first appeared – information from an unlikely source – a coded message? - disturbing thoughts - and how rationality shows they can (probably) be laid to rest - a modern stained glass window – an enigmatic owl

---

When the south wall of the chancel was being 'deconstructed', an area of a carbonaceous deposit was discovered – simply a damp black mess - underneath the internal sill of the small window at the east end of the wall. Was it of any significance?; it was certainly odd, but might have been no more than the remains of some sort of animal nest. So it was discarded.

Later on, we had cause to regret this. Because of the fairly short notice at the beginning of the project, not a great deal of research on the church had been carried out. There was time afterwards. So it was a month or two later that we came across a note on the church in the rather unlikely setting of a historical note by Canon Stevenson in the Urban District Council Handbook for 1946-8. It described the stained glass window – long before vandalised – that used to occupy this opening, and said that it was 'worthy of note'. It was of 'painted glass, probably Tudor' showing 'St Helen and a companion finding the "True Cross"; beneath was the intriguing inscription "Inventio Crucis, Retentio Lucis" which translates as 'the finding of the cross is the maintenance of light'.

This all sounded rather strange. The Tudor period, i.e. the time of the Reformation, would seem an unusual period for painted glass figuring such a subject. St Helen inevitably is often linked to relics of the True Cross. It might be argued that a chapel such as Eston was hardly likely to possess a relic, but might one have been brought here from elsewhere at the Reformation, when such objects were being destroyed, and hidden away inside the chapel, seen as an appropriate place on the strength of its dedication? The late Jim Lang considered that the spectacular St Helen Cross at Church Kelloe, in County Durham, which has carvings portraying the story of the finding of the cross, was probably brought from Durham Cathedral at the Reformation and concealed, perhaps together with an associated relic, simply because the church was 'off the beaten track' and possessed the correct dedication.

So was the St Helen window a coded clue to a concealed relic? Had we inadvertently discarded something that was at one time seen as of inestimable value? It was a disturbing thought, but the answer is 'probably not'. Canon Stevenson was probably not the most reliable of historians – his comments on Eston church having its origins in a 'Roman Garrison Chapel' have already been quoted – and the window is not shown on either the 1822 faculty plan nor on one late 19th/early 20th-century postcard. As the opening itself is clearly ancient, this would suggest that it was blocked up at this time. A slightly later photograph has been recently found by Jim Rees that does show this window, from the outside, and one can just about make out a figure and cross within it – however, it does look very like conventional 19th-century stained glass.

The window now contains new glazing, complete with a figure of St Helen and the cross (and an owl, the liturgical meaning of which is obscure) , below an inscription 'Ecclesia Helenae Populo Anno MMXIV' which translates as 'For the people of St Helen's Church in the year 2014'.

8. The Old Churches of Cleveland: A Gazetteer

An introduction to thirty-eight churches - twenty-five with standing medieval fabric – the others with ancient stones – brief accounts of each building – helpful aids to visitors - lists of points of special interest, both outside and inside

---

What follows are brief accounts of the medieval churches of Cleveland, hopefully set out in a form that can be used as a visitor's guide. A paragraph outlining the building's overall history is followed by a series of 'things to see', concentrating on evidence that allows that history to be reconstructed. The great majority of churches welcome visitors, although this is not a part of the country in which they are routinely left open outside of service times, apart from a few in tourist honeypots; people will have to make their own arrangements. This is usually best done by contacting a churchwarden, whose names and contact details are often displayed on notice boards, or can be acquired from the Diocese.

For those who wish to read up further, the best published accounts of each church building (albeit somewhat dated) are to be found in the Victoria County History of the North Riding (volume 2), published in 1923. The Pre-Conquest sculptured stones preserved in around half the churches described here have had the benefit of a masterly study by the late Jim Lang, published in 2002 in The Corpus of Anglo-Saxon Stone Sculpture Vol. 6 Northern Yorkshire (Oxford University Press). These early stones tend to get snaffled by museums; significant pieces from Crathorne, Easington and Ingleby Arncliffe are now in the Monks' Dormitory collection at Durham Cathedral, and several pieces from Kirklevington are in Preston Hall Museum, at Stockton.

Churches with extant medieval fabric

Crathorne, Danby, Great Ayton, Guisborough, Hilton, Ingleby Greenhow, Kirklevington, Kirkby-in-Cleveland, Liverton, Lythe, Marske-by-the-Sea, Marton, Newton-under-Roseberry, Ormesby, Osmotherley, Roxby, Rudby, Skelton, Stainton, Stokesley, Upleatham, Whitby, Whorlton, Wilton, Yarm

Churches on medieval sites with significant non-structural remains

Acklam, Bilsdale, Brotton, Easington, Egton, Faceby, Hinderwell, Ingleby Arncliffe, Kildale, Kirkleatham, Middlesbrough, Seamer, Westerdale

Acklam, St Mary

The present church comprises an 1874 building which now forms a south aisle – 'St Bede's Chapel' - to a larger building of 1956-7. The 1874 church is known to be at least the third on the site, but its form - a nave with a south-east chapel and a chancel - follows that of at least two predecessors. The previous structure is recorded as having been built in 1770, but old photographs show that its steep-roofed chancel was of quite different fabric to the remainder and may well, as at Eston, have been retained from the medieval building which is shown on a 1709 engraving of the nearby Hall, and was of very similar appearance right down to the positions of windows and doorways. The present church retains three medieval effigies:

* In a recess on the north side of the 1874 chancel; its hoodmould looks to be re-used medieval work. Lady, thought to be Margaret Conyers (d.1402), wife of Sir Thomas Boynton, with heraldry relating to the two families on the cushions that her head rests on.

* Under the arch between the old chancel and the new church, unidentified lady.

* In boiler room under sanctuary of new church, worn 13th-century female effigy, unfortunately broken into three pieces.

Bilsdale, St Hilda (Chop Gate)

Quite a remote rural church in an attractive upland valley; the signed access takes one through a farmyard. The present building, replacing an earlier one, is all of 1851, by the firm of Banks and Barry, an essay in rock-faced 13th-century Gothic with lancet windows and a western turret-cum-bellcote capped by a sharp little spire. A notice in the porch directs one to a key held locally.

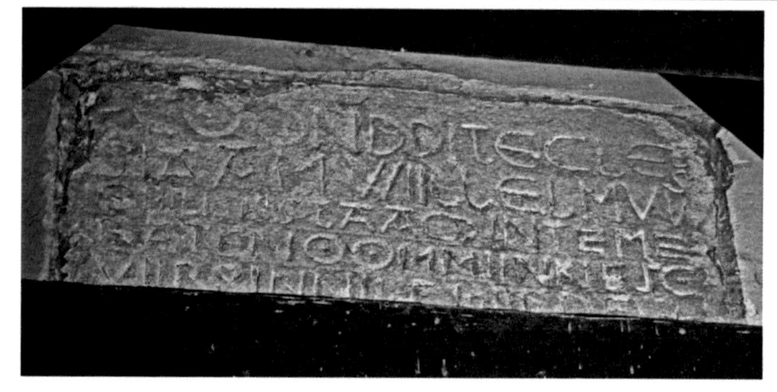

17 St Hilda's Church, Bilsdale. The dedication stone, a remarkable survival from the early 12th century - and now all that survives of the original building.

* In the south porch a plain ancient font, a bit like the supposed 'Saxon' one at Kildale.

* Also in the porch, but easy to miss – set high up over the outer arch (and needing a powerful torch to really see it) is a remarkable inscribed slab, claimed to be the original dedication stone of the first church on the site, and a unique and tangible link to the great Norman re-ordering of all things ecclesiastical – although it is a local Saxon saint who is invoked. It reads: COONDDIT EGLEE/ SIAM WIIELMVV/ NOBILIS ISTAAM INTEME/ RRATE NOOMMILINNE SC/ E VIRGINNIS HILDE', which, being translated from its 'barbarous Latin' reads 'This church was built by William the Noble in honour of the chaste name of the Holy Virgin Hilda'. William is thought to have been the father of Walter Espec who in 1145 gave this part of Bilsdale to Kirkham Priory (which he had founded in 1122), a gift perpetuated in the alternative names of the parish of 'Bilsdale Priory' or 'Bilsdale Kirkham'.

- * When the writer visited the church c1985 there were four small medieval head stones in the porch; on a second visit (February 2016) two were inside the church (one against the west wall, the other on the chancel arch step) but two could not be found. In addition there was a fifth and more elaborate stone with cup-shaped terminals to its cross, on the chancel arch step.
- * Against the font a carved human head, apparently set at the apex of the hoodmould of an arched opening, probably later medieval.
- * Just outside the south porch, beside the war memorial, are a few medieval stones – two fragments of the frame and tracery of a 15th-century window, a block with 13th-century dogtooth ornament and part of the head of an openwork cross which seems too big to be a headstone or gable finial; was it a churchyard cross?

Brotton, St Margaret of Antioch

Brotton is another place that demonstrates the typical Cleveland succession of churches – Norman, Churchwarden and Victorian, but here the later two phases were complete rebuildings, and the second saw the present church erected on a quite different site, up on the north side of the main street, whereas the old church – originally dedicated as at present but later to St Peter - stood c. 250 m to the south-west on the west side of Kilton Thorpe Lane, an odd position on the edge of the medieval village and distant from the manor. Was having a church here an afterthought, albeit one as early as the 12th century?

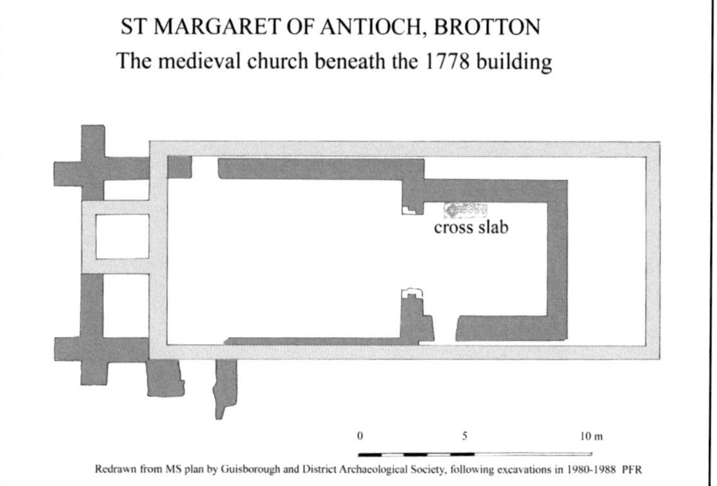

ST MARGARET OF ANTIOCH, BROTTON
The medieval church beneath the 1778 building

cross slab

0 5 10 m

Redrawn from MS plan by Guisborough and District Archaeological Society, following excavations in 1980-1988 PFR

18 St Margaret of Antioch (later St Peter), Brotton. Ground plan of the church as excavated in the 1980s, showing the 12th century building underneath the 18th century preaching box that succeeded it.

There is nothing medieval left to see in the cemetery where the old church stood; the site was excavated in 1980-1988 by the Guisborough and District Archaeological Society but sadly never published; such records as survive are held by Tees Archaeology. The Churchwarden building of 1778 had been replaced by the present parish church in 1891, and thereupon its story echoes that of Eston - relegation to use as a cemetery chapel followed by serious vandalism, and then demolition – this time without any happy postscript - in 1957. Twenty odd years later successive seasons of excavation revealed the ground plan of the original 12th-century church of nave (which unusually seems to have had north, south and west doorways), south porch and chancel; its walls still stood several courses high beneath those of its successor, a plain rectangular building with a small western tower. Old photographs show that it had plain round-headed windows and a pyramidal roof to the tower. In the chancel of the early church was uncovered a remarkable high-status 14th-century slab, with an elaborate foliate cross accompanied by a sword wound round with a sword belt, the design clearly copied from contemporary brasses, right down to the rivets. The writer saw and drew this when it was exposed; it is a pity that such a spectacular piece is once more concealed, as it really would merit conservation and display.

All visible relics of the old church are now displayed in the porch of its successor, a handsome neo-Perpendicular building by W. S. Hicks, surveyor to the Diocese of Newcastle and one of the best late Victorian architects in the region.

* A puzzling cross set upright against the west wall, but which may originally have been a recumbent monument; its reverse is absolutely plain. It had been re-used in the old churchyard and formerly bore a 1770 brass plaque but is probably early medieval.

* Several stones are all components of a very unusual 18th-century monument, clearly to a mariner, resembling a boat with an upright 'sail' itself bearing a rustic depiction of a three-masted sailing ship and a long and seemingly-garbled inscription.

* Two bells from the old church, a medieval one inscribed 'Thomas de Waldo me fecit' and one dated 1778, added at the rebuilding.

* An octagonal font bowl, worn and battered although the 'ihs' monogram in a quatrefoil panel has a very 19th-century look about it.

Crathorne, All Saints

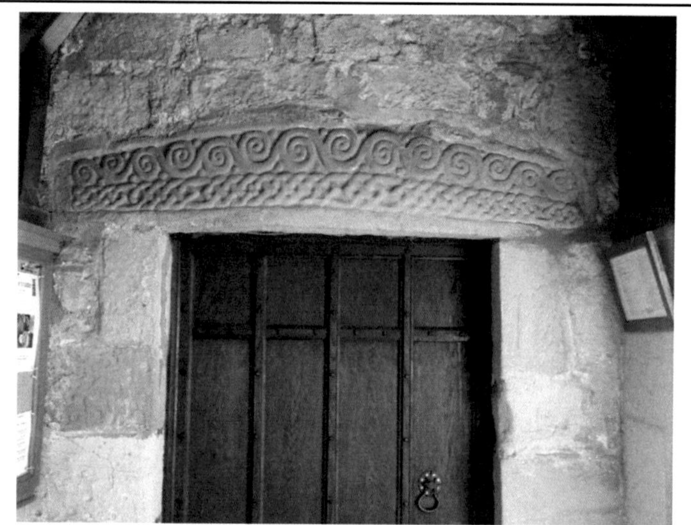

19 All Saints Church, Crathorne. The remarkable south doorway, its lintel formed by an Anglo-Scandinavian hog back grave cover, found in the 1887 restoration. A second similar hog back was spirited away to Durham Cathedral.

A handsome church with a cluster of other interesting buildings around it – the Georgian Old Vicarage over the road to the west, an 1824 Roman Catholic chapel to the west and the Old Hall to the north-west. The west tower, chancel and porch are all the product of a remodelling by C. Hodgson Fowler in 1885-6, leaving only the walls of the aisleless nave, which are thought to be of 14th-century date. The chancel had already been partially rebuilt in 1844.

Outside

* The south wall of the nave has three arched two-light windows with simple Y-tracery; their outer frames are old. The south door, inside the porch, has plain square jambs but a spectacular hog-back grave stone with plait and scroll ornament, placed here during the 1885-7 works, as its lintel. Above and slightly to the west of the ridge of the porch roof is a shield with the Crathorne arms.

* On the north of the nave are a blocked north door and a window of two cinquefoil-headed lights under a square head, both genuine 14th-century work.

* On the south of the tower lies the monolithic stepped base of a cross, probably Pre-Conquest.

* To the east of the south porch is a medieval stone coffin.

* Set on top of the north-east corner of the vestry is a shaped stone with the date '1688' and initials 'IP'; its upper part looks a little like a damaged wheel cross, but this would be unlikely at this date.

Inside

* A number of early stones, mostly cross slabs, are set in the side walls of the tower and west wall of the nave on either side of the tower arch.

* Part of an Anglo-Scandinavian cross shaft is mounted on the sill of the nave north window.

* A worn effigy of a deacon lies in the recess of the blocked north door.

* On the chancel floor is a slab with brasses of the Crathorne arms and an inscription in brass to Thomas and Elizabeth Crathorne; Thomas Crathorne was living in 1398.

* On the north of the sanctuary is an effigy of a cross-legged knight, his shield with the Crathorne arms; a modern brass plate identifies him as William de Crathorne, kt., slain at Neville's Cross in 1346.

* Displayed in the nave are several photographs showing the old church and the 1885-7 restoration.

Danby, St Hilda

If I was asked to choose the most attractive of Cleveland churches, it might well be Danby, beautifully sited in Church Dale far from both the present village and castle. Today the building is an amalgam of medieval, Churchwarden and good-quality restoration. The medieval church had a four-bay aisled nave with a south porch/tower and a chancel. In 1789 its nave was almost completely rebuilt as a preaching box, and in 1848 the chancel was rebuilt in a very Victorian geometrical Gothic. What makes the building memorable is the architect Temple Moore's contribution, of 1903, who respected all this multi-phase fabric and preserved the Churchwarden nave but reinstated its lost 13th-century arcades.

20 Danby. The outer walls of the medieval aisled nave were rebuilt - incorporating a little old fabric - as a Churchwarden preaching box in 1789, but the 15th century west tower remains. A wonderfully picturesque building.

Outside

* This is a highly unusual church building, picturesque to the extreme. The big Churchwarden nave with its low-pitched roof is barely overtopped by the squat medieval tower, and in complete contrast to the mid-19th-century Gothic of

the chancel. It has big round-arched windows; Temple Moore replaced their sashes with leaded glazing, but removed the eastern of the two gallery stairs on the north, leaving that serving the (surviving) 1808 western gallery. It looks as if he might have 'improved' the west end, with its buttresses, triple keystone to the central window and oculus in the gable above.

* The tower is perhaps 15th century, with a segmental-arched outer doorway, diagonal buttresses, and an irregular north-western stair projection.

* The only other medieval fabric visible outside is the lower parts of the buttresses at the east end of each side wall, and parts of the east wall of the preaching box on either side of the chancel – in effect the east end walls of the medieval aisles.

* Several old stones – including an arcade capital – lie outside the tower, and there is an interesting churchyard cross c. 8 m to the south, with a ?12th-century wheel head sitting on its truncated shaft.

* On the north of the nave an external stair to the western gallery; the north door and blocked door to the northern gallery have splayed lintels and tooled-and-margined dressings.

* You may well be greeted at the churchyard gate by a cat, which will escort you to the church door; I understand the animal regularly attends services. Feline piety is admittedly rare, and should be encouraged.

Inside

* The 'porch' is strange, a lofty space open to the heavy beams of the floor above. There are more old stones including a couple of cross slabs.

* The inner doorway has been like the outer, but has been cut square, and goes through a very thick wall; once through look up at the inner lintel, another cross slab.

* The arcades are Temple Moore's, incorporating a few pieces of the originals - the capital of the western pier of the north arcade and a few voussoirs. They are also twice the height of their predecessors, as the original western responds survive, and have been exposed in small openings against the west wall. There are also old stones in the chancel arch, and a few chevron-moulded voussoirs from the 12th-century church set above it, together with a cross slab that has the beginnings of an inscription (bring binoculars!).

* It is clear that thicker medieval walling survives at the east end of each aisle.

* Restored western gallery on octagonal timber piers.

* Some good later 19th/early 20th-century features such as the tiled floor of the whole chancel, and much of the stained glass.

Easington, All Saints

A handsome church in a 14th-century Gothic style by C. Hodgson Fowler, erected in 1888-9 replacing a 'plain and humble edifice' of 1771, but as at Lythe a treasure hoard of earlier stonework and monuments were uncovered during the rebuilding.

Outside

* A number of old stones lie outside the tower, including a worn cross base, two grave slabs, one with an incised sword and the other plain but of an odd slightly convex profile.

Inside

* Architecture, furnishings and fittings combine to make this an unusually attractive late Victorian interior.

* The base of the tower forms an entrance porch. Medieval cross slabs are set into the walls on the north and west, and at the north-west corner; set into the north wall is a beautiful little effigy of a baby girl in her cot, with an inscribed table above identifying her as 'Katheran' Conyers, d.1621, who died at the age of one month.

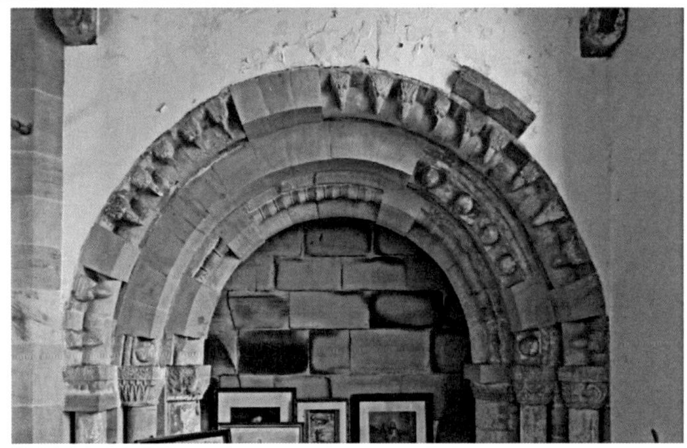

21 Easington. The resurrected Norman chancel arch, the stones of which lay discarded beneath the floor of the 1771 preaching box that replaced the medieval church, rediscovered and set into the wall of the tower of the new church in 1888-9.

* The stair on the north leads to a gallery room in the tower and here there is a surprise; built into the south wall is the partially-reconstructed 12th-century chancel arch; around half the arch survives, the missing voussoirs being replaced in plain stone. Some of the motifs on the capitals – the man with foliage issuing from his mouth, and a standing bird – are paralleled again at Liverton.

* Built into the west wall of the nave north of the tower arch is the upper part of another good cross slab.

* In the floor of the Sanctuary north of the altar is a splendid cross slab carved in relief with a marginal inscription, in leaded Lombardic capitals, to Robert Bushel, of c. 1300.

* In the north aisle are a collection of stones including a hogback in two pieces, part of an Anglo-Scandinavian cross shaft, an early cross head and a moulded stone from the jamb of a medieval window.

Egton, St Hilda

The original St Hilda's Church stood a kilometre to the west of the present village, and was a long low building with a nave, south aisle with a tower raised over its west bay, south porch and chancel. Sir Stephen Glynne's 1857 account describes a south arcade 'of five plain semicircular arches'; the chancel has windows in Decorated and Perpendicular styles; a 1439 dedication by the Bishop of Damascus may relate to its rebuilding. As usual there were post-medieval alterations – the tower is said to have been built in 1663 and Glynne called the nave windows 'modern and wretched'. Nevertheless, it was a tragedy that in 1886 this complex and interesting ancient edifice was pulled down and replaced by the present church in the village, a spiky Neo-Norman construction re-using a few token oddments from its predecessor to excuse what was really an act of vandalism. At the same time and under similar circumstances at Eston the old church, of less architectural merit, was retained as a cemetery chapel; here at Egton a cemetery chapel was built a mere decade or so later on the footings of the old chancel.

In the 'new' church notice:

* Three piers of the north arcade are said to be re-used from the medieval church, but they have been so re-tooled that it is hard to tell.

* The bowl of the piscina in the chancel is medieval, but this came from Grosmont Priory, 1.3 km to the east.

* In the exterior of the south wall are stones from the old church with the incised dates '1663' and '1704' which have been re-set, quite pointlessly. The hoodmould of the priest's door is also salvaged from its predecessor in the original building.

On the site of the old church:

* Go to the west end of the present chapel and walk about 10 m west on the line of its north wall. Level with the ground is the roll-moulded base of a circular pier, apparently an in-situ remnant of the medieval building – if indeed the present chapel is on the site of the old chancel, this must be a remnant of a north arcade that must have remained unnoticed in the building as it stood in the 19th century. Notes in the present church state that there are two more pillar bases, but they may have become buried.

* If you can gain access to the chapel (normally locked) there are three medieval cross slabs in the floor.

A little research work and maybe some minimal excavation would aid in the useful task of reconstructing the old church on paper.

Faceby St Mary Magdalene

Faceby Church is an attractive little Gothic building of 1875, with its chancel being extended in 1911, set on a slope so that the chancel has an undercroft. It replaced a much altered 12th-century chapel, a few relics of which survive inside.

* The arch of the Romanesque west door has been re-set on the internal face of the present south door. Slightly segmental in shape, it has an inner order with chevron and an outer with a roll-and-hollow moulding, under a hoodmould with raised saltire crosses.

* Eight chevron-moulded voussoirs have been re-used, four on each side, in the present chancel arch.

* A 15th-century window of two trefoil-headed lights, originally at the east end of the south wall of the old church, is now on the north side of the chancel.

* The head of a Pre-Conquest cross, ornamented with a series of incised circles, in the south porch.

Great Ayton, All Saints

The old church of Great Ayton, abandoned in 1876 when the present Christ Church was built, but now lovingly cared for and open in the summer months. At first sight a simple 12th-century nave-and-chancel church (with a big 14th-century south porch) but actually truncated in 1883 when the west part of the nave and west tower were removed; the nave had been extended in the 15th century, but its tower had been rebuilt in the 18th century. As at Eston the church was spared all Victorianisation save the replacement of its east window.

22 Great Ayton, All Saints. Like Eston and Skelton the old church was abandoned in the late 19th century. Shorn of its west tower and the west bay of its nave, which had been rebuilt in the late 18th century, it demonstrates a complex building history mixing Norman, later medieval and Churchwarden features.

Outside:

* The south porch is really interesting, in that it appears to have a subterranean charnel house beneath it. In the east wall is a low arch into which charnel (disarticulated human bones, such as might be produced by clearing a section of the churchyard) could be tipped into the chamber beneath. Above is a window, with a slot in its sill through which it is said holy water could be poured onto the bones beneath…

* The sharp-eyed will find several medieval cross slabs built into the porch walls, and a more obvious one re-set high in the 1883 west wall.

* The north wall of the nave, full of blocked openings, is an archaeological delight. Near the west end is the 12th-century north door, then a doorway higher up inserted in 1743 so that Thomas Skottowe, Lord of the Manor, could have a private access to his gallery, then another doorway was inserted in 1821 to serve a separate gallery, and finally a three-light Tudor window.

* On the south of the nave two big round-arched Churchwarden windows, and on the south of the chancel a possible Tudor window given a Gothick pointed arch in the later 18th century.

Inside

* Good 12th-century south door with the usual chevron ornament.

* In the nave the various blocked openings in the north wall, with two cross slabs set in the blocking of Skottowe's gallery door.

* Old pews with bases of the posts that carried the galleries.

* In the recess formed by the blocked window at the east end of the north wall of the nave, a number of Pre-Conquest carved stones including a crucifix dated to the later 9th century.

* Behind the 18th-century three-decker pulpit in the south-east corner evidence of a stair rising up the south wall, interpreted as providing access to the rood loft (or maybe to a post-medieval eastern gallery, as there is at Whitby).

* Good 12th-century chancel arch with a 14th-century recess on the north, with traces of wall painting, and a battered fragment of a statue of the Virgin Mary which may have originally stood here.

* On the north of the chancel, now opening inside the 1849 vestry, an original 12th-century window.

St Nicholas, Guisborough

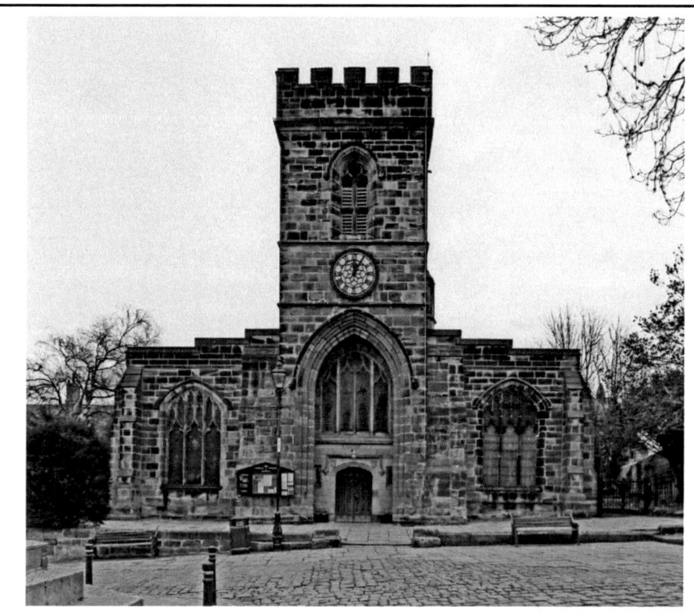

23 Guisborough, St Nicholas. The late medieval west tower stands within the nave, and straddles its west end, an oddly effective composition.

A big late medieval church, although when built it would have been dwarfed by, and quite literally lay in the shadow of, the great Augustinian priory church which stood alongside. There was almost certainly a church already here when Robert de Brus I founded the priory in 1119, but sadly no tangible evidence survives of any building prior to the present one, which has a six-bay aisled nave, with a contemporary slightly-narrower west tower built half-in and half-out of the western bay. The nave was rebuilt as a Gothick preaching box c1796, in this case keeping the old arcades, but when Temple Moore turned his attentions here in 1903-8 he erased a valid phase in the building's history, unlike his restorations at Danby and Kirkby where he imaginatively conserved Churchwarden work and combined it with both medieval and his own new work in a picturesque whole.

Outside

* The west tower is the best feature with its tall arch enclosing the (renewed) west door and window.

* A little bit of what looks like medieval chamfered plinth survives at the foot of the south aisle wall.

* The weathered masonry of the chancel is clearly ancient, although the swept pinnacles to its buttresses look like Gothick touches that have escaped the restorer. The vestry and organ chamber on the north are of 1889.

* The east window is Temple Moore but the windows in the side walls are odd, Perpendicular work with their tracery set within two-centred arches, but enclosed by clumsy outer arches of much shallower form. It has been suggested that they were re-used from some Priory building.

Inside

The interior, bar one remarkable monument, is a little disappointing. The four-centred arches of the arcades are old but much scraped, and panelling in the chancel hides any remains of old ritual features like piscinae and sedilia.

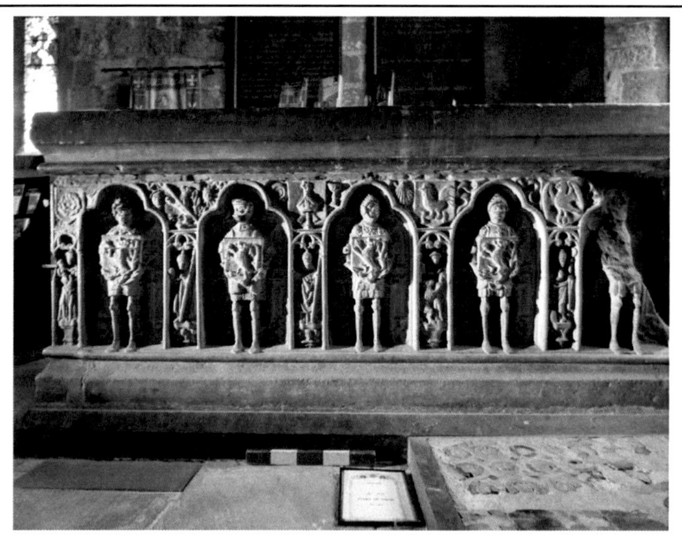

24 Guisborough, St Nicholas. A remarkable memorial to a remarkable family who distinguished themselves on both sides of the Border, given to the Priory, four centuries after its foundation by Robert de Brus I, by Queen Margaret of Scotland, perhaps as an act of reconciliation a few years after the disaster of Flodden.

* The one feature not to be missed now stands at the west end of the south aisle - the Bruce Cenotaph. It looks like a big altar tomb but never covered a burial; instead it commemorates the family who imprinted their presence on medieval Cleveland, founding the Priory, along with new towns like Hartlepool and Yarm. It is a remarkable piece of work, late Gothic bordering on the Renaissance, and is made of Teesdale limestone. The range of canopies on one side has figures of members of the local de Brus family, of Skelton Castle, and on the other side of members of the Annandale Bruces (of Robert the Bruce fame) from North of the Border. There is no inscription; instead one has to read the symbols and the heraldry, which suggest a date of around 1520. It is thought that Queen Margaret of Scotland gave the tomb to the Priory – it may be her figure at the east end of the north side, under a Tudor rose, perhaps as an act of reconciliation after the disaster of Flodden barely ten years before.

* On a much smaller scale, but also with a story to tell, is small cross slab now built into the internal face of the east wall of the south aisle, the distinctive cross of which has stylistic links to a far grander slab found in the 1970s at Brotton; at opposite ends of the scale of such monuments, they must be the work of the same hand.

* The glass in the west window of the south aisle is partly medieval and includes some entertaining, to modern eyes, figures from a representation of the Last Judgement.

High Worsall, Old Church

High Worsall is well known as a deserted medieval village – well known enough to have attracted the pop pseudo-archaeology of *Time Team* - and amidst its atmospheric green humps and bumps the little square of the old graveyard survives with a scatter of headstones and a little rectangle of low walls representing the tiny nave of St John's Church, partly stone and partly old brick. The church was rebuilt in 1710, re-using well-squared stone from its predecessor, then in the 1890s it was abandoned in favour of the new church of All Saints in the present village, and restored, after the removal of its chancel, as a cemetery chapel. However it fell into ruins and at some time since the walls were cut down to their present c. 1.5 m height except for a little gable left at the west end. The jambs of the narrow chancel arch can still be seen in the internal face of the east wall, but the outer face has been re-faced in twice-reused medieval stone. A plain early font and an 18th-century bell are in the new church.

Hilton, St Peter

The present church comprises the nave and chancel of what seems originally to have been a three-cell Norman building, now shorn of its sanctuary. It is perched on a raised mound, with an especially dramatic scarp on the west. Much of the walling is of well-coursed almost square blocks, very typical of the period.

The west wall has been rebuilt; on the outside it has been thinned back by c. 0.30 m above the lowest two or three courses and on the inside original masonry survives to c. 1.5 m; in the upper parts, inside and out, are several stones with knife-sharpening grooves.

* The windowless east end must be later as well as, inside, the jambs and imposts of the arch to the former sanctuary, perhaps apsidal, which survive. Inside is a square of old plaster with remains of wall painting, maybe early post-medieval work, in the form of stencilled foliate designs in red.

* Outside there are good Norman doorways north and south of the nave; the south door with two orders of zigzag is probably similar to the original south door at Eston mentioned in Graves' 1808 account.

* Above and to the east of the south doorway are two interesting stones, the first with faint remains of a sundial and the second with a Romanesque animal, perhaps an Agnus Dei, carved in relief in a sunk roundel.

* There are three absolutely plain square-headed windows, maybe of 18th-century date in their present form, on either side of the nave and on the south of the chancel. Inside, parts of their jambs are clearly older, and may survive from the original 12th-century narrow loops.

* On the north of the chancel is a 13th-century lancet, clearly inserted, with a trefoiled rear arch, now truncated by a later lintel.

* Inside there is an excellent original chancel arch, with variously carved capitals and bases to its responds.

Hinderwell, St Hilda

A preaching box of the late 18th and early 19th centuries, with Gothic windows of 1895 in the side walls, but with various tangible evidences of earlier origins.

Outside

* In the churchyard to the north, steps lead down to the holy well of St Hilda, although the little well house is of no great age.

* The west tower, dated 1817, is very reminiscent of that at Skelton, and contains the gallery stair.

* On the north, just east of a buttress, evidence of a gabled porch removed in 1895.

* The rather attractive east end is earlier; in a roundel above the Venetian window is an inscription 'This part of the church was built 1773. The south side and half of the East End stands on the old Chancel Ground & is repaired by the Rector'. Clearly this is the rector's defence against his ever having to repair the north half of the chancel…

Inside

* Under the western gallery of 1818 lies the discoidal head of a free-standing cross, a little large to be a headstone, which Lang tentatively dates to the later 11th century.

* Set against the east wall is a 12th-century pillar piscina (with stylistic affinities to some of the corbels found at Eston) now set on top of what looks like a section of a later medieval crocketted pinnacle.

* Lying alongside the pillar piscina is a strange little stone with an attractive cross made up of eight interlaced loops, carved in relief, yet the shape of the stone suggests a post-medieval headstone. Is it a re-worked 12th-century piece?

Hutton Rudby (or Rudby-in-Cleveland), All Saints

Lying below the River Leven, this is, unusually for the area, largely a 14th-century church. The nave has a four-bay south aisle, with a porch carried up as a tower, and the chancel has a Victorian north vestry. One needs to seek for 'hints and allegations' in the fabric to try and unravel a complex building history, the last phase of which was a 'de-churchwardenisation' in the 1920s when a low-pitched 18th-century roof which spanned both nave and aisle was replaced in a return to the assumed medieval design.

25 Hutton Rudby, All Saints. Quite a complex church largely of 13th century and later date, with a porch/tower like Danby and Whorlton.

Outside

* The handsome porch-cum-tower is probably of 15th-century date; the very odd grid-like tooling at the base, seen again on the east end at Stokesley, is the product of some late 18th or 19th-century restoration.

* The north wall of the nave is especially interesting, and the moulded plinth and a good two-light window near the east end seem early 14th century. But an earlier (perhaps 12th-century) chamfered plinth appears below it.

* The north wall of the chancel is set outside the line of that of the nave – very odd! Chancels were almost always narrower than the nave – so this would seem to imply that the chancel, which seems 13th century, is later than the nave, and that this has been rebuilt on earlier foundations.

* The external walls of the south aisle, and parts of the chancel, have been re-faced in the 19th century.

Inside

* The three-bay south arcade has attractive quatrefoil piers, with a short length of wall at the west end and then a fourth arch, product of a westward extension; there is a clear break between the well-squared masonry above the main arcade and the rubble over the western arch. It is difficult to work out what this means – the plinth evidence shows the nave was not extended to the west as some have thought. Was there an earlier western tower that collapsed?

* Near the east end of the aisle is a fine tomb recess containing a low-relief effigy of a priest, with cross-slab like floral decoration sprouting around his head; to the east is an altered piscina with a deeply fluted bowl.

* The chancel has simple Y-tracery windows on the south but those on the north (one intact, two with rear arches visible internally) seem to have been lancets, indicating a 13th-century date.

* Below the intact lancet is what may have once been a doorway to a vestry, now containing a few interesting carved stones.

Ingleby Arncliffe

A very pretty little church of 1821, in the shadow of the mid-18th-century Arncliffe Hall, nestling at the foot of the wooded Cleveland escarpment away from its village, which is on the other side of the busy A172. It replaced an older building of roughly similar form, but which stood a few metres further to the south-east. There are significant Pre-Conquest stones but the normal visitor will not see them; the better were spirited away to Durham Cathedral and others are incorporated in the internal walls of the belfry.

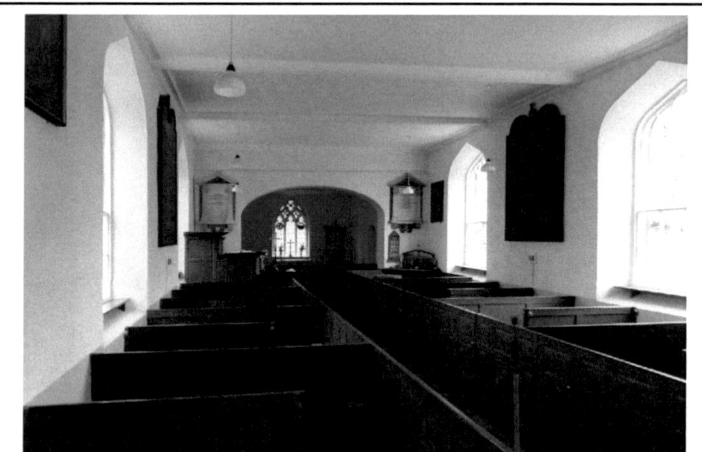

26 Ingleby Arncliffe. A little-altered late Georgian interior, a slightly upmarket version of how Eston must have once looked. A few medieval features were recycled from the earlier church which stood alongside.

Outside

* Almost exactly contemporary with, and of virtually identical proportions to, Eston, and differing only in that the relics of medieval fabric are not retained but re-used. This remains inside and out a late Georgian church that has escaped restoration. The proximity of the Hall means this is a slightly more genteel

building than Eston. The only touch of Gothic is in the four-centred arches of the nave windows, which still have their sashes.

* The simple Norman west door is more of a copy than a transplant. The arch is of two orders with narrow chamfers (like the Thornaby chancel arch) but in reality little more than the fluted capitals, which vary in detail, looks old.

* The 14th-century east window of three trefoiled ogee lights is also re-used, although its stonework has again been partly renewed.

Inside

* In the porch, under the tower, part of an early cross slab, crudely carved in relief.

* The nave retains its original box pews (with some partitions removed), now painted purple (which sounds more bizarre than it actually appears).

* Three-decker pulpit with a nodding stick, an implement a bit like an elongate billiard cue with which churchwardens could assist the congregation in resisting any temptation to somnolence.

* On either side of the altar are effigies of c. 1300 thought to represent Sir William Colvill and his brother Sir Robert. They have the very rare feature of ailettes – an item of knightly armour peculiar to this period, consisting of rectangular plates of leather or wood fixed to the shoulders. Whether they were functional or simply decorative, experts disagree.

* At the head and foot of each effigy are slabs, each with a pair of shields. These may come from some other medieval monument.

* The east window retains some medieval glass, the shields of Fauconberg and St Quintin, bearings of the two wives of Sir William Colvill.

Ingleby Greenhow, St Andrew

At the south end of the village, at the foot of Church Lane next to Ingleby Beck, stands an archetypical Cleveland church, a classic combination of 12th-century Norman and 18th-century 'Churchwarden' combining to produce a building which almost defines 'picturesque' but will never appear in any architectural textbook. It consists of a nave with a south porch and five-bay north aisle (now with a north vestry), a small western tower, and a chancel. As at Danby the 18th-century work owes its survival to restoration coming late – 1906 – and at the hands of the same tactful architect, Temple Moore.

Outside

* Most of the exterior of the church - the walls of nave and aisle, the east end of the chancel and the south porch, are all of 1741 (datestone on porch) and in characteristic herringbone-tooled sandstone, with big segmental-headed windows with keystones.

* The little west tower is 12th century, but its oversailing belfry, with mutilated openings, is probably 15th.

- The proportions of the elongate chancel and one mutilated lancet window mark it out as of 13th-century date, although the fabric of the south wall has been partly recut to try and match it in with the 1741 nave walls, when the priest's door was altered to receive a 'Classical' outer order. But what does the big ungainly plinth on the north mean?

Inside

- The 12th-century north arcade is the most memorable feature, of two heavy square orders on alternating round and octagonal piers, but their capitals are a real oddity, cut to a cruciform plan with carvings of beasts and heads at the corners. Nobody seems quite sure of their date; they can hardly be genuine 12th-century work. Are they the handiwork of some late 18th or early 19th-century mason with antiquarian tastes?

- The very plain tower and chancel arches, the latter flanked by squints, are genuine 12th-century work. Temple Moore discovered the foundations of a presumably 12th-century apse which at one time could be seen by lifting a trapdoor.

- Under the third and fourth arches of the arcade are two medieval effigies, one a 13th-century priest (with the inscription ' VILKS DE WRETTON, CAPELLANUS') and the other a later knight under a big cusped arch and canopy, with a black-letter inscription now illegible.

- In the sides of the 1906 plinth of the priest's effigy and beneath that of the civilian are a whole series of medieval cross slabs and slab fragments; there are others in the internal face of the north wall of the aisle, and the external face of its west wall, a collection of over twenty in all.

- What has happened to the simple 12th-century font under the west end of the arcade? Its mouldings do not go all the way round... your guess is as good as mine.

Kildale, St Cuthbert

Kildale was a medieval seat of the Percy family. This is a church with an intriguing approach, perched on a little ridge and now reached via a narrow footbridge over a railway cutting. As it stands today it is a very Victorian rock-faced building in a Decorated Gothic style, designed by Fowler Jones of York and built in 1868, replacing a church that had been at least partly rebuilt in 1714 (and altered in the earlier 19th century) although old plans show thicker walling on the north of the nave suggesting that some early fabric had survived.

Outside

- There are a number of medieval grave slabs and other stones in the churchyard, two against the south churchyard wall a few metres west of the gate, and others against the south side of the tower.

- Look west from the churchyard and the site of the manor house forms a raised platform, with a later farmhouse on its south side, and medieval ashlar walling showing through the turf in places.

- The gable of the south porch incorporates several medieval stones, two headstone crosses and higher up a slab with a 'marigold' flanked by two with incised decoration of c1100.

Inside

* In the south porch are four big medieval grave slabs to members of the Percy family, two having their coat of arms. Two have swords, one a possible pair of shears (at the foot of the cross) and one a hunting horn on its carrying strap (baldrick), now quite hard to make out.

* Under the tower is a big and very plain tub font, supposedly Saxon, and several early stones including a Saxon cross arm and several medieval head stone crosses.

* The present font has an odd ribbed bowl, a bit difficult to date but possibly 12th century.

Kirkleatham, St Cuthbert

Kirkleatham was the seat of the illustrious Turner family; their Hall did not survive the mid-20th century, but a cluster of other notable buildings did; the Free School – now called the 'Old Hall' - is now a museum. There was a medieval church here but little of it survived the Turners – the tower was rebuilt in 1731, then the spectacular Baroque Turner Mausoleum, a pyramid-topped octagon, was built onto the north side of the chancel in 1740, and finally the rest of the medieval fabric was replaced by the present quite grand Classical building in 1763.

Outside

* The Victoria County History believes the lower part of the medieval tower may be encased in its successor but there seems no tangible evidence of this; however those with keen eyes can spot a re-used piece of medieval cross slab in the south wall of the stair turret, about 5 m above the ground.

* The Mausoleum has dressings of Vermiculate stone – a conceit found in Classical architecture, where the stone is cut to look as if worm eaten – but is set on a plinth of irregular pieces of genuinely worm-eaten (or technically mollusc-drilled) stone, presumably from the same local foreshore, perhaps under Huntcliff, east of Saltburn. In the churchyard a little to the north is a pile of similar blocks, some packed with fossils. Three cross slabs which lay against the west wall of the (old part of the) churchyard in 1991 seem to have disappeared.

Inside

* At the north-west corner of the nave is a 13th-century effigy of a lady. Nearby is a small and roughly-hewn stone coffin.

* In the central aisle of the nave is a large blue limestone slab with indents for a brass effigy of a priest, shields and a marginal inscription. Adjacent to the east is a slab with a 15th-century brass that has a worn black-letter inscription in memory of Thomas Lambert and Agnes his wife.

* On the south side of the chancel is a fine 14th-century chest with a traceried front, and beside it a small cross slab with a foliate cross and sword, ascribed (but on what grounds?) to Sir Thomas de Thweng d1374.

* In the tower ringing chamber, another cross slab forms the lintel of the north window.

Kirkby in Cleveland, St Augustine

Quite a memorable building; this is a church of two halves, the 1815 Churchwarden preaching box nave and west tower, and Temple Moore's lofty Arts-and-Crafts Gothic chancel of c1905 which has three-bay aisles and an aisleless sanctuary with a vestry on its south, which is a medieval survival, datable by documentary evidence to 1458. The pre-1815 church is said to have been a cruciform building with a central tower, but geophysical survey has located a possible earlier building under the churchyard to the north.

Outside

* The Churchwarden nave remains unaltered, except that, as at Danby, Temple Moore replaced sash windows in the big round-arched openings with leaded glazing.

* The 15th-century vestry is an oddity; old photographs show it simply hinged to the corner of the previous (1815) chancel.

* Temple Moore re-set medieval headstone crosses at the western angles of his chancel aisles, much as he did on the east gable of the nave at Newton-under-Roseberry.

27 Kirkby-in-Cleveland, St Augustine. An old drawing shows a cruciform medieval church with a central tower, but all that survives of this, oddly, is the vestry, at one corner of the chancel of 1900; the rest of the church is Churchwarden work of 1815.

* Some distance from the church on the north are the sadly-decayed effigies of a late 14th-century knight and lady. It was near here that the putative Pre-Conquest church stood.

Inside

* The interior is as dramatic as the exterior, with the soaring verticality of the Gothic chancel a total contrast to the big box of the nave.

* The 1815 western gallery, with its access in a projection on the south of the tower, has been allowed to remain intact.

* Several early stones, including some Pre-Conquest pieces and a medieval cross slab and headstone, have been set into the internal face of the east end of the south chancel aisle.

* There are other stones stored in the first floor of the tower

Kirklevington, St Martin

A church of threefold character; south door and chancel arch are excellent Norman work (although dismantled and re-set in 19th-century walls), the chancel is of the 13th century and the nave an 1883 rebuild, although its distinctive bellcote is more or less a copy of its predecessor. The church has a splendid collection of carved stones, both Pre-Conquest and medieval cross slabs.

Outside

* A medieval coffin lies to the east of the south porch.

* The chancel has good 13th-century features – a priest's door and lancet windows, as well as an inserted 14th-century window, in its side walls.

* Beneath the 1883 eastern lancets two medieval grave slabs have been re-set, with swords.

* Quite a lot of interesting stones, including chevron moulded voussoirs, probably from the former north door, have been re-set in the walls of the 1883 north vestry.

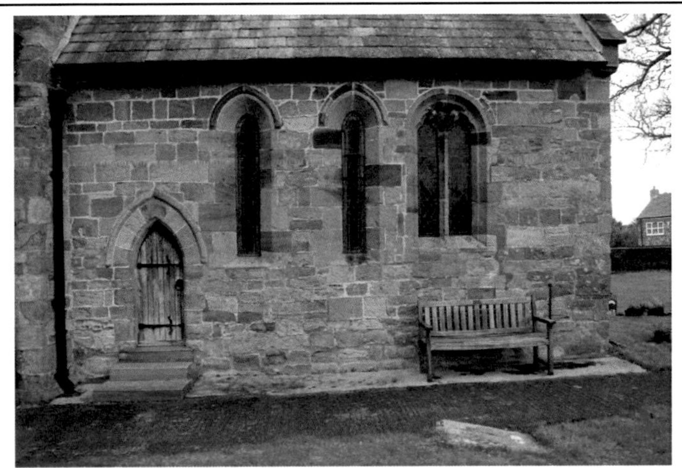

28 Kirklevington, St Martin. The 13th century was a good one for new and more elongate chancels over much of Northern England, but Kirklevington is Cleveland's only example.

Inside

* On either side of the porch are fine medieval cross slabs; the south door is a good 12th-century piece, with two orders of chevron, the inner continued down the jambs.

* The nave is all of 1883, except for the chancel arch, again with two orders of chevron. The carved capitals of the outer order of shafts, together with adjacent panels facing the nave, show the symbols of the Evangelists – from north to south a lion (St Mark), a man (St Matthew), an eagle (St John) and an ox (St Luke).

29 Kirklevington, St Martin. In the chancel some outstanding pieces of Anglo-Scandinavian sculpture - or so it appears. Actually they are very convincing fibreglass casts, and the originals are in Preston Park Museum.

* Inside the chancel there is an original piscina – with a restored bowl – at the east end of the south wall. Set in the west end of the north wall is a splendid 14th-century priest's grave slab, with a chalice, book and (much more faint) a circular paten.

* Lots more cross slabs have been re-set in the internal walls of the vestry, although some are partly hidden by furniture.

* The old font, replaced by the High Victorian one at the west end of the nave, long lay in the churchyard but has been brought in and stands by the pulpit. Its shaft, with weathered dog-tooth ornament, is 13th century but the bowl may be post-medieval.

* Most of the Pre-Conquest carved stones, largely Anglo-Scandinavian ('Viking' in popular parlance) are currently removed to Preston Hall Museum, but not all are on display. One important stone, with a deer and hound, is set in the north wall of the vestry along with the medieval cross slabs. Carbon fibre casts of three more – convincing at least to the eye – are now set against the west wall of the chancel north of the chancel arch.

St Michael, Liverton

The little church stands on its own down a lane at the north end of the village; at one time it was dedicated to St Martin. A 12th-century two-cell church was remodelled out of all recognition in the late 18th century and then restored in 1902-3.

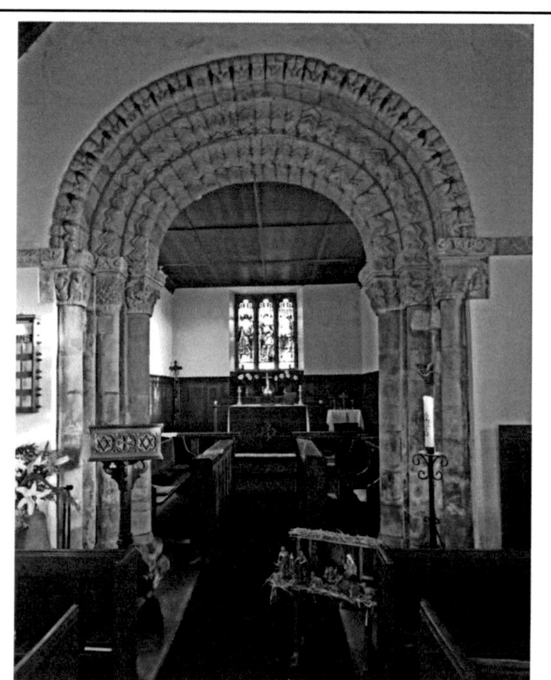

30 Liverton. The superb mid-12th century chancel arch, a real surprise inside a small and much-altered church. The puzzle is why such a grandiose piece is here; it is considerably more sophisticated than the chancel arch at Whitby in what was a much larger and higher-status building.

Outside

* Early masonry in the west part and eastern angle of the south wall of the nave, and in rather more of the north wall where the jambs of an early door are visible – its round-arched internal head was seen in 1902/3 but is again plastered over. The bluish stone of the early fabric contrasts with the olive herringbone-tooled fabric of the later remodelling.

* A blocked square-headed window in the west end, largely covered by the 1902-3 porch, is probably post-medieval.

* The chancel is all rebuild, but stands on earlier footings; a worn chamfered plinth at the east end looks like 12th-century work.

Inside

* The spectacular chancel arch is remarkable both for its richness and for its fine state of preservation – it had been plastered over in the 18th century and was disinterred in 1902-3. It has two orders of chevron and an outer one of paired masks with foliage looping from their mouths. The carved capitals are a delight – on the south the Fall of Man and a Boar Hunt, on the north birds, beasts and foliage. All is interpreted in a 2006 article by Rita Wood[27] who reads it as embodying a teaching scheme, based on two sermons by St Augustine, and suggests that it was designed by a canon of Guisborough; she speculates that it may represent a 'gift of sculpture' made in return for a grant of access to local ironstone.

* On the north of the sanctuary a good medieval cross slab with the arms of the local Fitz Conan family.

---

[27] 'The Romanesque Chancel Arch at Liverton, North Yorkshire', Yorkshire Archaeological Journal 78, 111-143.

Lythe, St Oswald

Both a landmark and a seamark, the church lies to the east of the village at the top of the long descend to Sandsend, commanding a tremendous prospect towards Whitby. It combines elements familiar to Cleveland churches, genuine medieval fabric, a very good Edwardian restoration, and a tremendous collection of early lapidary material which has recently been made the subject of an impressive exhibition.[28] Unusually for Cleveland, the church is normally open, although one needs to contact a churchwarden to see the additional stones in the tower basement.

Outside

* Approaching the church from the south-west, all that one sees is the product of Sir Walter Tapper's c. 1910 remodelling. He found a preaching box formed by knocking together the main body and full-length north aisle of what was apparently a largely 13th-century church, with its west tower rebuilt in 1768, and left an Arts-and-Crafts no-expense-spared Gothic building so splendid that one can hardly begrudge the loss of some historic fabric, although this had apparently been so much altered that it was impossible to reconstruct the original form of the building.

* On the north it is a different matter. Medieval fabric survives for the full length of the wall, supported by a plethora of buttresses of varying shapes and sizes. Both north aisle and vestry (later joined) have diagonal buttresses.

* The east elevation is old as well; the chancel has a pair of 13th-century lancets and there is a restored two-light window round the corner on the south, but the south aisle is all Tapper's work.

Inside

* Architecturally virtually everything here is Tapper's work; old photographs are displayed showing the building before, and during, the c1910 works. A piscina and recess alongside on the south of the sanctuary, both with trefoiled arches, are in situ 13th-century work.

* The works produced around 40 Pre-Conquest stones (mostly Anglo-Scandinavian, i.e. 10th and early 11th century, when there was clearly a very significant graveyard here), along with some medieval ones. The best are displayed at the west end, along with instructive modern illustrations showing how the graveyard might have looked when its hogbacks and crosses were fresh and decorated with painting. There are also 12th-century stones including a capital with a 'green man' and part of a tympanum. Most of the re-used stones apparently came from the 1768 tower.

* There are many more stones displayed on benches in a basement beneath the tower, along with a collection of relevant literature, and catalogues of all the lapidary material. Would that other churches displayed their stones as well as this!

[28] See the excellent and informative website www.stoswaldslythe.org.uk.

Marske-by-the-Sea, St Germain

31 Marske. The 12th century font, a sophisticated piece of carving demonstrating the Norman love of abstract geometric patterns; a very similar font from Upleatham is now in the old church at Skelton.

On a wind-blasted site right on the coast, only the graveyard and tower now survive of the medieval parish church. In 1808 Graves saw the church in a ruinous state; it consisted of an aisled 12th-century nave, a chancel he thought to be 13th century, and an 'embattled west tower surmounted by a short stone spire' - which is all that survives today. The nave arcades consisted of circular piers supporting round arches and were apparently of 12th-century date, while the chancel is said to have been an addition of the 13th century. The chancel arch was pointed, but the windows had been altered probably in the 18th century. The body of the church was rebuilt in 1821 and then the building, like Eston, was relegated to use as a cemetery chapel in 1867 when the new church of St Mark was opened, and lasted until the 1950s when it was demolished.

* The tower is clearly of late 18th/early 19th-century character, despite a current information board at the entrance to the churchyard stating that it was 'largely built around 1160 AD'. The fact that it pre-dates the 1821 rebuilding is shown by the existence of two roof lines on its east face, that of the medieval nave symmetrical with the tower, and at a higher level that of the 1821 preaching box nave, the ridge of which was in line with the north side of the tower.

* What could be genuine 12th-century work is the old west wall of the nave, which clearly pre-dates the tower – very much the same scenario as at Eston. Again, as at Eston, this has later openings (including a Gothic-arched doorway to a former gallery) and sockets for gallery floor and church ceiling.

* The remainder of the outline of the building pulled down in the 1950s is outlined by the surviving base courses of its stone walls which have a couple of substantial bases of buttresses, and may in part survive from the medieval building.

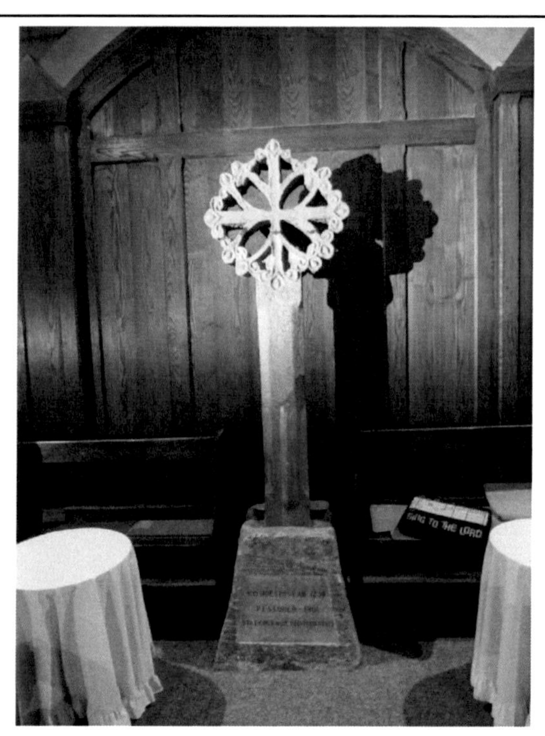

32 Marske, another treasure now in St Mark's Church, a splendid 13th century cross, the well-preserved head having been found buried in the coastal dunes.

Other relics are now in St Mark's Church, beside the impressive Marske Hall of 1625.

* A fine geometric-patterned 12th-century font rather like that at Skelton.

* Set against the west wall of the nave is a splendid free-standing 13th-century cross, its openwork head of clustered fleur-de-lys very reminiscent of cross slab designs.

* Now set in the internal face of the west wall of the north aisle (in what is now a kitchen) a fine 12th-century capital with a mask with foliage scrolls issuing from its mouth, the traditional 'Green Man'.

* Four old hatchments, retrieved from the old church, are set on the west wall of the nave.

33 Marske, St Mark's Church. A relic from the old church of St Germain, a capital, probably from the chancel arch, with the familiar Norman motif of a Green Man - perhaps an allusion to the medieval legend of Seth burying his father Adam with a seed from the Tree of Life in his mouth, although pagan interpretations are more trendy.

Marton, St Cuthbert

Originally this was quite a big Norman church with aisles, transepts, and, if a sketch on an old map is to be believed, a west tower as well. The chancel was probably rebuilt or extended in the 13th century. At some later period the tower, and the south aisle and transept, were all lost; the latter were reinstated in the 1840s, the architect being J.B.Rudd, of Tollesby Hall, 'an amateur' in sharp-edged spiky neo-Norman. It is probably fair to say that he did his best, and admit that after a century and a half his work is just beginning to take on a charm of its own.

Outside

* The south wall is of the 1840s, bar a 17th-century armorial panel now perched on the parapet of the south aisle.

* Go round to the west end; again all the stonework looks restoration but notice the broken-off plinths of the buttresses; are these the stubs of the side walls of the lost tower?

* It is only on the north that older fabric survives. The pilaster buttresses and lower courses of the embattled aisle wall look old (although Ord writing before the restoration says the 'aisles' had been destroyed).

* The north transept is intriguing, with two pilaster buttresses on the north. And odd little arched recesses a course above the plinth at each end of the wall. The two-light window on the west looks 14th-century work.

Inside

* The north arcade is 12th-century work, with interesting carved capitals (although there is some doubt as to their authenticity); there is a four-bay part (the western arch rebuilt) then a gap and a separate arch, perhaps a little earlier, to the transept.

* In the chancel the only genuinely old feature seems to be the 13th-century piscina with dogtooth ornament.

* In the north transept floor is a big medieval cross slab with remains of original lead inlay (cf. Easington), with a sword and another emblem which might have been a book.

* On the chancel floor, against the south wall, a late medieval floor stone with a black-letter inscription, little of which is now legible.

Middlesbrough, St Hilda

All that can be seen of the medieval church of St Hilda, and its associated Benedictine Priory, can be viewed by visiting the Dorman Museum in the centre of the modern town. By 1130 Robert de Brus had granted a church here to Whitby Abbey, and a small priory was established. Its church seems to have remained in use until the 17th century. A 1618 plan shows a tiny representation of a church, with a tower and some sort of spire, alongside a substantial house; more informative is an 18th-century drawing showing a large house which clearly has medieval features, with the ruins of the church adjacent. By the early 19th century all this seemed to have gone, and one farmhouse 'The Old White House' remained, which the new town grew around in the 1830s; when this was pulled down in 1846 the shell of the chancel was revealed, with remains of 15th-century windows in the side walls. Some architectural fragments were retained, and subsequently had a remarkably chequered history. Built into the wall of a brewery that arose near

34 Middlesbrough Priory. A late-18th century drawing showing the remains of what appears to have been a fully-fledged monastic house, with the ruins of a substantial church and an attached house, perhaps the medieval west range.

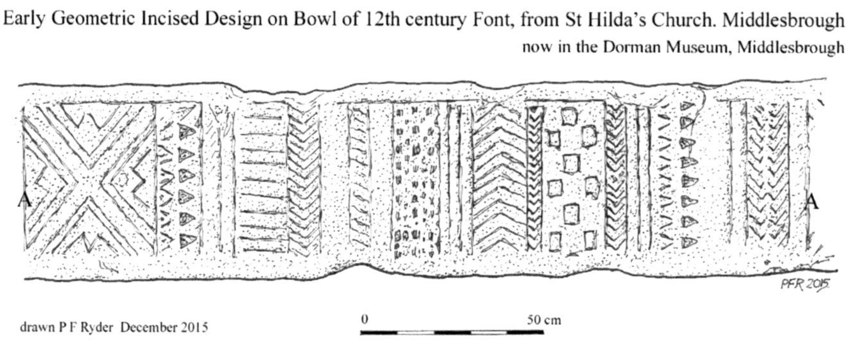

Early Geometric Incised Design on Bowl of 12th century Font, from St Hilda's Church. Middlesbrough
now in the Dorman Museum, Middlesbrough
A
A
PFR 2015
drawn P F Ryder December 2015
0
50 cm

35 Middlesbrough Priory. The priory church seems to have also functioned as a parish church, at least after the Dissolution, and its font has managed to survive. It is circular; its incised geometric patterns are here drawn as a continuous band, and are much cruder than the (later?) Marske and Upleatham fonts.

the site, they were retrieved when this was pulled down in c1900 and then incorporated into an ornamental arch in Albert Park, but in 1911 taken to St Hilda's Church (built in 1838-40) and finally, when this in turn was demolished in 1969 brought to their present resting place. There are a number of small architectural fragments, of various medieval dates, all now safe in glass cases, but there is also a fine early Norman font, also from St Hilda's, with crudely incised 'early geometric' ornament.

Newton-under-Roseberry, St Oswald

A Norman nave, mid-Victorian (1857) chancel and a good west tower of 1901 by the redoubtable Temple Moore.

Outside

* Nave of coursed squared blocks with a chamfered plinth; blocked north door with a carved tympanum, much worn but an upright cross is visible. Windows altered, probably enlargements of originals.

* The south porch is probably of the 14th century, and has an outer arch with shouldered lintel re-using a fine cross slab with a recumbent hound at the base of the cross – maybe an echo of the beasts under the feet of effigies. The porch gable has a 12th-century headstone utilised as its finial.

* Another headstone cross now set on top of the south-east corner of the nave.

* In the south wall of the tower stair turret a fine carved block, perhaps of c1100 and originally an impost, with a dragon confronting what might be a wolf.

* Outside the south wall of the nave a stone coffin, and a weathered cross slab.

Inside

* Good Norman chancel arch of two moulded orders, springing from an impost band, chamfered beneath, which returns the full width of both faces of the wall.

* Recess on the south of the sanctuary re-using a medieval headstone as its rear wall and another slab with a cross as its head.

* 12th-century font, from Ingleby Arncliffe, with intersecting round arches and a band of cable moulding above; looks to have been re-cut.

Ormesby, St Cuthbert

The parish church at Ormesby is a larger but in some ways very similar building to its former chapel of St Helen's at Eston; Graves' 1808 description tells us it had a nave, a strong square tower and chancel, the nave being the oldest part and having a circular chancel arch and a south doorway with zigzag ornament, partly built up – a description so similar to what he wrote about Eston that one wonders if he confused the two buildings. The ghost of Ormesby's Norman nave survives but most of what we see today is 1875 reconstruction by Hicks and Charlewood, or the 1907 tower and spire by Temple Moore, all reputable architects.

Outside

* Norman masonry survives on the south of the nave, with the original plinth and buttresses.

* The south-west vestry (where one would expect a porch) has a plain square-section plinth and looks Georgian.

* The external south walls of the church are a treasure house of carved stones; in the eastern bay of the nave wall, east end of the chancel vestry and chancel wall beyond the vestry are 14 cross slabs along with several Pre-Conquest fragments.

Inside

* At the east end of the north aisle the effigy of a 14th-century lady, who has been identified as Lady Juliana Percy. On the windowsill alongside is part of a coped-and-tegulated grave cover (cf. Yarm), representing the tiled roof of a 'man's last house' and probably of the 12th century.

* Beside the pulpit are the moulded base of a medieval column (implying the church once had an aisle?) and the bowl of a holy water stoup.

* Under the tower an impressive fragment of a male effigy – just a pair of feet resting on a fine lion. On the windowsill above is the head of an Anglo-Scandinavian cross.

Osmotherley, St Peter

An attractive church in a pretty village. Apart from the west tower and (rebuilt) south porch almost all one sees is either late 18th/early 19th century (walling on north, with a typical shallow plinth) or 1892 when C. Hodgson Fowler restored and remedievalised the building, adding the south aisle and replacing all the windows. He uncovered the foundations of an apsidal east end, said to have been Saxon although such a feature could equally well have been a late 11th or early 12th-century one.

Outside

* The west tower is probably of 15th-century date although its west window may be a century later; the angle buttresses have some unusual detail in their triangular projections.

* At the foot of the north wall of the nave a medieval chamfered plinth is just visible, below the Georgian one, showing that the wall was rebuilt on old footings. Near the west end of the Georgian wall part of a medieval cross slab has been re-used, with the shaft and stepped base of a cross.

* The south porch, moved out and rebuilt stone-for-stone by Hodgson Fowler, has a range of little chamfered square-headed windows reminiscent of those in the 1458 vestry at Kirkby-in-Cleveland.

Inside

* In the south porch quite a collection of Pre-Conquest and 12th-century stones, several now in a sadly deteriorating state; the hogback on the eastern bench has disintegrated in recent years.

* The south door, moved out to its present position in 1892, is a good Norman piece, with an inner order of beakheads and an outer of chevron.

* The nave arcade is of 1892 but the chancel arch is 13th or 14th-century work; notice in particular the very short triple-shafted responds.

* The two-bay south arcade of the chancel is of c. 1540, when Sir James Strangways gave money in his will 'to make an aisle on the south side of the choir'. At its east end it cuts into a 13th-century recess for a piscine or sedilia, just one side of which survives.

* Plain circular font, probably Norman, at the west end of the aisle.

Roxby, St Nicholas

A strange little church, unusually a late medieval foundation of c1520, in a remote hamlet 3 km south-west of Hinderwell (in which parish it lies); the Boulby Potash Mine is now an inescapable feature of the expansive landscape it commands. A simple rectangle with a western tower; much is of 1818, and Churchwarden Tudor in style. It was abandoned and derelict in 1894 but restored and returned to use in 1909.

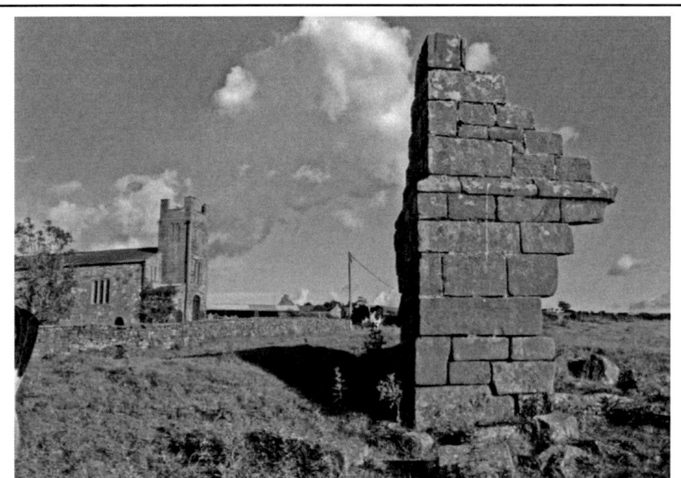

36 Roxby. A puzzling little church that seems to be late medieval in part, remodelled as usual in the Churchwarden era; here it is seen from the surviving fragment of Roxby Hall which lies in the field to the north-west.

Outside

* There are clearly different builds in the fabric; Pevsner and the Victoria County History see the earliest parts as 17th-century fabric. On the north the walling of the west part of the wall looks older but on the south a blocked priest's door with a round arch and blind tympanum could be late medieval; this is a building that needs more study.

* A gallery stair survives on the south of the tower, which looks typical early 19th-century work.

* In the field to the north-west, a single lonely crag of masonry of the medieval or 17th-century hall.

Inside

* In the chancel floor a brass to Thomas Boynton, d. 1523, who founded the church and who 'was ye first corsse to be beryed in yt', totally in the medieval tradition with his figure in armour and shields at the corners, somewhat vernacular in its craftsmanship (Pevsner just says 'bad').

Seamer, St Martin

A neat little Georgian Gothick church of 1821-2, replacing one described by Graves as 'a low structure apparently of remote origin', consisting, like the present building, of chancel, nave and tower (*Cleveland*, 186).

Outside

* The south elevation is of herringbone-tooled olive/brown sandstone, with detail typical of the period – square-headed windows of two lancet lights under Tudor-style hoodmould with turned-back ends, and a tall but shallow square-edged plinth.

* The slender west tower is glanced by high-level lancet windows, now blocked, which, as at Eston, would have lit a western gallery.

* The north elevation of the nave is quite different, re-using older stone. The eastern of the two windows is clearly a re-used medieval piece as well, a square-headed onc of two trefoiled ogee lights. The north side of the chancel is of rather browner stone, but with the same plinth as on the south; the arched head and uppermost stone of each jamb of the priest's door look more recent than the lower jambs. So does any medieval fabric survive in situ? The fact that both nave and chancel walls have the same Georgian-style plinth would argue for a total rebuilding.

Inside

* The font bears a plate inscribed 'The gift of Sir Cuthbert Heron, Baronet, to the parish of Seamer, county of York. This marble pillar was taken from the ruins of a church at Alexandria, in Egypt, at the glorious battle of the Nile, in the year 1798, and brought to England in the ship Antelope, Captain William Rayne.'

* Wall tablet with bust, in memory of Stephen Attlay, 'late of Jamaica,' d.1786.

Skelton, All Saints (Old Church)

All Saints church stands at the west end of Skelton village, beside the entrance to the grounds of the Castle, once a de Brus stronghold although, as with the church, the medieval was all but swept away at the end of the 18th century. It was always 'the squire's church' and when parish and squire fell out in the 19th century and the parish built their own church, another All Saints, in the village, the old church was abandoned and left completely unmodernised, to be rescued by judicious repair in the late 20th century as a building frozen in time, frozen in fact since 1785.

The church is now in the care of the Churches Conservation Trust; a notice directs the visitor where to find the key a few houses away.

Outside

* The exterior is classic Cleveland Churchwarden, a simple embattled west tower, a three-bay nave with round-arched windows still preserving their intersecting Gothick glazing bars, and a chancel with a Venetian east window.

* Go round to the north side and the masonry of the chancel is quite different. It has one big stepped buttress – so something of the medieval church did survive the rebuilding by John Hall Stevenson (the squire). What looks like a north transept is in fact his private pew.

Inside

* A remarkable interior. The nave is full of original box pews, and the three-decker pulpit, half way along the south wall, faces the squire's pew - complete with fireplace - on the north. The Word was indeed predominant over the Sacrament, but there was no equality under the Word...

* Note the pew holders names painted on the panelling alongside the wall. Skelton was taken as a model for several features in the Beamish reconstruction of St Helen's, Eston.

* One incongruity calls one back to the medieval origins of the church. The chancel is markedly skew, to the south; whatever the reasons for this, one would not expect to find this misalignment in a post-medieval church, nor indeed would one expect a preaching-box nave to be accompanied by a chancel of these dimensions.

* The aforesaid chancel is now empty, bar for altar and altar rails, but is home to a collection of Pre-Conquest and medieval stones, along with old creed and commandments boards and wall memorials.

* In the centre of the floor is a blue limestone slab with indents for brasses and an inscription, probably of 15th-century date and commemorating members of the Fauconberg family who then held the Castle.

* Three stone coffins (one with remains of a lid with a central raised shaft) are survivors of a 'vast number' that Ord in 1846 records as having been found north-west of the church.

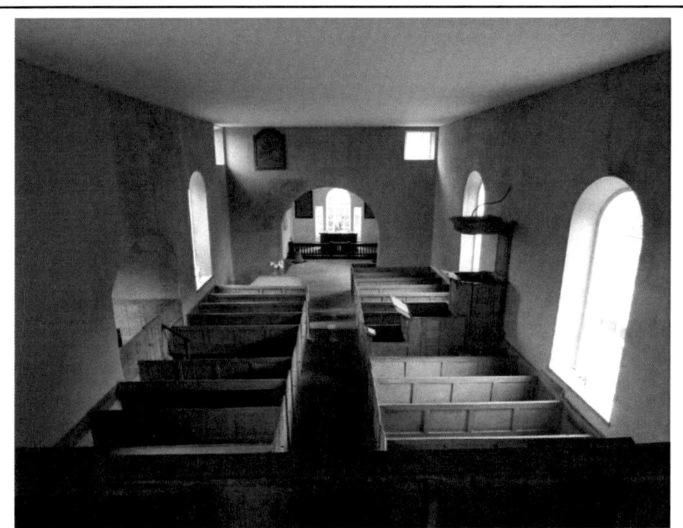

37 Skelton, All Saints (Old Church). Apart from the remarkable Whitby, Cleveland's best-preserved Churchwarden interior. Only the skewed alignment of the chancel betrays the survival of some medieval fabric.

* Other stones include one end of a crude hog back, with a bear's head, and a couple of small pieces (within the altar rails) that actually came from a 1970s excavation at Upleatham. An elaborate 13th-century piece with a petalled roundel seems to be part of a window head, and rather grand for a small church – did it come from the Castle?

* In the north-west corner of the nave is a very fine 12th-century font, square and with geometrical patterns on its faces, very like that at Marske. It comes from St Andrew's Church at Upleatham.

* In the present parish church, part of an inscribed Saxon sundial.

Stainton, SS Peter and Paul

Another typical Cleveland church with the threefold character of medieval origins, Churchwarden remodelling then Victorian gothicisation. All we know of the medieval church is that it had a c1200 chancel arch, a later medieval north-east chapel to its nave ('the Hemlington aisle') and a west tower. In 1765 the nave was rebuilt as a Churchwarden preaching box, then a Gothic chancel was recreated in 1861; the nave received Gothic windows in 1900. The 'Millennium Room' replaced a Victorian vestry on the north of the chancel, in 2001.

Outside

* The late medieval west tower built around by the western corners of the preaching box, just as at Stokesley. The tower is an odd mix of 15th century (belfry openings, parapet) and late 17th/early 18th century (west door, the Classical-section string course below the belfry).

* The preaching box was built on the footings of the medieval nave. Sections of original chamfered plinth are visible on both sides, rather more on the north with what looks like the base of the medieval north door visible.

* The north chapel has medieval plinths and masonry in its lower walls.

* On the north of the 2001 extension are re-used 19th-century features (and an 1899 rainwater hopper) but the big quatrefoil window re-set in the gable (it had been re-used in the earlier Victorian vestry) is a puzzle; is it a genuine medieval piece?

* The chancel is all Victorian Gothic; look at the 'tegulated' ornament on the big buttresses. Outside the south-east corner is a stone coffin claimed as 'Saxon', but with no real dating evidence.

38 Stainton. A mysterious feature re-set in the north wall of the new Millennium Hall, and previously in the north wall of the mid-19th century chancel; is it a genuine medieval piece, perhaps a quatrefoil window?

Inside

* The tall narrow round-headed tower arch, plastered over, looks 18th-century work; was the tower rebuilt, re-using old materials?

* The arch to the transept is simple 15th-century work in parts.

* The chancel arch is the best medieval feature, pointed rather than round but still with some Romanesque feel in its imposts and semicircular jamb shafts.

* In the chancel, standing upright in the recess of the priest's door in the south wall, a good (but weathered) effigy of a medieval priest, along with some other interesting carved fragments.

* The oldest stones are now inside the 2001 extension. High in the south wall are a crosshead and a piece of shaft, and re-set on the north side of the east window a simpler cross head and the bear's head terminal of an Anglo-Scandinavian hogback.

Thornaby, St Peter ad Vincula

A rare dedication, 'St Peter in Chains'. Now standing alone on a large expanse of hummocky greensward that represents Thornaby's ancient village green – although there is now modern suburbia all around – this is the mutilated and abraded nave of a Norman church, restored in 1908 when box pews and a three-decker pulpit were removed.

Outside

* The west end has two big stepped buttresses, set asymmetrically, with a late square-headed door between; above it is the head of a late medieval window of two round-arched lights, and the gable is topped by an old bellcote.

* The side walls show a patchwork of fabrics, with three plain square-headed windows on the south – very like those at Hilton – and one on the north, which retains one old chamfered jamb. The east jamb and turn of the arch of an old north door are visible.

* The eastern quoins rather oddly have a narrow vertical chamfer.

* One long quoin a metre above the plinth at the east end of the south wall is a medieval grave slab, with an incised pair of shears.

* The east end has a slab of walling added in 1908 to allow the chancel arch to be opened out and restored. Prior to this there was an east window, with built into the wall below it a stone allegedly with a Runic inscription which had been read as 'The Best of Bistwick'. What this means, and what happened to the stone, no-one seems to know.

Inside

* The chancel arch, now framing the altar, is by far the best feature, semicircular and of two orders, with acanthus foliage carving on the capitals.

* The walls show many patches and irregularities; it is not clear which breaks are remains of earlier features, and which simply represent structural failure. The south wall is very irregular in plan, and the eastern half of the north wall better-quality squared fabric than the western; does it represent a mid-12th-century extension of an shorter early 12th-century nave? Detailed

39 Thornaby, St Peter ad Vincula. All that survives is the much-altered nave, its best feature the Norman chancel arch.

recording and analysis might be useful.

* Re-used in the eastern splay of the central window on the south are three carved stones, a base, a 12th-century capital with beasts, and a sinister standing figure, perhaps a devil.

* West of the window is a shallow square-headed recess which might represent an earlier south door, although there is no sign of one externally.

* The round-arched north doorway is better seen internally than outside.

* The font at the south-west corner of the nave has a moulded base of 12th-century character, and a very plain shaft and bowl.

Upleatham, St Andrew

A highly-picturesque little building, on its own beside the road away from the present village, and most famous for being (incorrectly) claimed as 'the smallest church in the country'. At the time of writing it feels a bit abandoned; the only gate into the churchyard is seized up, and visitors have established a path through a hole in the churchyard wall; as at Whorlton, the interior is only glimpsable through peep-holes in a locked door.

40 Upleatham, St Andrew. A seriously-shrunken building. Only the western half of the nave - with its tiny west tower - remains roofed. The low walls to the left enclosed the 18th century Lowther vault, but seem to include the south wall of the medieval chancel and the east end of the former south aisle.

The small size of the building is a result of its being seriously abbreviated. All that remains roofed is the western half of what was once a four-bay aisle, with a small 17th-century west tower, solid at its base. Excavations in the 1970s , never properly published, revealed parts of the walls and several medieval monuments.

Outside

* The south wall is an instructive piece of archaeology; one and a half arches of the Norman nave arcade are visible, with a blocked window in the first bay and a blocked door in the second.

* The east wall is probably 18th-century work; note the keystone in the course above its lintel, typical of the period. Higher up three old corbels have been re-set.

* The north wall has a 13th-century doorway and weathered Norman corbels.

* Quite high up on the west side of the tower is a stone inscribed 'WILLIAM CROW BVLDED STEPEL 1684'.

* East of the church are the ruins of the 18th-century Lowther Vault, which in fact incorporates medieval walling; its north side is the south wall of the old chancel (with a big buttress at its south-east corner) and its west wall the east end of the nave and aisle, complete with what looks like the base of the eastern respond of the arcade, but is probably a re-set stone.

Inside (One needs to make arrangements with Redcar and District Council to inspect the interior, although it can be glimpsed through peering in through the little loops in the door)

* There are two intact cross slabs and the head of a third, of quite high quality.

* In the east wall is a re-set trefoiled recess, now decaying badly, enclosing what looks like a small carved figure.

* In the west wall is the splayed recess of the medieval west window, later covered by the tower.

* The 12th-century font is now in the Old Church of All Saints at Skelton.

Westerdale, Christ Church

A little Gothick church, rebuilt in 1838 and so the very earliest Victorian, but with various later Victorian alterations such as the tracery in the east window (1875) and the porch on the south of the tower (1896).

Outside

* Built into the west wall of the tower is a stone that looks like an altered early Norman door head, with a segmental arch studded with rudimentary nail-head, incised chevron patterns, and '1838' carved in relief on the tympanum.

* In the churchyard c. 8 m west of the tower a coped and moulded medieval graveslab.

41 Westerdale. Little is known of the medieval church, except that it must have had a 12th-century doorway, the head of which was re-used (and re-dated) in the west wall of its successor.

* South of the south-east corner of the nave a big stepped-and-moulded block, probably medieval, but a bit difficult to interpret. Is it part of the base of a churchyard cross?

Inside

* Inside the church, in the porch, there are six medieval grave slabs (including two head stones), an attractive little collection of varied designs.

Whitby, St Mary

Surely the best-known of all Cleveland churches, and for character and atmosphere second to none, perched with the Abbey on its headland. It is thought that most of the Anglo Saxon settlement was up here – and maybe a Roman signal station as well – but much has been consumed by the crumbling cliff edge now nibbling at the boundaries of the churchyard; every so often a fresh scatter of bones on the eroding slopes below prompt lurid headlines. The church also suffers from its associations with lurid 19th-century fiction and consequent late 20th-century Goth culture.[29]

Always subordinate to the Abbey towering over it to the east, this is nevertheless a big church, although in its original medieval form it was no more than a nave and chancel – the nave surprisingly long for a church of this date. Later came the western tower and transepts, then the post-medieval transformation which left it what it is today. The nave was extended to the north in 1818, and the Gothick south porch built in 1823-4. All this miraculously escaped the hand of the Victorian restorer, perhaps because the better-off townsfolk of the West Cliff - Whitby is very much a town of two halves - were able to build their own churches.

Outside

The church is best seen from the slightly-higher ground to the east, from which it manifests itself as a sprawling jumble of a building, a bizarre mix of embattled parapets, Gothick-glazed windows and upthrusting roof dormers.

42 Whitby. Perhaps the most remarkable of all Cleveland churches, a strange amalgam of the 12th, 13th and 18th centuries, here seen from the north-east; note the external stairs giving access to the various galleries within.

* The original mid-12th-century fabric is best seen in the chancel with its corbel table and round-arched windows (and the only high-pitched and slated roof in the building, a product of 1905 restoration) and in the south wall of the nave with its Norman door (with evidence of a former gabled porch) and two more windows.

* The massive but squat west tower is an addition of the later 12th century. It is said to have lost its top in the 17th century; if so, were the large belfry openings reconstructed at a lower level?

* The transepts are 13th-century additions; the northern still has three lancets in its end wall and the south a larger window that has lost its tracery. On the east side are a variety of external stairs serving the various galleries within.

---

[29] Despite its name, its devotees sadly do not seem to demonstrate any great interest in the medieval architectural style characterised by pointed arches.

Inside

This is a church frozen in time, and the first impression of the interior brings total bewilderment; are we in a church, a nonconformist chapel or on board ship? The liturgical focus might either be the towering three-decker pulpit or the stove (still cleaned out every day by the Church Maid), with galleries all around and above that the clerestory and roof lights carried on broad basket arches supported by big lobed piers.

* The actual medieval architecture is largely hidden by the galleries (to which the visitor does not normally have access). In the nave the upper parts of the tower arch and the zigzag rear arches of the southern windows are hidden from the ordinary visitor, as are parts of the 12th-century chancel arch. In the chancel the original windows have roll-moulded surrounds.

43 Whitby. The interior; stand in awe and wonder, there is nowhere else quite like this in the country.

* A pair of late medieval fonts – at least, octagonal bowls with panelled and traceried sides which look very like fonts – they were found at Newbiggin Hall near Aislaby.

* The Cholmley Pew which arrogantly spans the chancel arch, with its barley-sugar piers and cherub-studded frieze is of later 17th-century date. The west gallery with its Doric pilasters is of c1700 and the north gallery of 1764.

* The pulpit of 1778 originally straddled the central aisle of the nave, and was moved into its present position in 1847. The attached ear trumpets helped an early 19th-century vicar's wife, who was deaf, hear her husband's sermons; it is not recorded whether they were installed at his or her request.

* The box pews are of 17th and 18th-century dates; their faded inscriptions distinguish between 'free' sittings and those intended specifically for 'strangers'.

* At the west end of the north aisle a considerable collection of 12th-century architectural fragments are displayed; which part of the church do they come from?

* There is another 'museum corner' in the south transept where several medieval grave slabs can be examined.

* Only in the chancel can one escape into what feels like a medieval church, thanks to a 1905 restoration by W. D. Caroe, who thankfully came late enough, and under an architect wise enough, to not interfere with things further west. The roof structure is his, and is rather good.

Whorlton, Holy Cross

Whorlton is a memorable place, of departed consequence and present tranquillity, and very early origins – Roman pottery has been found in the churchyard. Its village has long since has migrated downhill to a streamside setting at Swainby, leaving the picturesque ruins of its church and castle, and a host of intriguing earthworks – now seen as primarily those of the Castle gardens. The Castle was the home of the Meynell family, and its 14th-century gatehouse is largely intact. Holy Cross Church has a wonderfully complex history, beginning as a substantial Norman church with a three-bay north aisle; around 1200 a south aisle was added (still with round arches) and later the nave was lengthened a bay to the west, a south aisle added and the chancel extended, with a new northern chapel. However, the vicissitudes of the 14th century, be they some unrecorded Scots raid or population depletion after the Black Death, cost the church its south aisle which had gone by c. 1400, and a new south porch-cum-tower (cf. Danby and Hutton Rudby) had been built. The north aisle may have lasted until c. 1810. In 1876 the church was abandoned and partly demolished to provide materials for its replacement in Swainby; the old arcades were found embedded in the nave walls, and left standing along with the tower and chancel, which served as a cemetery chapel and remains roofed. Archaeological recording was carried out in conjunction with repair work in 1996-7, and further light shed on the complex story of the building.[30]

44 Whorlton, Holy Cross. Half-ruined and the epitome of picturesque; the village migrated downhill to Swainby and left the church, ruined castle and a landscape of earthworks, best seen in low sunlight on a summer evening.

Outside

* The western corners of the nave and the arcades survive. Three 12th-century arches of the north arcade with scalloped capitals, a (fallen) western arch with nail-head, three taller round arches to the south arcade of c1200 (the tower built over the western) and a later medieval western arch. The rather odd cinquefoiled heads of a two- and a three-light window that now sit on top of the south arcade are from windows that were once inserted in the blocked arches.

* The tower was once a porch but its outer arch has been blocked up. Weathered medieval cross slabs are re-used in its east and west walls – with many more in the internal walls, although it is kept locked. Its relation to the adjacent arch of the arcade is a piece of instructive above-ground archaeology; it is clear that the arcade was first blocked, and then the tower built on.

* Good Norman chancel arch with quite elaborate mouldings, now blocked by a wall of 1877; the wall above (capped by a bellcote) a Victorian rebuild as well. Blocked opening skewed through the wall to the north which formerly linked to the lost northern chapel.

---

[30] See Vyner, B. (1999) Whorlton Old Holy Cross Church, Swainby, North Yorkshire. Yorkshire Archaeological Journal 71, 129-153, a most useful account.

* The chancel has some good c1300 windows and a priest's door; a three-light window at the west end of the south wall (above a blocked 'low side') has the arms of the Bates family (of Easby) (which occur again inside) and a '1593' inscription on its lintel. On the north is an 1877 projection backing the Meynell tomb. In the buttress north of the chancel arch is the head of a cross slab carved in high relief, just above an '1891' datestone.

Inside

There is quite a lot to see inside the chancel; contact the present church in Swainby village to make arrangements for a visit. Otherwise its interior can only be glimpsed, through a small grilled opening, rather as at Upleatham.

* Unless you can arrange for the door to be unlocked, the interior of the chancel can only be glimpsed through a small grilled opening. In the chancel are a piscina, an aumbry and various corbels.

* On the north is a cusped recess with heraldry pointing to a date in the early 15th century, moved in from the former north chapel demolished in the later 19th century. It contains an older knight's effigy of timber, which is thought to be one of two Sir Nicholas de Meynells, of either 1299 or 1322. Lying loose beside it is an early medieval headstone cross.

* In the floor is a tapering medieval slab, without any carved design, of crinoidal limestone, an unusual import from the Pennines.

* Set against the west wall (upside down) is a grave slab of c1100 found in the 1996-7 work re-used in the foundations of the former north-east chapel.

* Remains of medieval glass in the east window.

Wilton, St Cuthbert

Wilton is all contrasts; the old village in the Castle grounds south of the main road, the modern ICI complex on the north. And the church itself is a building of contrasts, medieval, Georgian Gothick and then as often a good-quality restoration in 1907 (when much of the fabric was apparently carefully taken down and re-erected stone-for-stone). The quite elongate nave is Norman, the chancel a bit of a puzzle but most likely 13th century.

45 Wilton, a remarkable rural siting despite Teesside industry only a few hundred metres away. A typical nave-and-chancel church of the 12th century which has survived sundry later changes and restorations.

Outside

* Much of the nave masonry is characteristic squared 12th-century fabric, above a chamfered plinth; some of the small round-headed windows are restoration, but that near the west end of

the north wall looks genuine; it has strangely notched jamb stones.

* The fabric of the chancel and its weathered corbel table look Norman, but the diagonal buttresses at its east end must be later – although they seem to tie in with the fabric. On the south a low-side window, priest's door, and a pair of lancets.

* The west wall of the nave has a quite different plinth, and a window of two ogee-headed lights; was it rebuilt in the 14th or 15th century? Stones with grooves made by sharpening implements have been re-used quite high up (as at Hilton).

* The south porch must be 17th-century work, with its moulded Tudor arch.

* Sir Robert Smirke designed Wilton Castle in 1810; did he remodel the church as well? The west end has short wing walls ending in square turrets with tall pyramidal caps, and a little central bell tower (stone on the west, whitewashed brick on the other sides) with a lead spire; one account saw it as being in 'pseudo-Swiss taste to suit its pretty background of rock and wooded hill'. An old picture in the church shows further Gothick spikes on the eastern corners of the nave as well.

Inside

* Excellent Norman south door with two orders of chevron, the outer on capitals with spiral patterns and masks.

* On either side of the porch early 14th-century effigies of members of the Bulmer family which lay long in the churchyard and are now much weathered.

* In the nave, a triple-arched arcade of early 19th-century ashlar carries the bellcote.

* The chancel arch is relatively recent – three stones which may be from the original one – two capitals and a moulded voussoir – have been re-set in the recess of the blocked priest's door.

Yarm, St Mary Magdalene

Yarm is set in a meander of the Tees much as Durham is in one of the Wear, and, further north, Warkworth on the Coquet. The find of a 7th-century stone here in the 19th century points to an early settlement, which is hardly surprising on such a site, but the church one sees today is that of a new Norman town planted by the de Brus family. It was founded as a Chapel of Kirklevington, and stayed one until the 19th century, but was a high status building from the first. Sadly all that survives is the west end of a broad but aisleless nave, with turrets at its angles, and (presumably) a central bell cote replaced by a later medieval tower. The rest of the church is Georgian, rebuilt after a serious fire in 1730.[31]

Outside

* The best view of the Norman west end is from the west (County Durham) bank of the Tees. The central of the original three windows has been altered, and in the gable above it is a big vesica window of the 13th century.

---

[31] For an excellent account of the early parts of the church see D.H.Heslop (1990) The Church of St Mary Magdalene, Yarm, Cleveland in Durham Archaeological Journal 6, 35-43.

* In the churchyard about 15 m south of the east end of the south aisle is an interesting coped grave slab, with a halberd (a combined spear/battle axe) on one side. The '1647' inscription probably marks a later re-use.

Inside

You will have to make arrangements to view the rooms at the west end which are historically the most interesting part of the church, but are not usually open to the public.

* A newel stair in the south-west turret leads up to a mural gallery, a highly unusual feature perhaps once serving as a 'private pew' for the manorial family. There was another stair, which only survives in part, in the north-west turret; both turrets were once taller than they are now.

* In the vestry, a 1906 addition on the south of the western chambers, are two panels of re-set medieval stones including some pieces of real interest, 12th-century coped-and-tegulated grave covers (simulating ‘a man's last house' with a shingled roof) and later medieval headstones and cross slabs.

* In the main body of the church, at the west end of the north aisle, a pair of rather small recumbent effigies, a civilian and his wife, and an inscription dated '1638'; is this a medieval monument reused?

* Octagonal 15th-century font of Teesdale limestone.

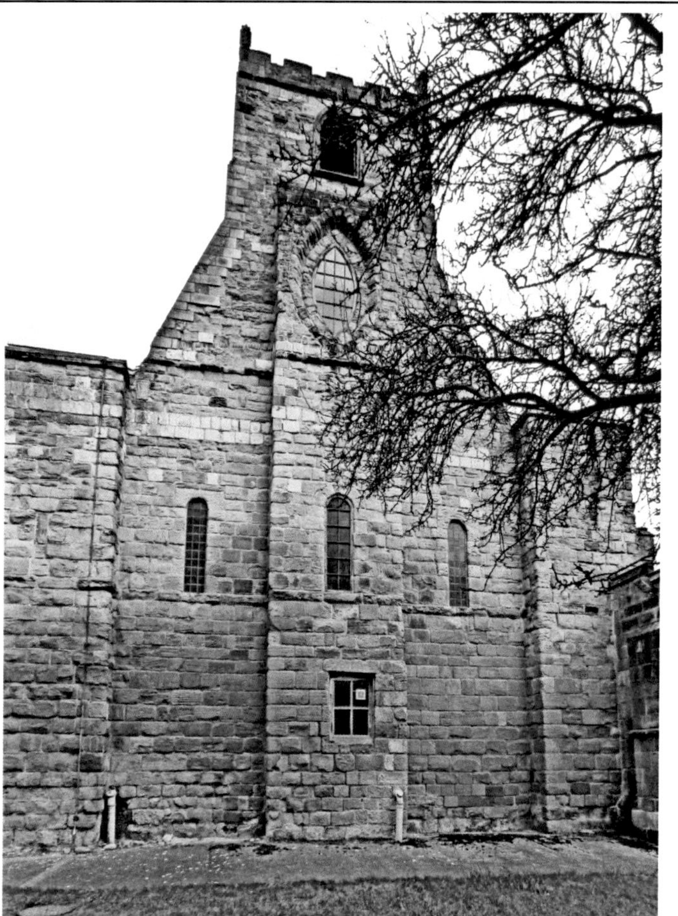

46 Yarm, only the west end survives of the church of a new 12th century town founded by the Brus family, but it is full of interesting features; the rest of the building was rebuilt in the early 18th century after a fire.

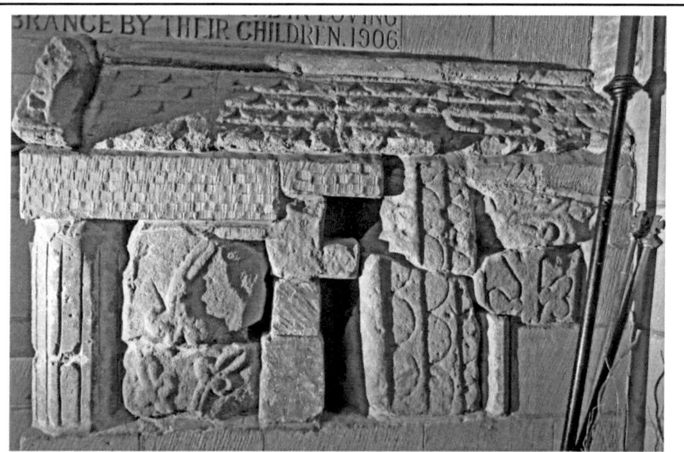

47 Yarm, stones found during restoration work and set into the vestry wall in 1906, including 12th-century coped-and-tegulated grave covers along with later medieval cross slab fragments.

9. Cleveland Churches, Norman to Churchwarden – a Unique Regional Character

Before the Norman Conquest – carved stones but no surviving church buildings – an explosion of 12th-century church construction – the landscape reorganised – new castles and monasteries - Norman church plans - later medieval changes – the Churchwarden era – Victorian restoration – the Arts and Crafts movement

---

Twenty five churches in the area – including Eston despite its migration northwards – have standing medieval fabric, ranging from relatively complete medieval buildings like Hutton Rudby and Wilton to almost mute fragments like Marske-by-the-Sea and Ormesby. Another 13 have been completely rebuilt but retain significant stones from their predecessors.

No church retains any fabric that has been identified as pre-dating the Norman Conquest, but 12 have carved stones – mostly crosses, or grave stones of some form – that do, and documentary evidence attests to the existence of another 8 by this time. No less than 16 have fabric dating between the Norman Conquest and c. 1200 – Norman or 'Transitional' in style - and at least 4 more are known to have had work of this period now evidenced by ex-situ stonework. Later medieval work is much more scarce; Guisborough and Hutton Rudby are the only two substantial buildings, whilst an early illustration suggests there was another at Kirkleatham.

Significant work of the 'Churchwarden' era – often the rebuilding of naves as 'preaching boxes' – survives at a surprising number of churches, around 16 – and it is this, together with the extensive survival of Norman work, that really marks out Cleveland churches as a distinctive group.

An oft-repeated traditional mantra is that the first Christian missionaries in the area raised preaching crosses, to be followed by timber churches and only stone buildings late in the Saxon period, or even after the Norman Conquest. The only real evidence for church origins would come from excavations, and these have been limited – some works at Brotton, Upleatham and Whorlton – and none of these revealed Pre-Norman structural remains.[32] Surviving stones of this period are largely sepulchral monuments, often showing Anglo-Scandinavian influence, as in the collection of hogback grave covers at Lythe, now displayed at the west end of St Oswald's Church in an impressive new exhibition.

The majority of Pre-Conquest churches, be they stone or wood, would thus appear to have been swept away in a veritable explosion of Norman building, which probably commenced around half a century after the actual Conquest, at the same time as new monastic houses were being founded, such as Gisborough in 1119; Whitby, apparently abandoned during the Danish onslaughts of the 9th century, had already been refounded c. 1084. The Normans brought about a complete reorganisation of the landscape, founding new villages and completely reorganising the church; an excellent analysis of how this happened in Cleveland (at least in the wapentake of Langbaurgh West) has been published by Robin Daniels.[33] The majority of Norman churches were built by the new lords – the Brus and Meynell families between them were responsible for about 20 of the churches – and Daniels pointed out that 'the new stone churches were... potent symbols of Norman power and control… people now had to go to church in a Norman building, grander than anything that had gone before, and to listen to Norman clergy expounding

---

[32] Parts of the early monastery at Whitby, including a number of stone buildings, are known from excavation.

[33] 'The Church, The Manor and the Settlement: Evidence for the Tees Valley, England', in the European journal Ruralia (1996; the paper is available online at http://www.ruralia.cz/sites/default/files/doc/pdf/102-114.pdf.

the rightness of the current order'. The churches at Skelton and Whorlton were closely associated with castles of the Brus and Meynell families respectively, and with planned settlements which were intended to be towns; at Guisborough St Nicholas' church stands close to the gateway of the Augustinian Priory – a Brus foundation, which the town grew up around, and at Whitby St Mary's Church stands in a very similar relationship to the Benedictine Abbey. The now-lost St Hilda's Church in Middlesbrough seems to have begun as the church of a small Benedictine priory.

It is this imposition of a new ecclesiastical order that is still evident in the buildings that stand today, and it is worth looking at these Norman churches, and their original plan types:

Brotton	Nave and chancel
Egton	Nave with 5-bay aisles
Eston.	Nave with ?4-bay north aisle, chancel
Faceby	Nave and chancel
Great Ayton	Nave and chancel
Hilton	Nave, chancel and ?sanctuary
Ingleby Greenhow	Nave with 5-bay north, chancel, west tower
Kirklevington	Nave and chancel
Liverton	Nave and chancel
Marske?	Nave with aisles, chancel
Marton	Nave with aisles and transepts, perhaps west tower
Ormesby	Nave and presumed chancel
Stainton	Nave and chancel
Thornaby	Nave and chancel
Whorlton	Nave with 3-bay north aisle, chancel
Whitby	Nave and chancel
Yarm	Nave and presumed chancel

It is notable that the presence or absence of aisles does not seem to relate to size or status. Eston, a mere chapel, had an aisle, Whitby, by far the largest church of all, had a simple nave-and-chancel plan. Yarm, technically a chapel but an unusually high-status building, had an aisleless nave with a western gallery and angle turrets. Only Ingleby Greenhow has an original Norman tower, although Whitby received its very substantial west tower within half a century of its original construction.

Later medieval alterations are to some extent conspicuous by their absence. Over much of Northern England the 13th century was a time for rebuilding and lengthening chancels, as seen at Kirklevington and Lythe, and also perhaps at Ingleby Greenhow and Marton, although here later alterations have confused the picture. Whorlton is one of the few churches to demonstrate a multi-phase expansion – originally having a three-bay north aisle, this was matched by a three-bay south one c. 1200, and then later nave and aisles were extended a further bay to the west. Only Hutton Rudby and Guisborough have later medieval aisles. Such towers as exist are generally later medieval, and three are unusually sited over south porches, at Danby, Hutton Rudby and Whorlton. Whorlton is an unusual case in that the tower was built after the church contracted in size again, standing on the site of the demolished south aisle. Quite a number of churches were reduced in size, although it is not always clear when; Eston and Egton had also lost aisles, Marton had lost an aisle and transept, Thornaby its chancel and Upleatham had been reduced to a mere remnant. Whether these losses were the result of medieval vicissitudes such as Scots raids or the Black Death (Whorlton at least must have been) or post-medieval neglect is not clear.

Coming to the Post-Reformation years, the 17th century saw Upleatham, and perhaps also Eston, receive new towers, and then in the 18th century, in the 'churchwarden' period proper, came a whole series of remodellings to suit the changing needs of church practice. At Kirkleatham the money of the Turners allowed a complete rebuilding, to the glory of the family as much as of God; a medieval manorial family might well endow a new chantry chapel, whereas here a Baroque mausoleum was first added to the old church and then the church rebuilt as well in a dignified Classical manner; John Carr, who worked on the adjacent Hall (sadly demolished in the mid-20th century) may have been the architect. Elsewhere naves were re-cast as 'preaching boxes' with far less architectural finesse. Brotton (1778), Easington (1771), Hinderwell (1773), Ingleby Arncliffe (1821), Kirkby-in-Cleveland (1815), Loftus (1811), Marske-by-the-Sea (1821), Skelton (1785) and Stokesley (1771) all join Eston (1822) as more or less total reconstructions made during the reign of George III; Danby (1789), Gisborough (c. 1796), Great Ayton (1790), Ingleby Greenhow (1741), Loftus (tower rebuilt 1769) and Whitby (nave rewindowed c. 1764, north aisle 1818, south porch 1821-3) all underwent substantial alterations or additions. Most of these were very simple buildings, the earlier with round-arched sash windows (e.g. Great Ayton), the later (the north aisle and porch at Whitby) verging on a rudimentary Gothic. The Eston nave had paired lancet windows; the almost-contemporary one at Marske had similar openings but set awkwardly under quasi-Tudor hoodmoulds, a design seen again at Seamer, also of 1822.

It is difficult to find a reason for this degree of Georgian rebuilding, which is unusual for the North of England; perhaps it was because, as already explained, the Norman churches had seen relatively little later enlargement and were inadequate for a population which grew as alum and then ironstone mining were developing in the area. Perhaps, as elsewhere, the Anglican establishment felt a need to counter the growth of nonconformity, in particular Wesleyan Methodism.

That this 'Churchwarden' or Georgian work survives to such an extent today may also reflect a lack of the usual Victorian restorations, which usually aimed to erase what was then seen as 'debased' work and replace it in a more appropriate Gothic style. It might be that the late 18th and early 19th century had produced substantial and sound structures which did not cry out for attention in the manner of patched and decaying medieval fabric elsewhere. Another factor may be that that the sort of prosperous landowners who would finance such restorations were rather thinner on the ground than say in parts of the East Riding. Much of Cleveland remained a 'working class' area, with its fishing and extractive industries, and there were few great country houses and estates with the exception of Kirkleatham and Wilton, close together on the south of the Tees Estuary. The Turner's Classical rebuilding of St Cuthbert's Church at Kirkleatham has already been mentioned; the church at Wilton, dedicated to the same saint, lies close to Wilton Castle, a house remodelled c1810 by architect Sir Robert Smirke for Sir John Lowther, who seems to have prettified the Norman church at the same time by adding a steep spirelet to the belfry balanced by further spikes on corner turrets. This was no reconstruction to allow more tenants to sit under the Word, simply aesthetic improvement. The very last of this wave of rebuildings was the simple little Gothic Westerdale of 1838, just after Victoria came to the throne, preserving nothing of its predecessor save a few stones – albeit interesting ones – now in its porch.

Now we come to a quite separate phase, and a country-wide one, Victorian restoration, often fuelled by the doctrines of architects such as Pugin who claimed to 'have revolutionised the taste of England', and the developing High Church movement. Gothic, as opposed to the Georgian Classic style (with its pagan overtones) was once more seen to be uniquely suited to Christian architecture, and the medieval centuries were perceived as an ideal to be regained rather than a dark age of superstition.

This great wave of remodelling and refurbishment barely affected St Helen's at Eston; all that happened there was that the east window received some basic Gothic tracery c1870, but then again by 1883 the old building was to be replaced by the new brick-built Christ Church. The same thing happened at Great Ayton where another Christ Church, again on a different site, was erected in 1876, and the old church was allowed to survive, shorn of the west bay of its nave and tower (which had been rebuilt in the 18th century). At Acklam in 1876 a new church replaced what was either a Churchwarden or very much Churchwardenised predecessor. Faceby was one medieval church totally rebuilt in 1874-5, although a few old features were re-used in the new fabric. Danby received a new and very Victorian chancel in 1848 as did Newton-under-Roseberry in 1857, Stainton in 1861 and Crathorne (which also was given a new west tower to replace its bellcote) in 1887-8. At around the same time Hodgson Fowler, an architect with a genuine interest in historic fabric, rebuilt the wholly-Churchwarden All Saints at Easington in a Decorated Gothic style, quite alien to the area. However, much as at Eston a century or so later, he found a host of earlier lapidary material re-used in the 18th-century building, and was able to reconstruct the 12th-century chancel arch inside his Victorian tower; he also found some splendid cross slabs which were carefully preserved. This respect for the past was not always the case; elsewhere in the North of England some clergy reacted against the antiquarianism of others (perhaps reflecting the growing Low Church/High Church divide). At Bolam in Northumberland one vicar took exception to the Norman grotesques on his chancel arch – the Rev S. S. Meggison (1817-1879) who 'time and time again...saw boys imitating the naughty little stone faces - putting out tongues and pulling their ears - until one day in a rage he took hammer and chisel and hacked them all off'. At Satley, in Durham, in 1870 the vicar ordered churchwardens to break up recently-discovered medieval cross slabs.

Around the turn of the century a new era dawned, at least to modern eyes, when the final phase of restorations came at the hands of a new generation of architects. Under the influence of the Arts-and-Crafts movement, they no longer slavishly imitated copy-book versions of medieval Gothic, and they also had greater respect for earlier fabric, even the despised 'Churchwarden'. This new approach is well seen at Danby, where in 1903 the preaching box nave was remodelled by Temple Moore, respecting its exterior but reinstating the lost 13th-century style arcades, albeit considerably taller than they had been, whilst assiduously preserving surviving remnants of their genuine predecessors. Temple Moore was also responsible for the chancel at Kirkby-in-Cleveland, where he left the Churchwarden nave and tower alone, and for a complete rebuild at Carlton (1896-7) and the towers at Newton-under-Roseberry (1901) and Ormesby (1907), all good-quality work. One of the best restorations was Sir Walter Tapper's 1910 remodelling of Lythe, although here his Arts-and-Crafts influenced Gothic entailed the sacrifice of the picturesque but ramshackle Churchwarden nave and tower; the extant 13th and 15th-century fabric in chancel, vestry and north aisle was carefully preserved, along with a fine collection of early carved stones that his works brought to light. The church is one of the few kept open, and its stones have very recently been made the subject of an impressive modern exhibition, which demonstrates just what can be done with the resources of historic artefacts that many buildings have.

Post Script

Summing up – some personal opinions - is a church 'only stones and mortar? – does the whole St Helen's project await a final consummation?

This has been the story of a humble but historic church building, which, after being abandoned and trapped in a deprived urban area, found last-minute salvation in being uprooted and reconstructed at a leading open air museum, restored to its pristine Georgian condition to be visited and appreciated by tens of thousands. Obviously very much a one-off, but one that prompts a few further thoughts, which being a free agent the writer is entitled to give (but you, dear reader, can of course skip this page if you want). To put my cards on the table, as well as being an Independent Buildings Archaeologist, among other things I am also a Reader in the Church of England.

The church, it is often said, is people, 'ecclesia', the assembly. Its buildings are 'only stones and mortar' – and those stones and mortar are often, quite fairly, seen as a millstone around its neck. But is anything ever 'only'? Might there be something non-quantifiable, opaque to contemporary science, about an ancient structure like this which has been the focus of a community and its worship for centuries? Even in the few weeks since St Helen's has been re-opened something has been noticed in the reaction of visitors – and museum staff as well - to the re-erected church. The museum authorities have no plans for it to become a consecrated building again – this was spelled out by the Bishop of Durham at the opening ceremony – 'if it were then the museum would become entangled in archaic church faculty law'[34] – although the building can be licensed for services if need be. The 'Church Times' reported the re-opening as 'Church resurrected as Museum Piece' … and that rankled with me, again on the implied 'only' in this phrase.

Beamish (and in particular Jim Rees) have done a splendid job. But I feel we are still one step short of a proper consummation to the whole project. The Museum are, I believe, planning a Georgian coaching inn where people can actually stay, they have erected a traditional fish-and-chip shop where the length of the queues testifies to the quality of the fish-and-chips. What about a church that can be used for its proper purposes? With a bit of enterprise on the parts of both the Museum and the current church authorities St Helen's could serve as a church again, complete with a chaplain.[35] The Church has a story to tell (which happens to centre on Death and Resurrection) and part of this story is told through its historic buildings. St Helen's is, true, now a Museum Piece and a very creditable one. It could yet be more.

Peter Ryder March 2016

[34] Fair enough. Church faculty law is only understood by wizened ecclesiastical gnomes who live in deep crypts and rarely see the light of day. This is true.

[35] The Metro Centre has its own on-site chaplain. 'The church should be where people are'. Visitor numbers at Beamish have doubled over the last five years; there were over 654,000 in 2014, making this the region's most popular museum.

Appendix: The Cross Slabs of Cleveland

The cross slab grave cover is by far the most common form of monument to survive from the medieval period, but one which by reason of its a very ubiquity has received relatively little attention, at least since the days of Victorian antiquaries. What follows is not an academic treatise but a brief account to go with scale drawings of all the cross slabs in Cleveland, which is rich in such monuments. As the name implies, most slabs are carved with a full-length cross, often in an elaborate foliate flower-like form – the cross the archetypal Christian symbol, its flowering symbolising the Christian belief of new life given through the death of Christ. Quite often the cross is accompanied by another emblem as well, relating to the person commemorated – a sword for a man, a pair of shears for a woman (or housewife, shears being the equivalent of modern kitchen scissors). A priest's slab usually showed his particular badges of office, the chalice and a clasped book.

One of the most attractive features of these monuments are the many and varied forms of crosses depicted, and this is what allows an approximate date to be ascribed – very few indeed bear any inscription, and even fewer a written date. Simple crosses, with straight or splayed arms, or perhaps made up of four circles, probably date to the 12th century; more elaborate forms with fleur-de-lys terminals, or more naturalistic foliage (cf Upleatham) are later medieval. But a warning is needed here – as with architectural features in church buildings, archaeologists have been keen to ascribe quite close dates based on stylistic changes, in the belief that design follows a steady evolutionary pattern. There is increasing evidence to show that this was not always the case; a mason would be commissioned to carve a stone, or make a new window, and he might well choose, or be asked, to copy an existing example rather than be bound by an up-to-the-minute design.

The majority of the slabs recorded here are tapering in form, and most would have probably lain in the churchyard, either forming the lid of a stone coffin, or a grave marker on the surface above it. A few high-status stones would have lain inside the church, perhaps in a tomb recess in an aisle or chancel wall. In the later medieval period what we term floor slabs – larger rectangular stones which would fit better into a church pavement – became more common, although there are few examples in Cleveland other than the impressive priest's slab at Kirklevington (3). Sometimes a slab in a churchyard might be accompanied by small upright crosses at its head, or head and foot; these are called headstones, and are included along with conventional full-length cross slabs in this survey. They are common in Cleveland; many are often sub-circular (discoidal) in form (e.g. Crathorne, Eston, Ingleby Greenhow, Kirklevington, Kirkby, Newton-under-Roseberry, Westerdale, Whorlton); others are more like small upright pillars (Bilsdale, Lythe).

In the later medieval period new monuments – inscribed slabs, brasses and effigies – came into favour, at least with those who could afford them, but the use of cross slabs continued lower down the social scale – although there are few examples we can date to the last century or so before the Reformation. Whether this is because less were made, or that earlier designs were copied (so we simply do not recognise their late date) is uncertain. There are some interesting hybrids between the higher-status forms of memorial and the cross slab. At Brotton a superb stone, alas again buried, showed a cross that was clearly copied from a brass prototype, right down to the rivets; at Hutton Rudby a priest's effigy is combined with a foliate cross, the arms of which literally sprout out of the figure's head. Both of these are of 14th century date.

In Cleveland there are around 190 cross slabs – and allied monument types – at 25 of the 35 or so churches which stand on medieval sites, a much higher survival rate than in many parts of the country.

This is partly due to the fact that suitable stone for carving, almost always a local Jurassic sandstone, was readily available throughout the area.

In Cleveland the use of cross slabs seems to have stopped at the Reformation, and indeed by the time of the Civil War even a simple cross was seen as a 'Popish' symbol by Puritans, and many stones were deliberately broken. At Eston headstone (7) was found broken into three pieces, each being re-used in a different part of the fabric, possibly reflecting a superstitious belief that the stone might re-form itself if given the chance! Many, if not most, were simply utilised as building stones, often forming lintels or treads in stairs, as at Danby and Whorlton. With Victorian restorations and rebuildings such re-used slabs were brought to light again, and were either re-set in walls so they can be appreciated today (Crathorne, Kirklevington, Ingleby Greenhow, Ormesby etc) or lie loose in porches or even scattered around churchyards. Unsecured stones are sadly vulnerable; two interesting coped stones which lay in the porch at Kirklevington 'disappeared' a few years ago and there have been other losses at Kirkleatham and Upleatham.

A Note on the Drawings

In practice cross slabs, being relatively two-dimensional objects are better recorded by drawings than photographs, where lichen, damage and discoloration of the stone can obscure the carved design, and which are highly dependant on an appropriate angle of lighting. The stones are drawn in a fieldbook, with running dimensions locating all elements of the design, and then photographed as well (hopefully with side-lighting; powerful modern LED torches are a great help here), then drawn up, usually at 1:10 scale, first in pencil and then inked in with fibre-tip pens, checking minor detail with photographs.

All these drawings, along with descriptions of the slabs will be available online as part of the database for the project 'Cross Slabs in Northern England', held by the Archaeology Data Service at the University of York (http://www.archaeologydataservice.ac.uk). The complete database contains over 4,000 cross slab monuments, covering the historic counties of Yorkshire, Durham, Northumberland, Cumberland, and Westmoreland.

Bilsdale (Chop Gate)

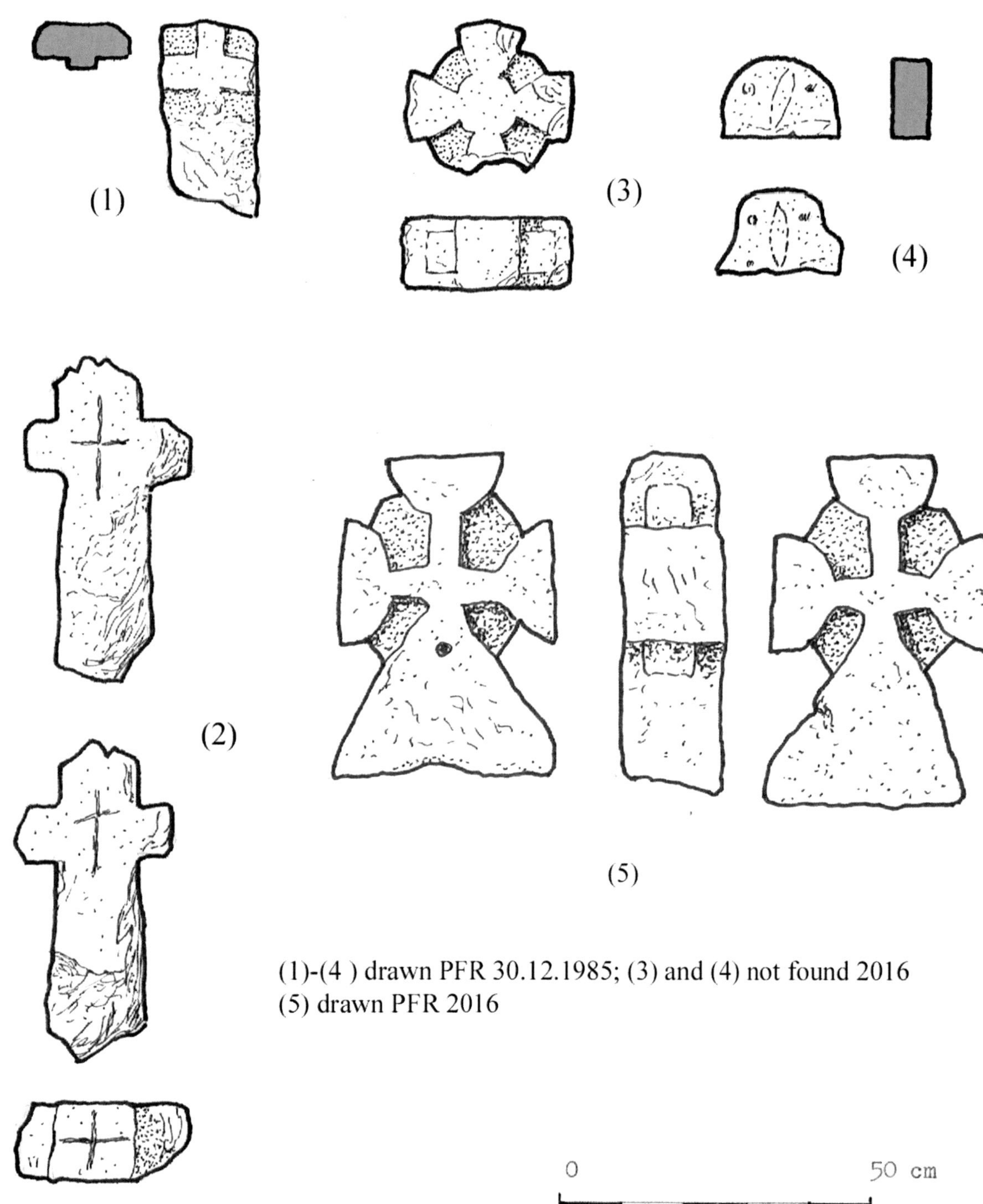

(1)-(4) drawn PFR 30.12.1985; (3) and (4) not found 2016
(5) drawn PFR 2016

Brotton

Medieval Cross from St Peter's Churchyard
now in the porch of St Margaret ofAntioch, Brotton

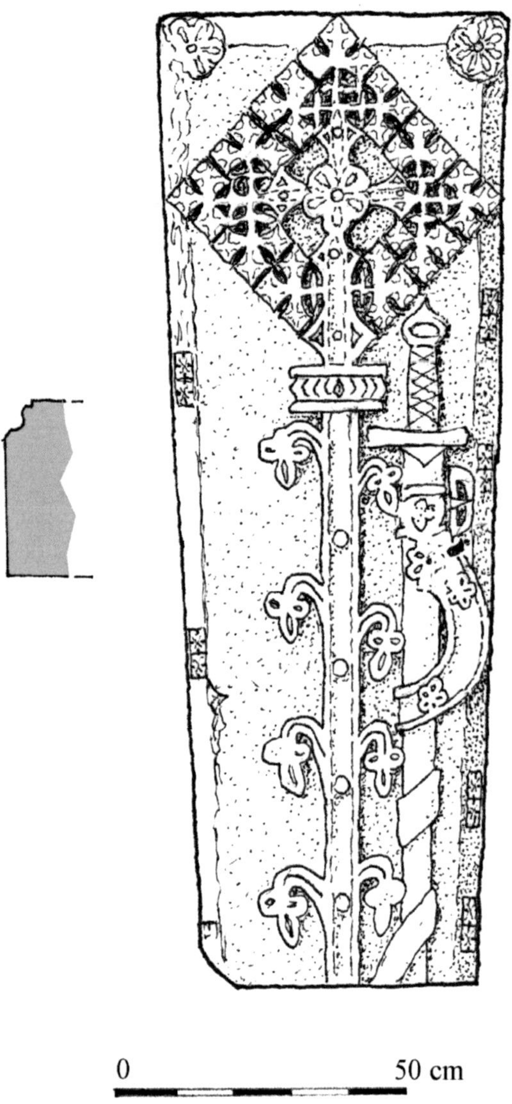

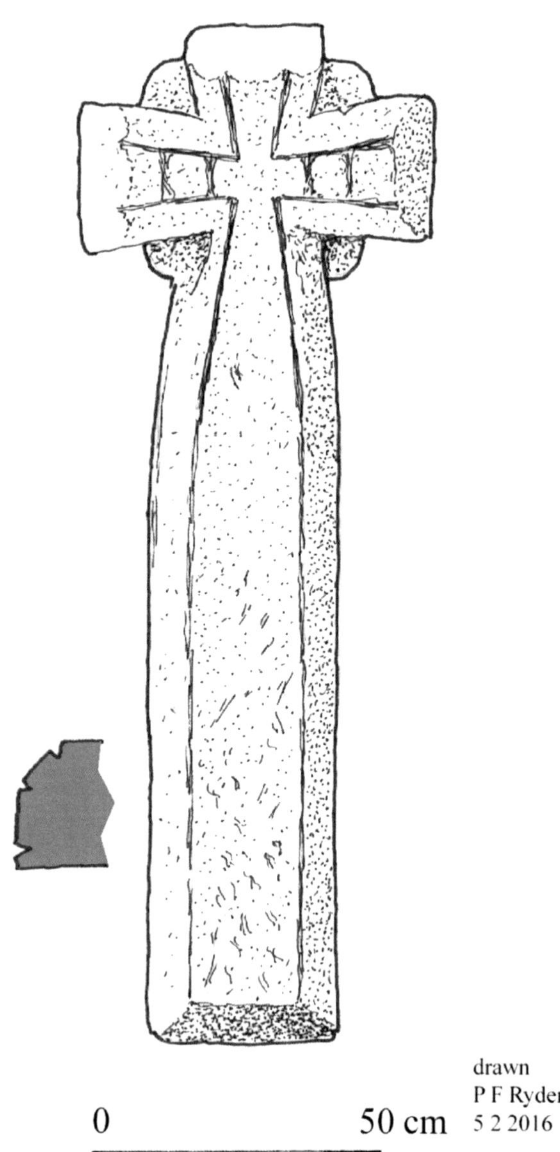

Crathorne

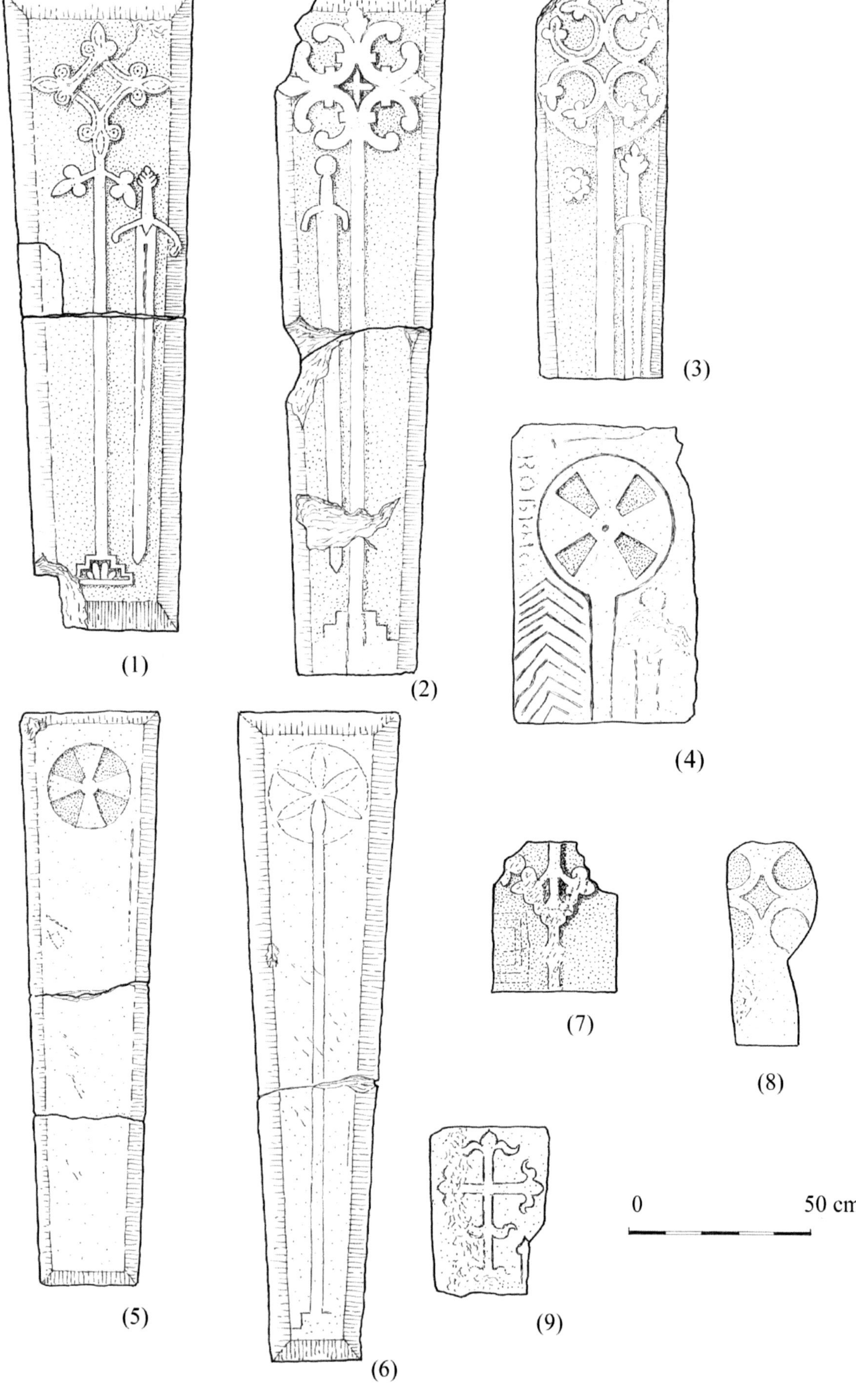

Danby

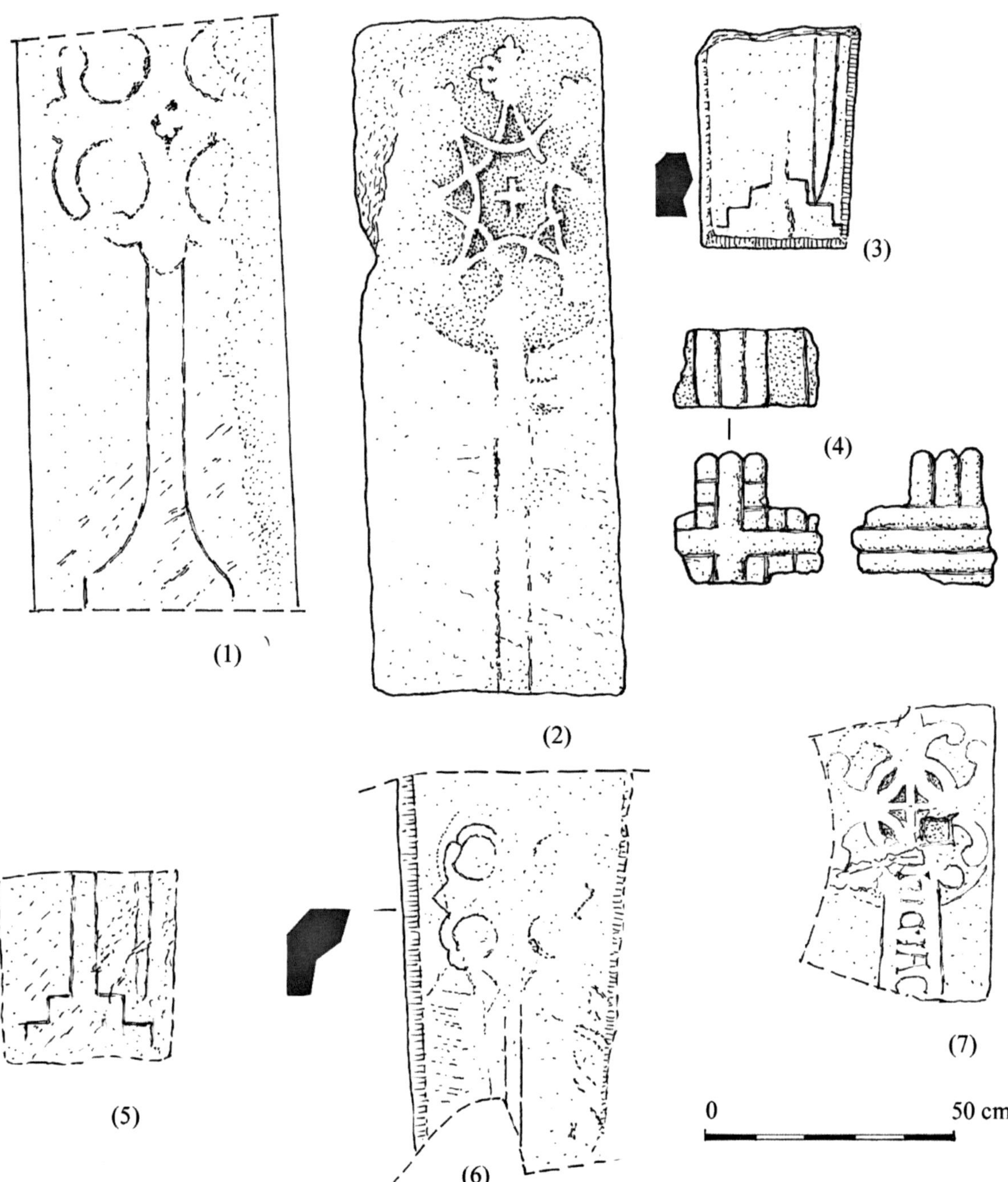

Easington

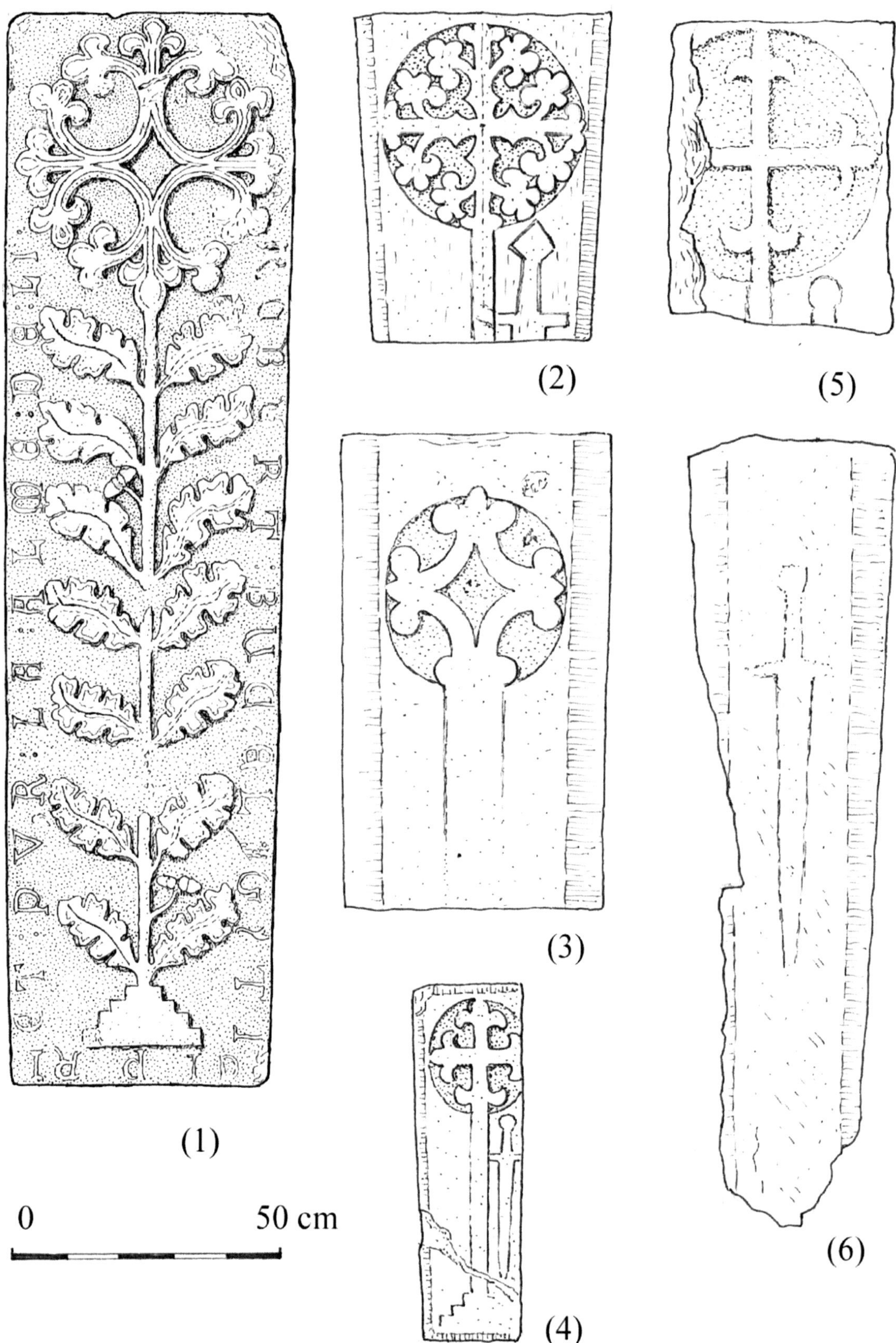

Egton (now in cemetery chapel)

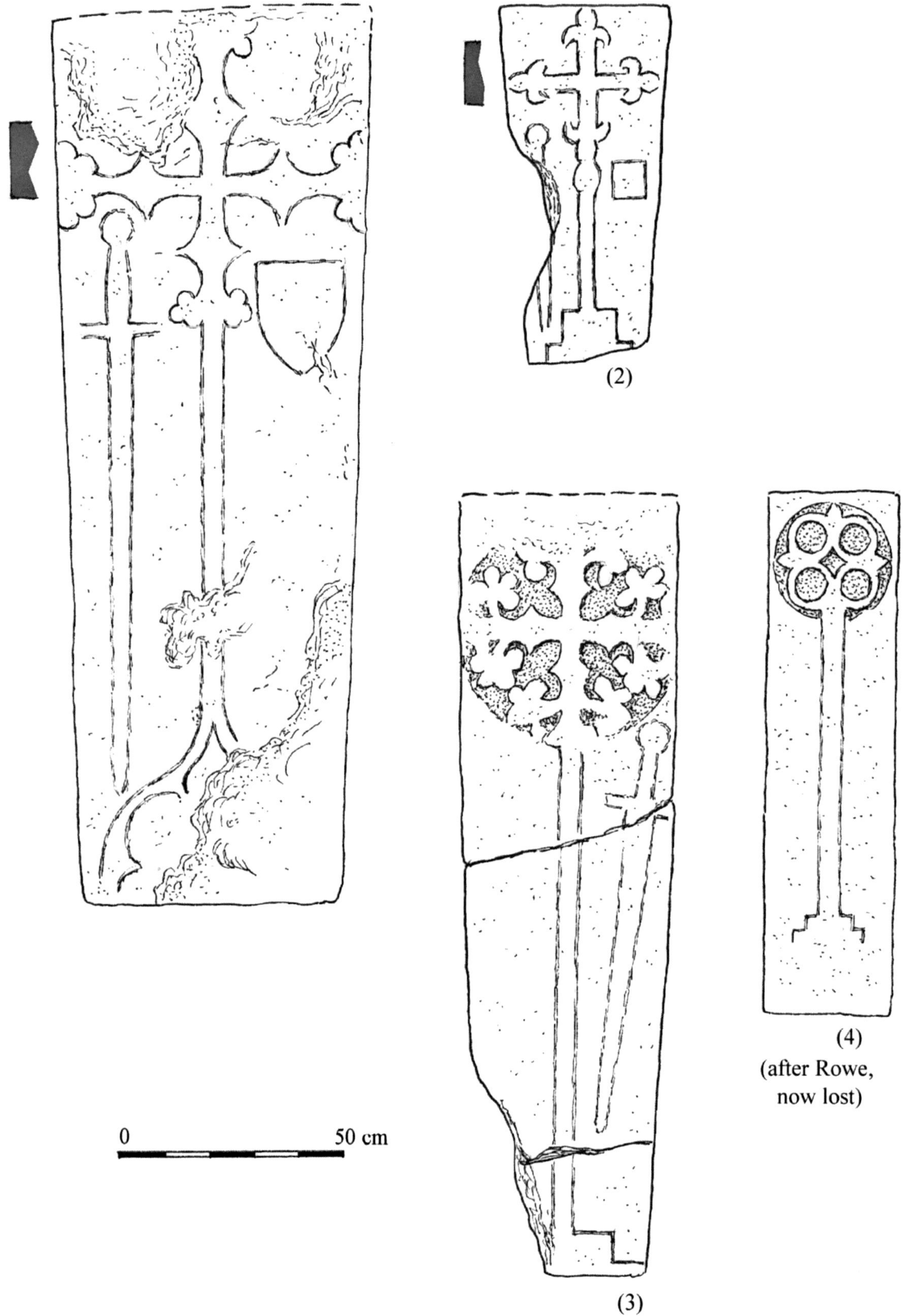

Eston

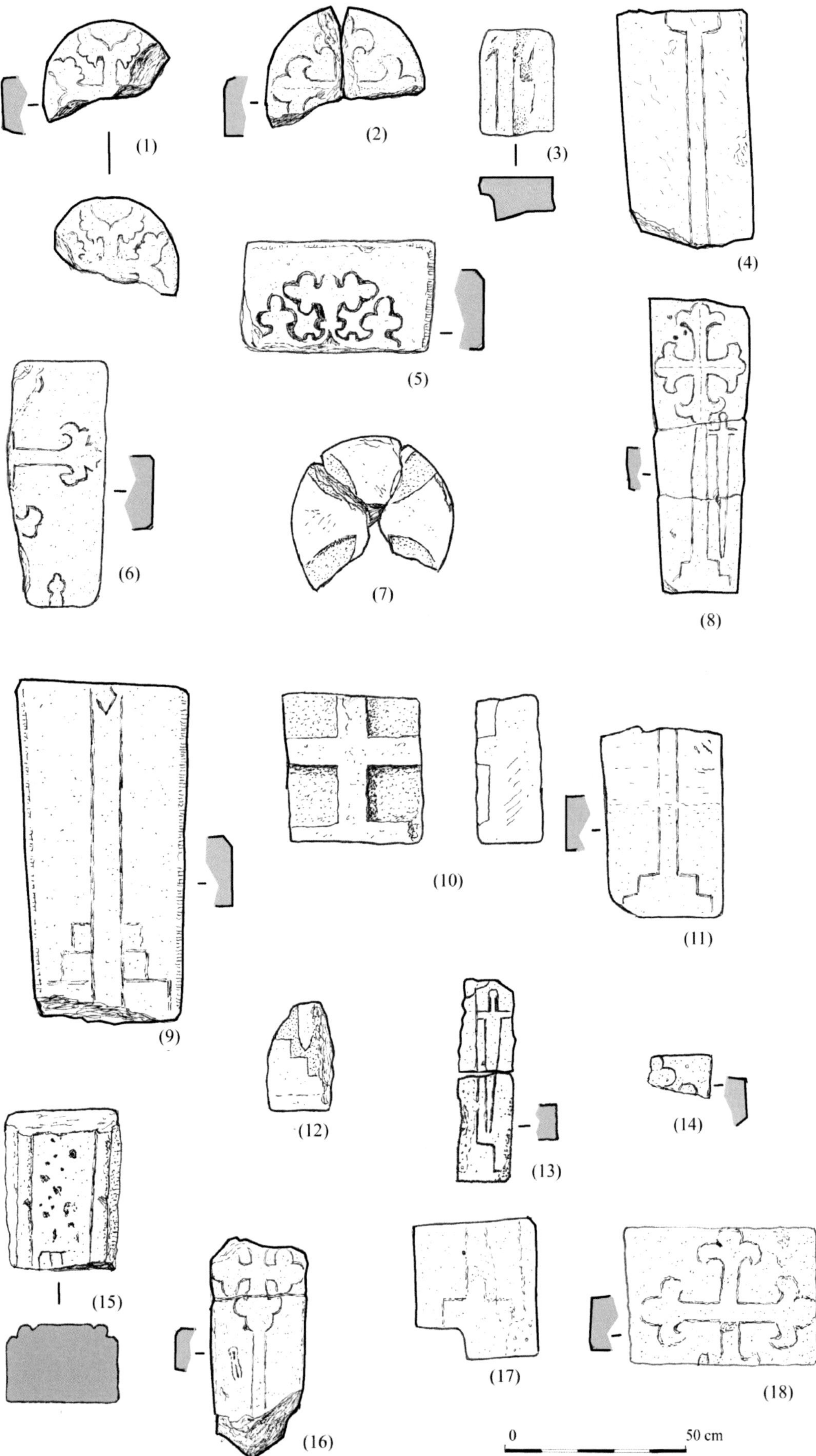

Guisborough, St Nicholas

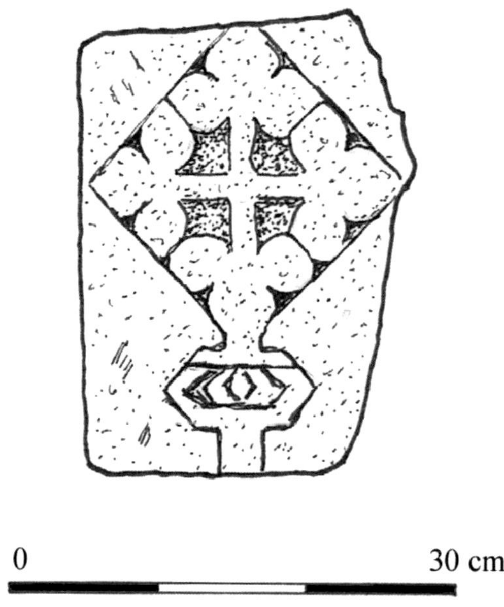

Hinderwell, St Hilda

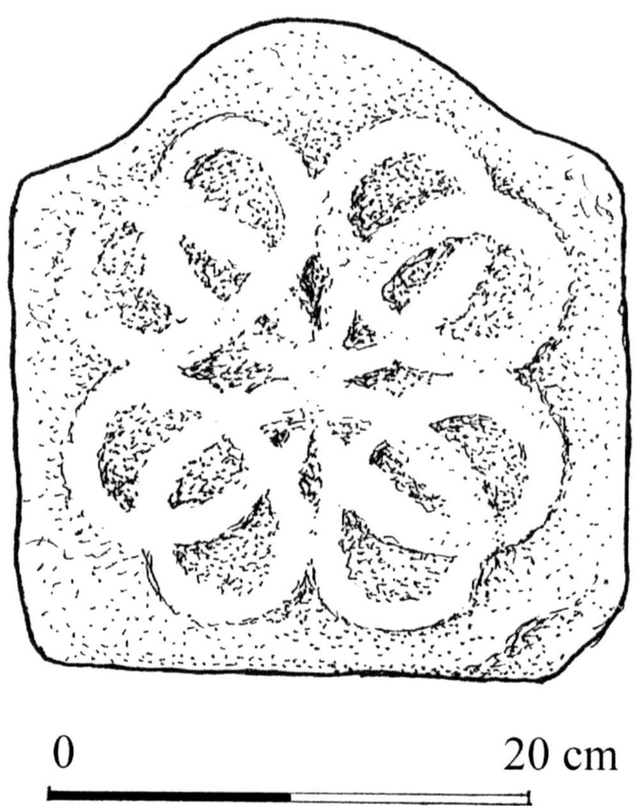

Gisborough Priory

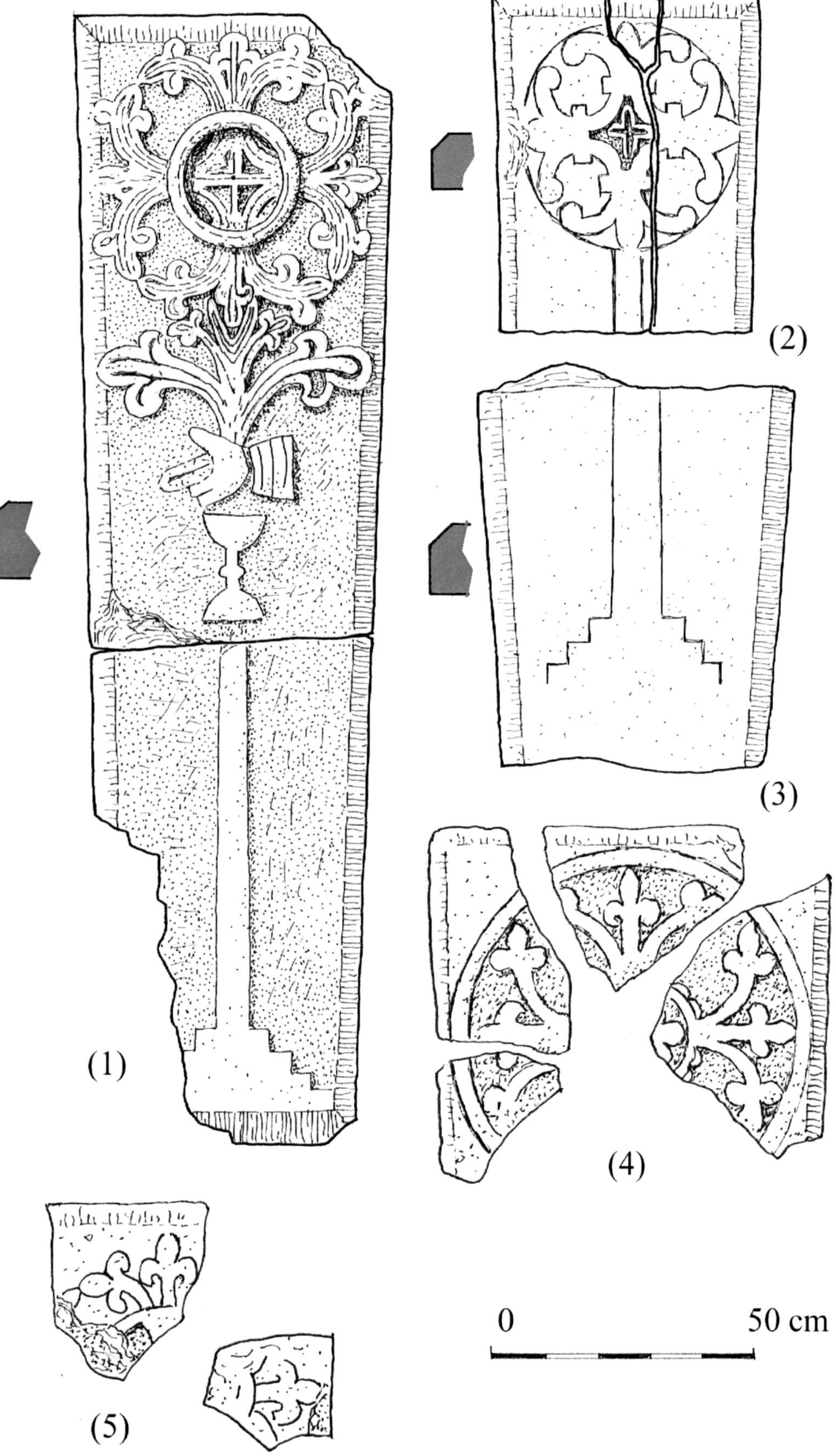

Great Ayton

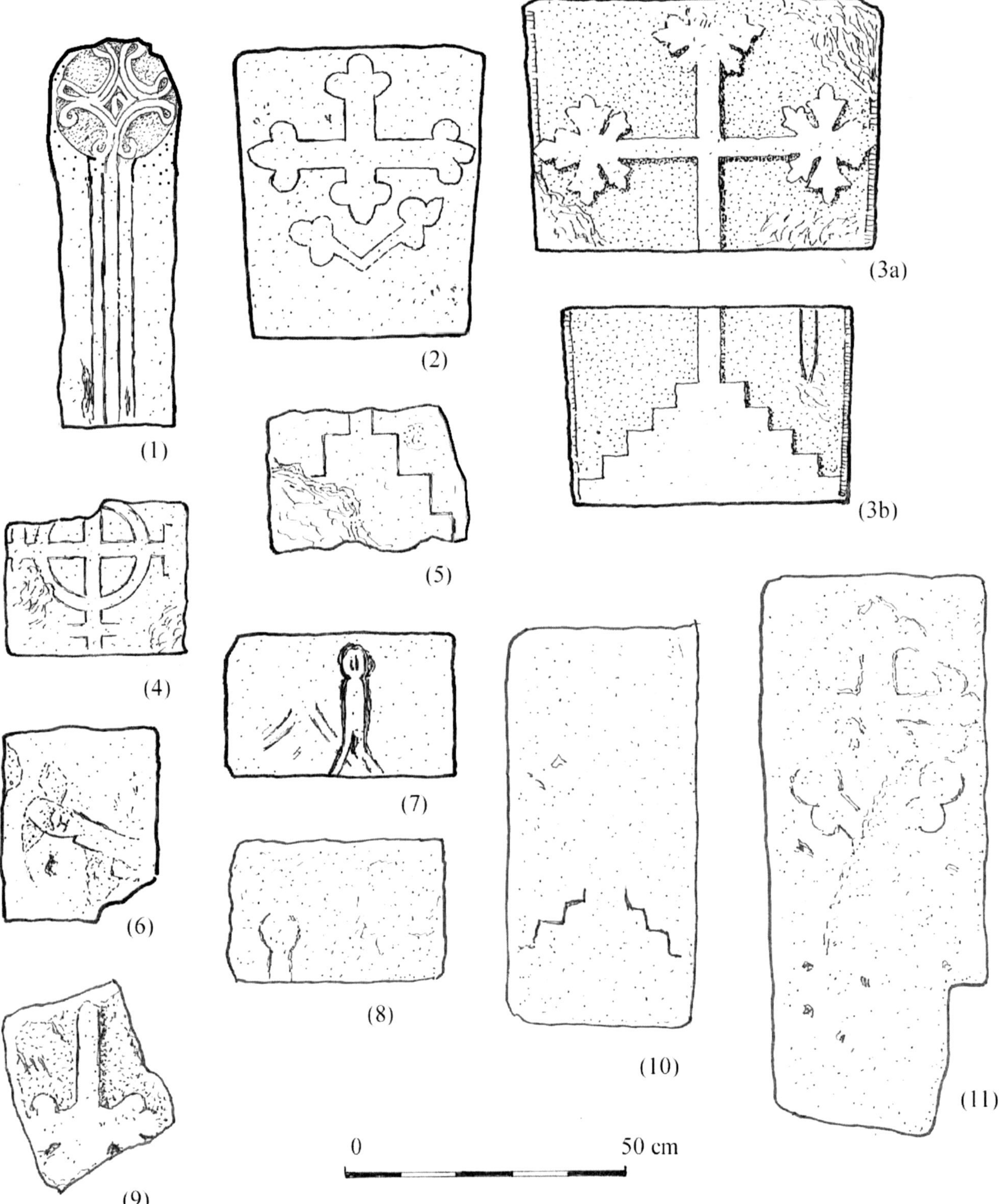
(1)
(2)
(3a)
(3b)
(4)
(5)
(6)
(7)
(8)
(9)
(10)
(11)
0
50 cm

Hutton Rudby

(1)

drawn PFR Nov.2015

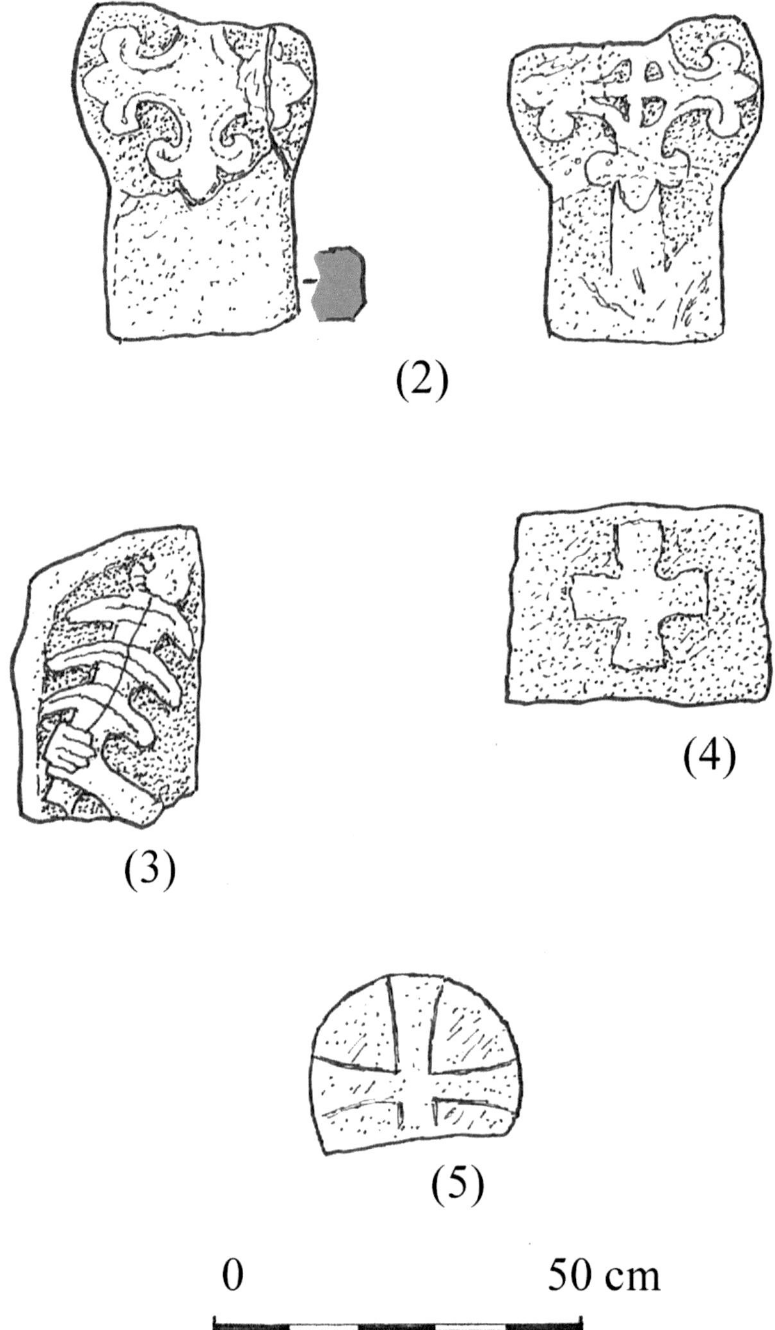
(2)
(3)
(4)
(5)
0
50 cm

Ingleby Arncliffe

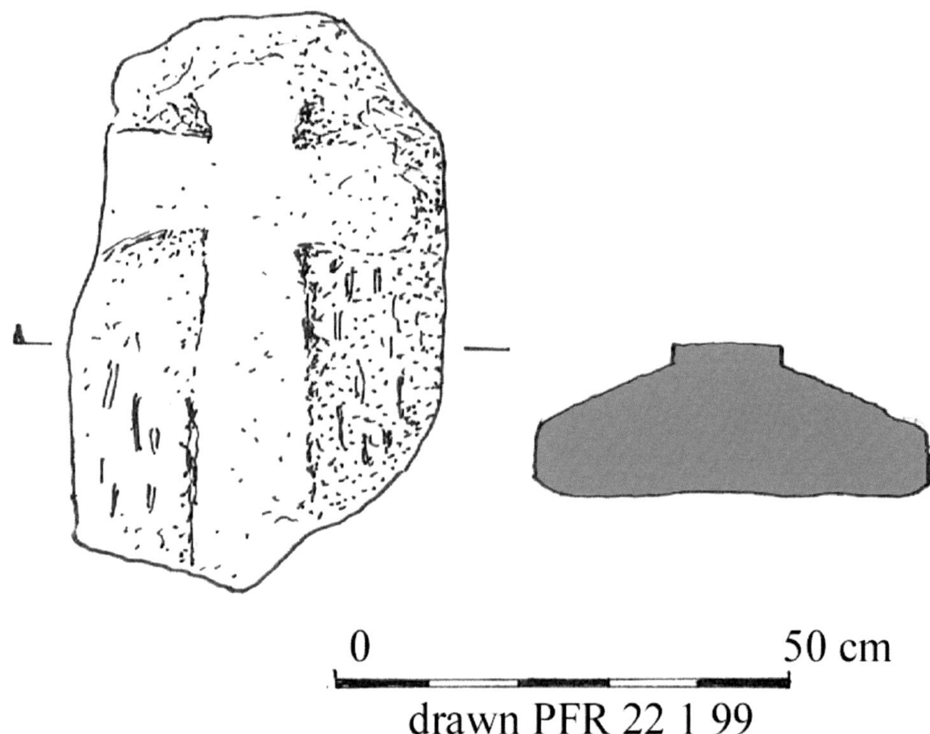

Ingleby Greenhow

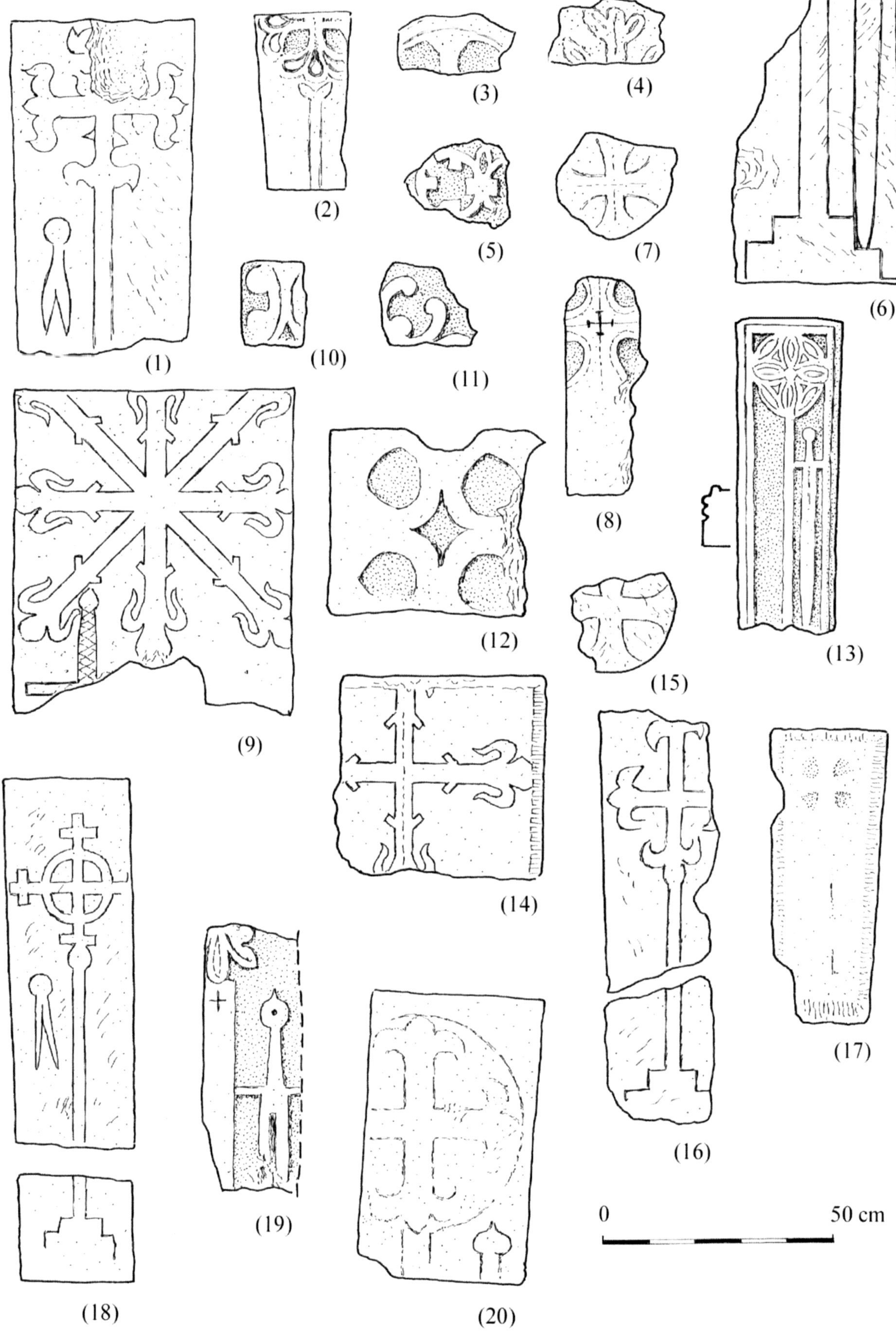

Kildale

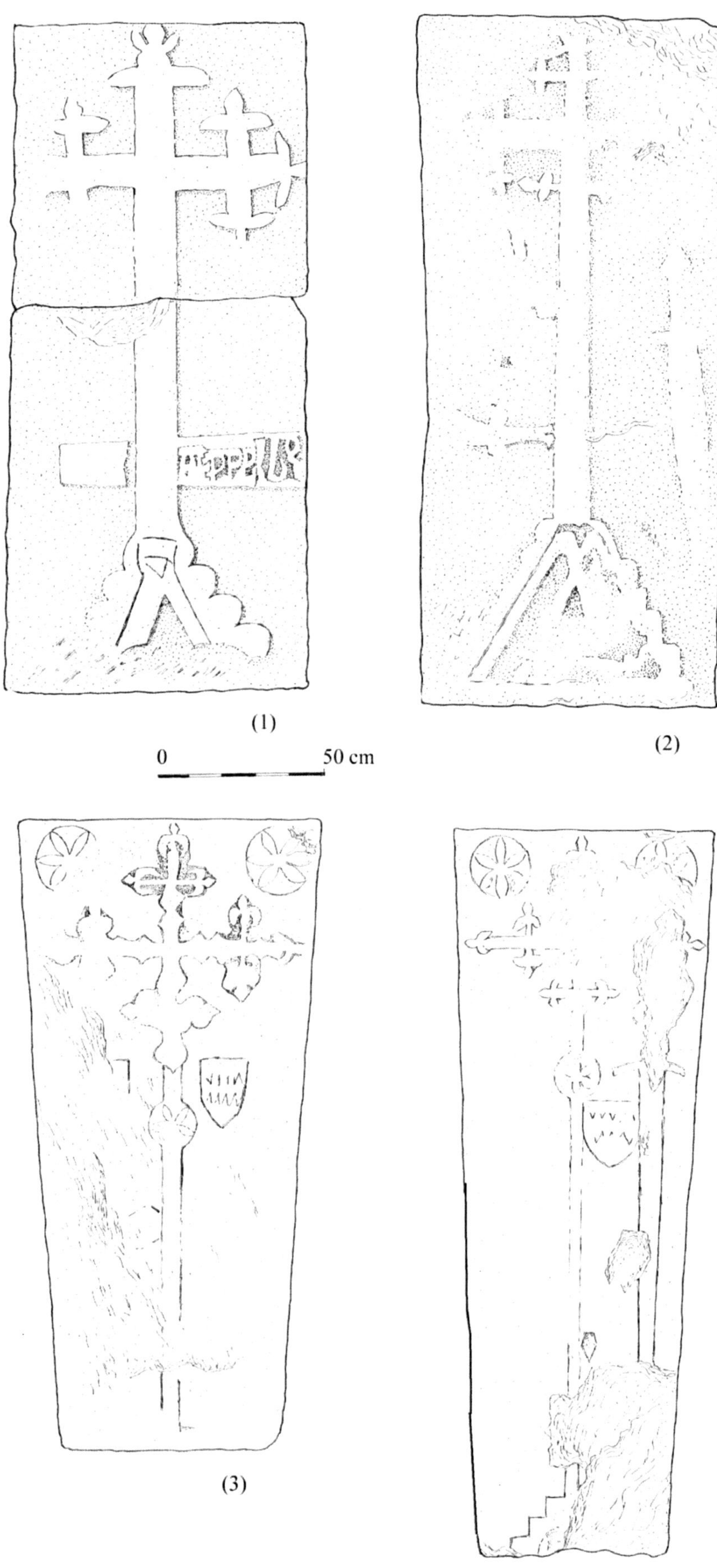

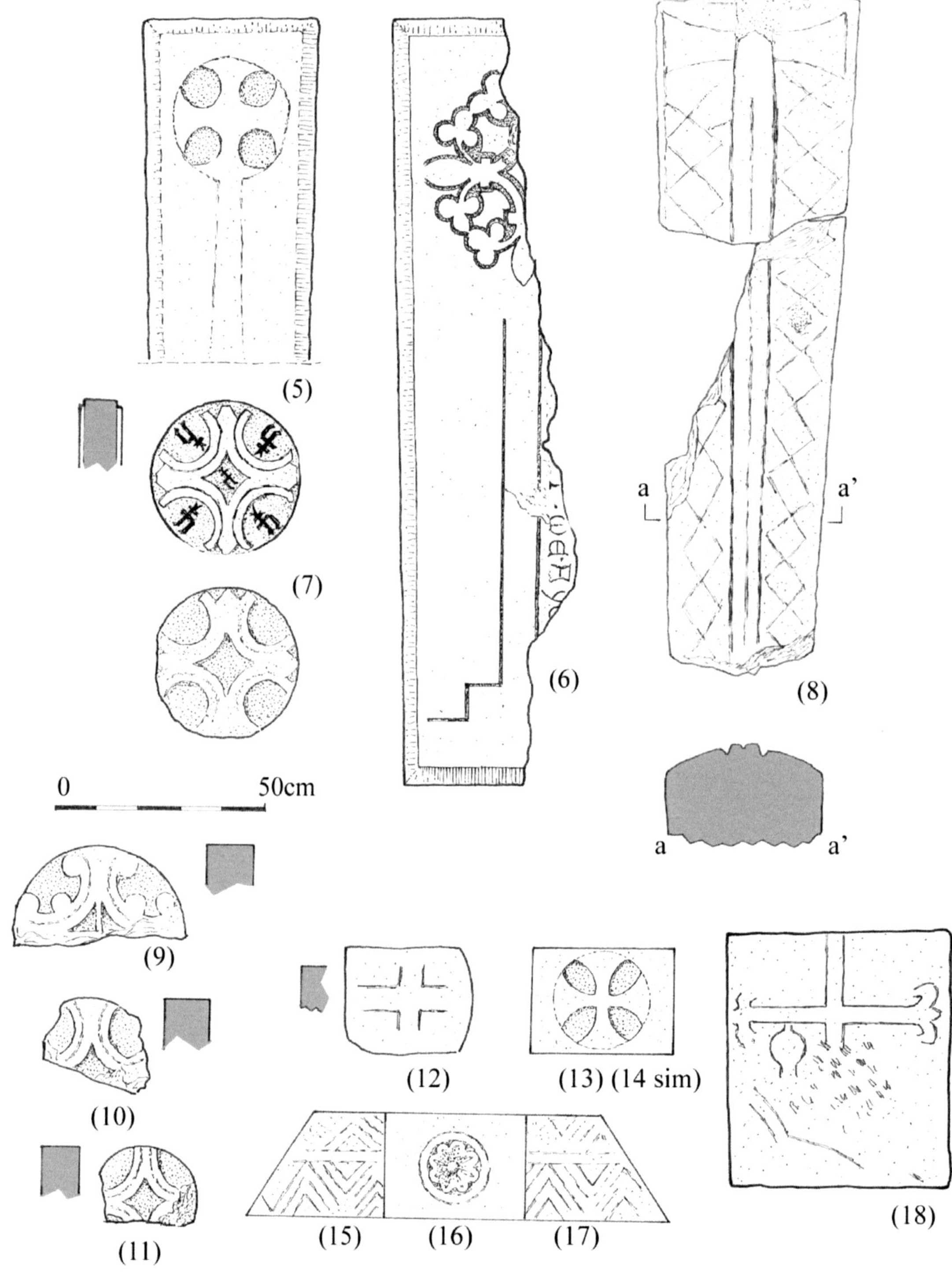
(5)
(6)
(7)
(8)
a
a'
0
50cm
a
a'
(9)
(10)
(11)
(12)
(13) (14 sim)
(15)
(16)
(17)
(18)

Kirkby in Cleveland

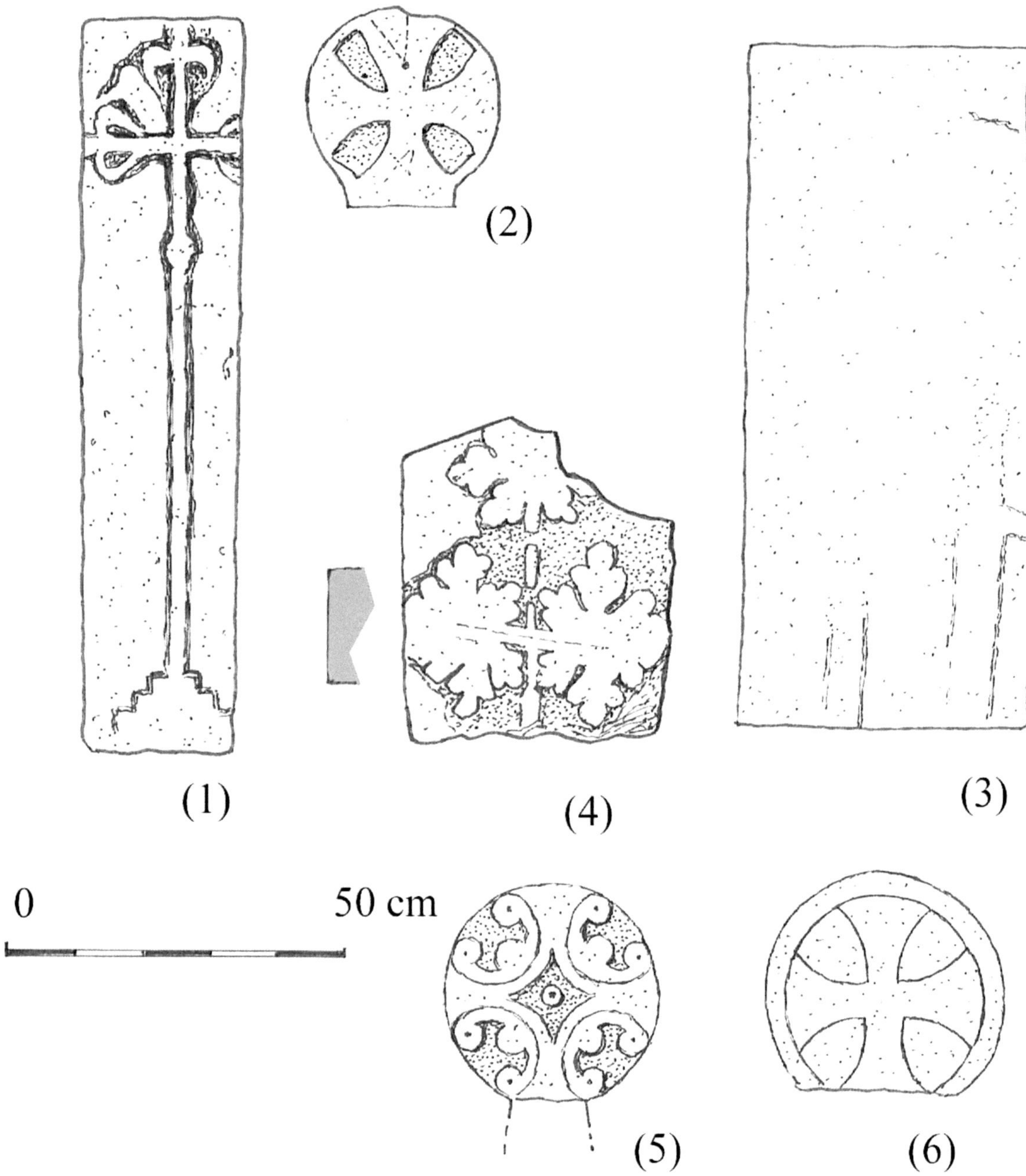

Kirkleatham

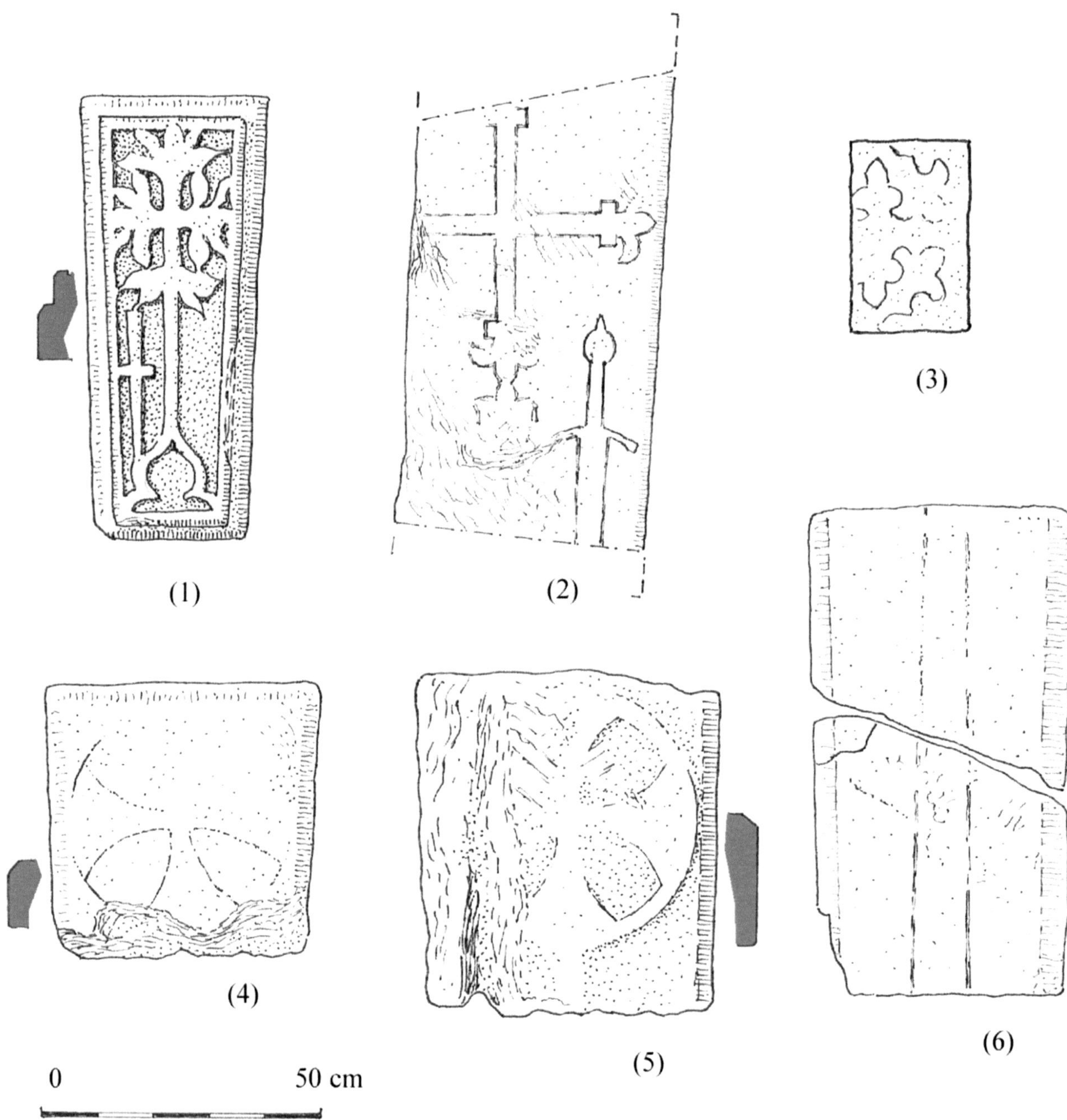

Kirklevington

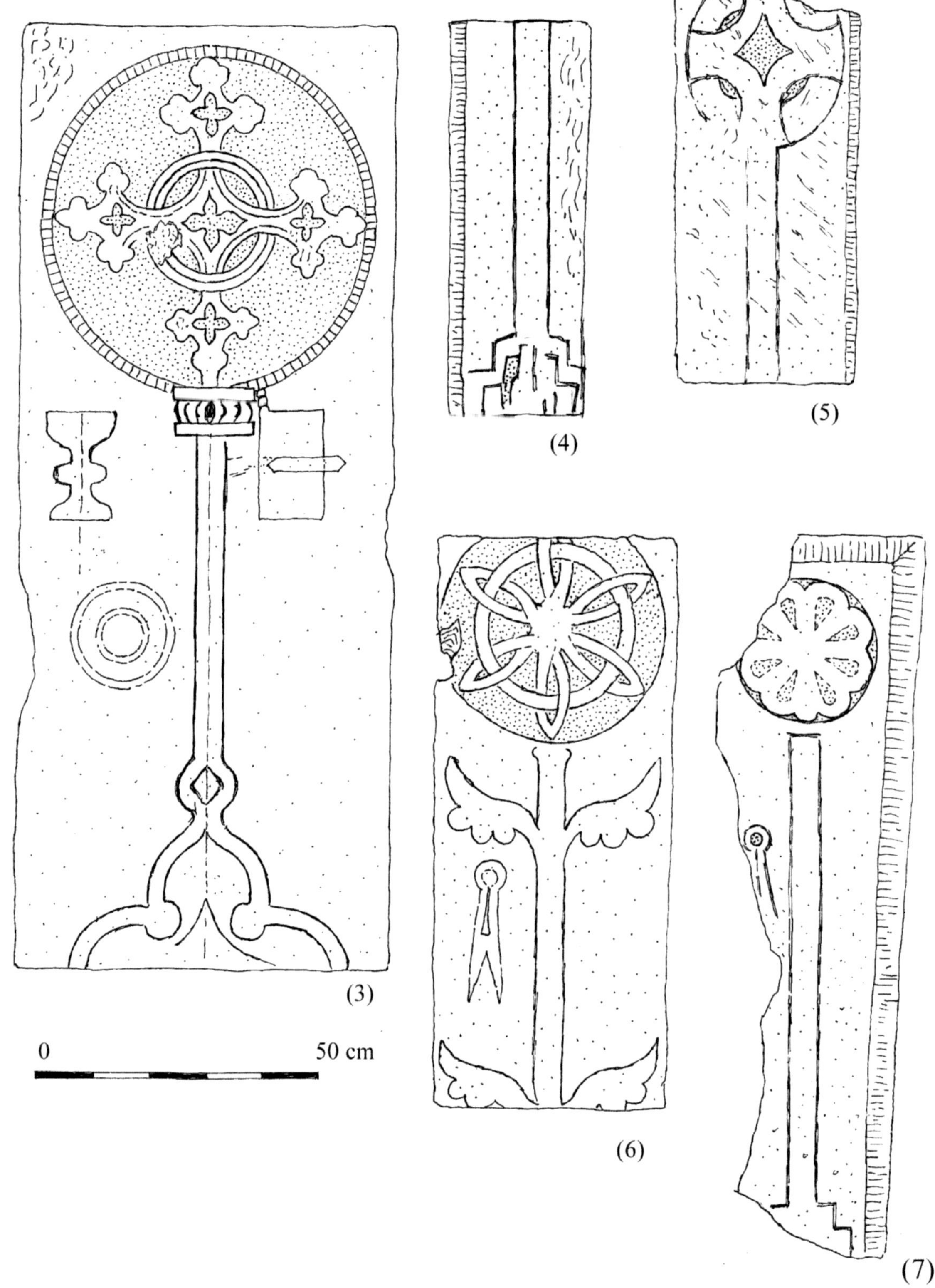
(3)
0
50 cm
(4)
(5)
(6)
(7)

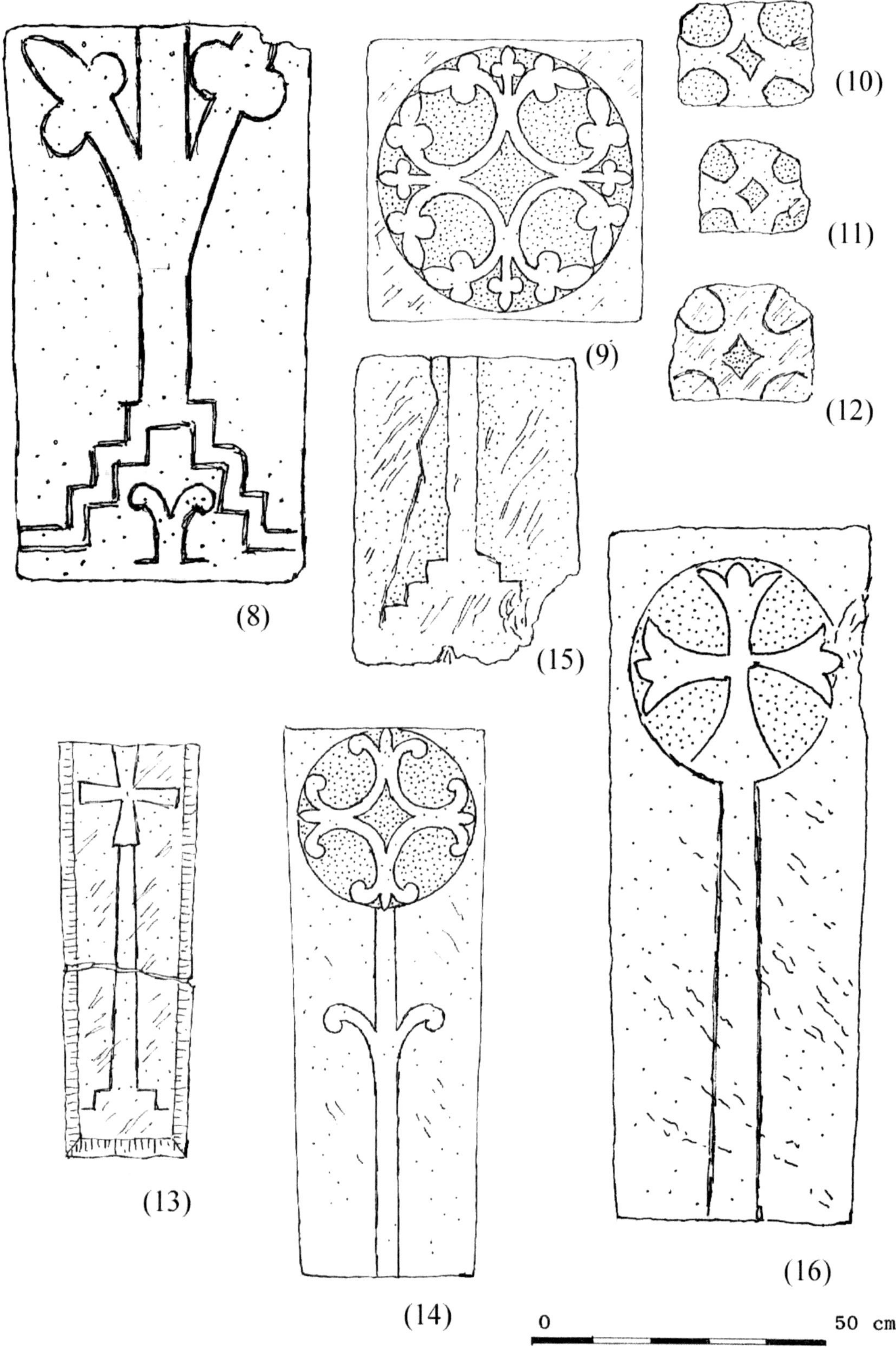
(8)
(9)
(10)
(11)
(12)
(13)
(14)
(15)
(16)
0
50 cm.

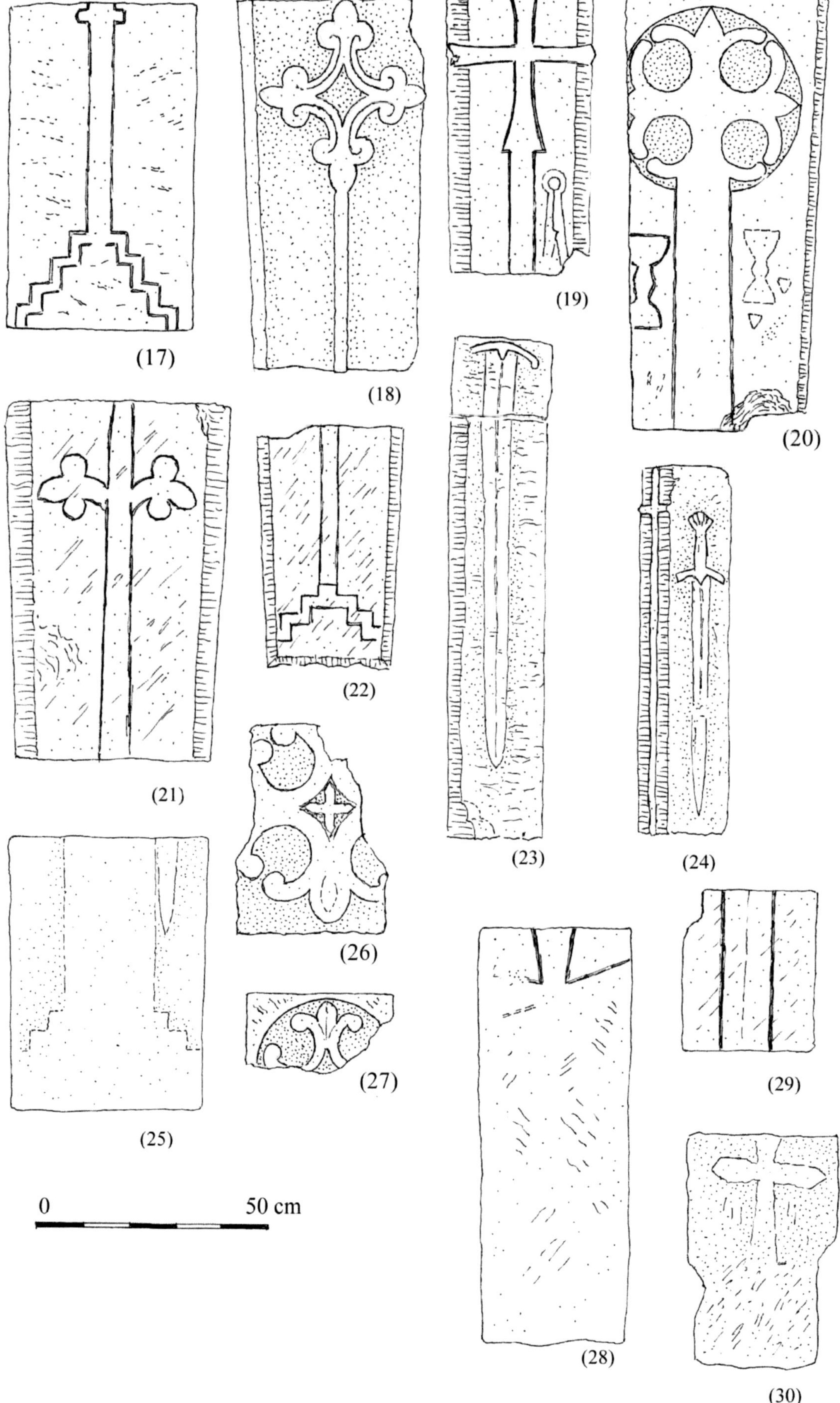
(17)
(18)
(19)
(20)
(21)
(22)
(23)
(24)
(25)
(26)
(27)
(28)
(29)
(30)
0
50 cm

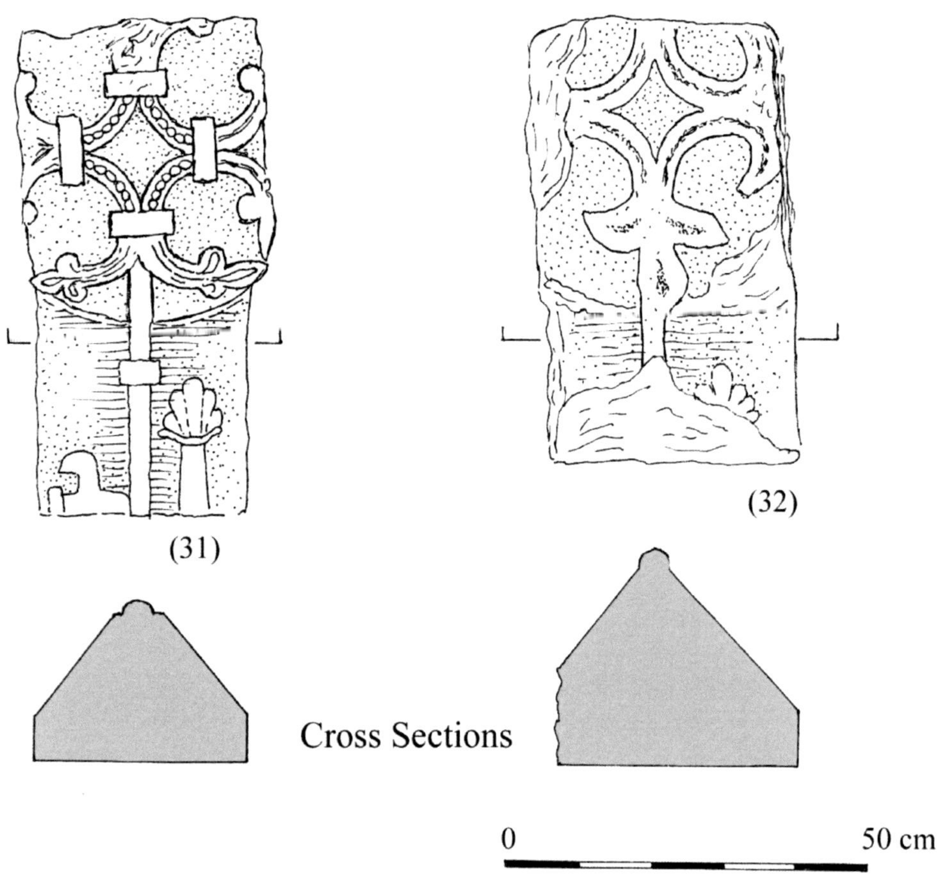

Kirklevington: Coped slabs, now lost

drawn P F Ryder October 1981

Liverton

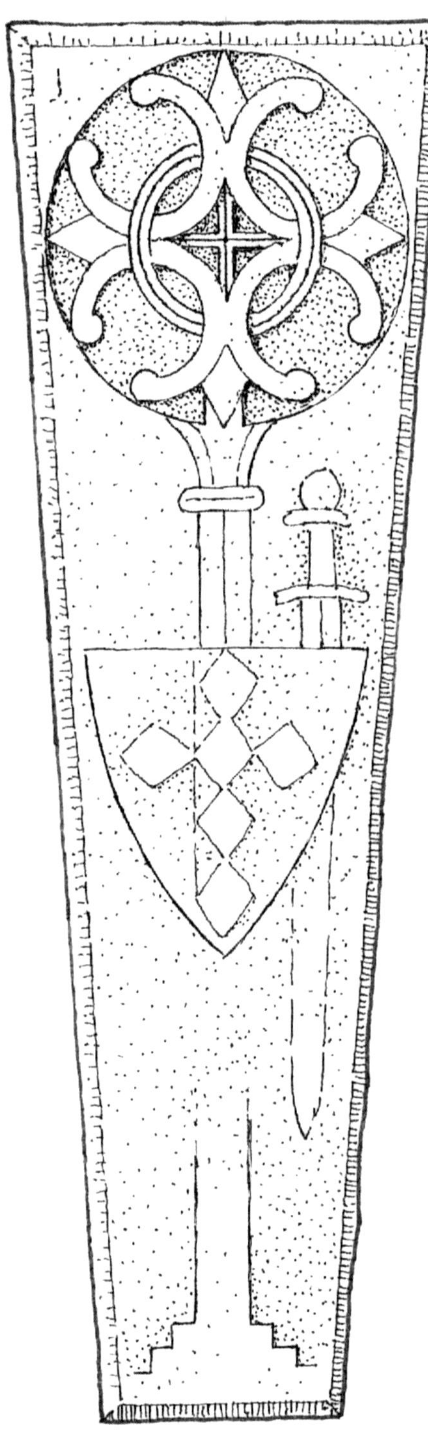

0 50 cm

Low Worsall

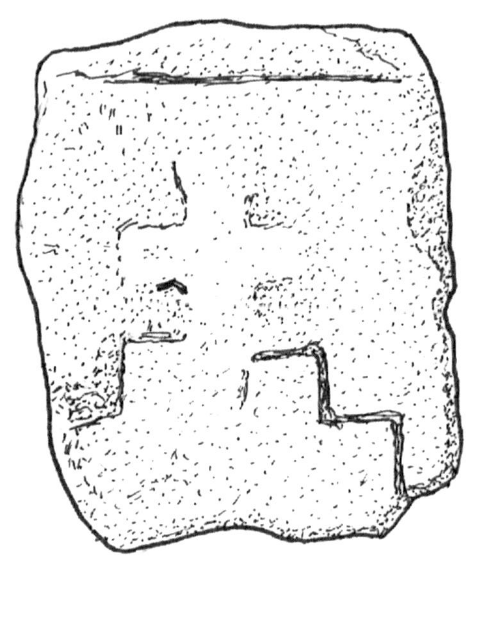

0 30 cm

Headstone or grave marker found in excavation on Low Worsall green, 2016

Lythe

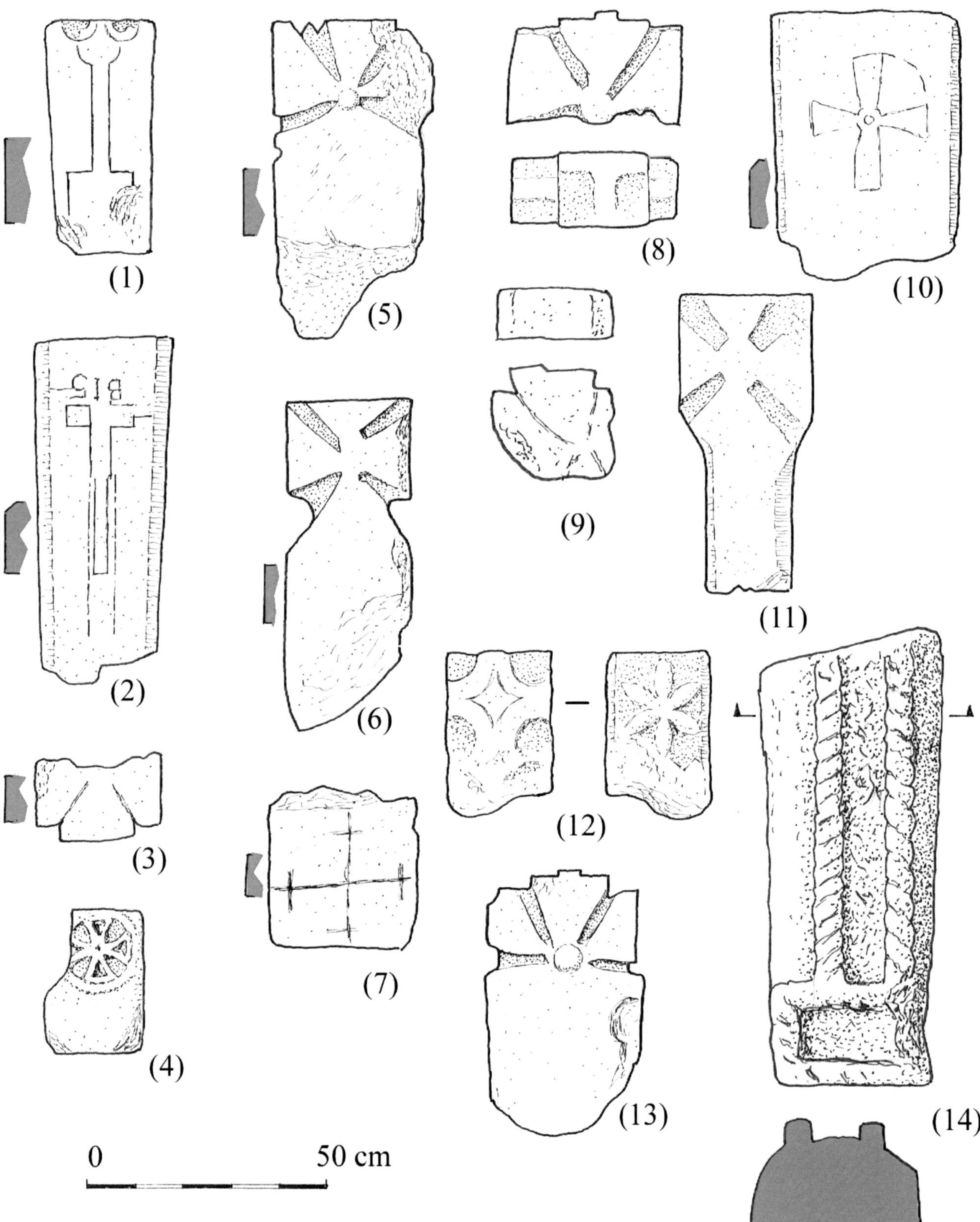

Marton

Newton under Roseberry

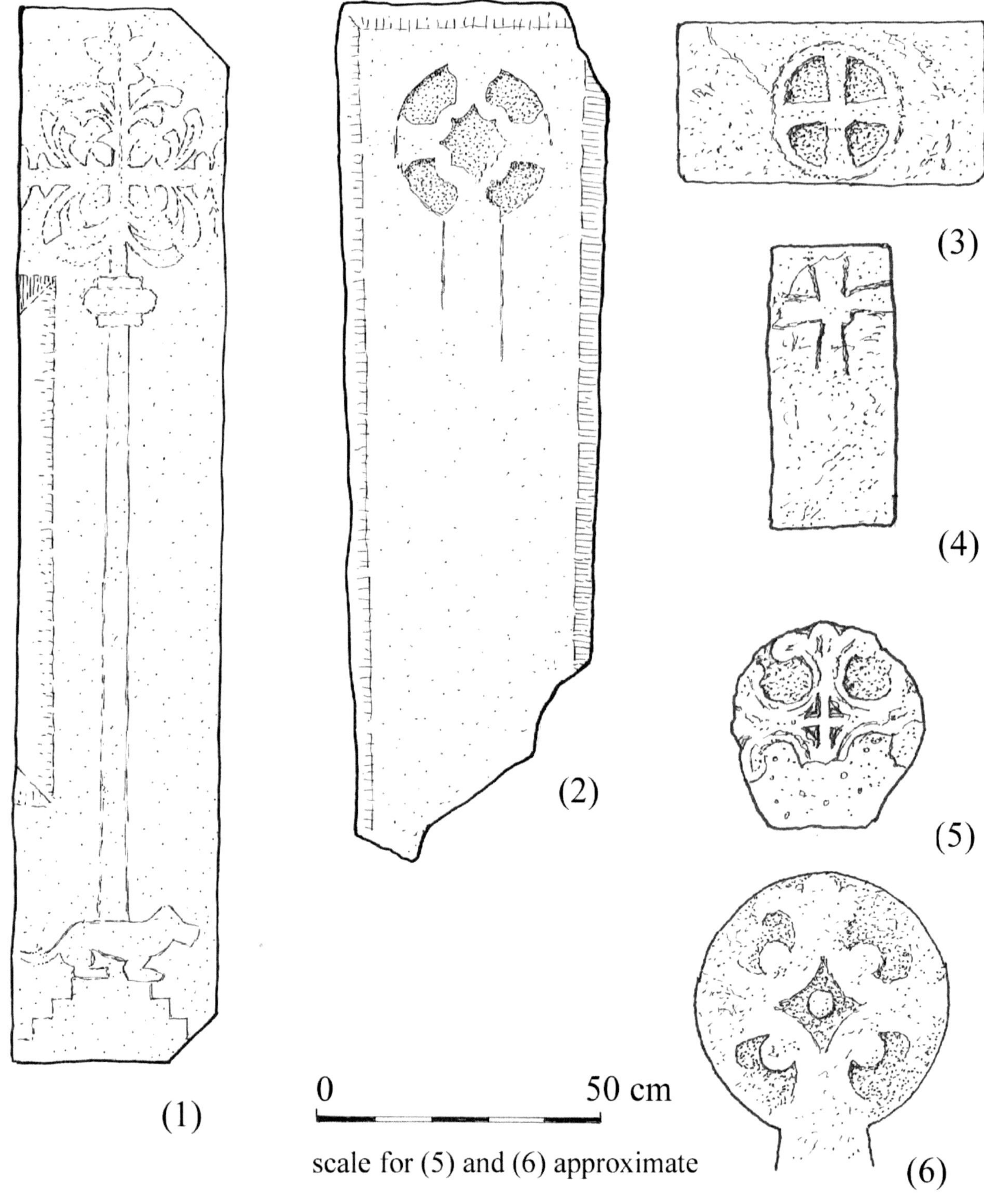

Ormesby

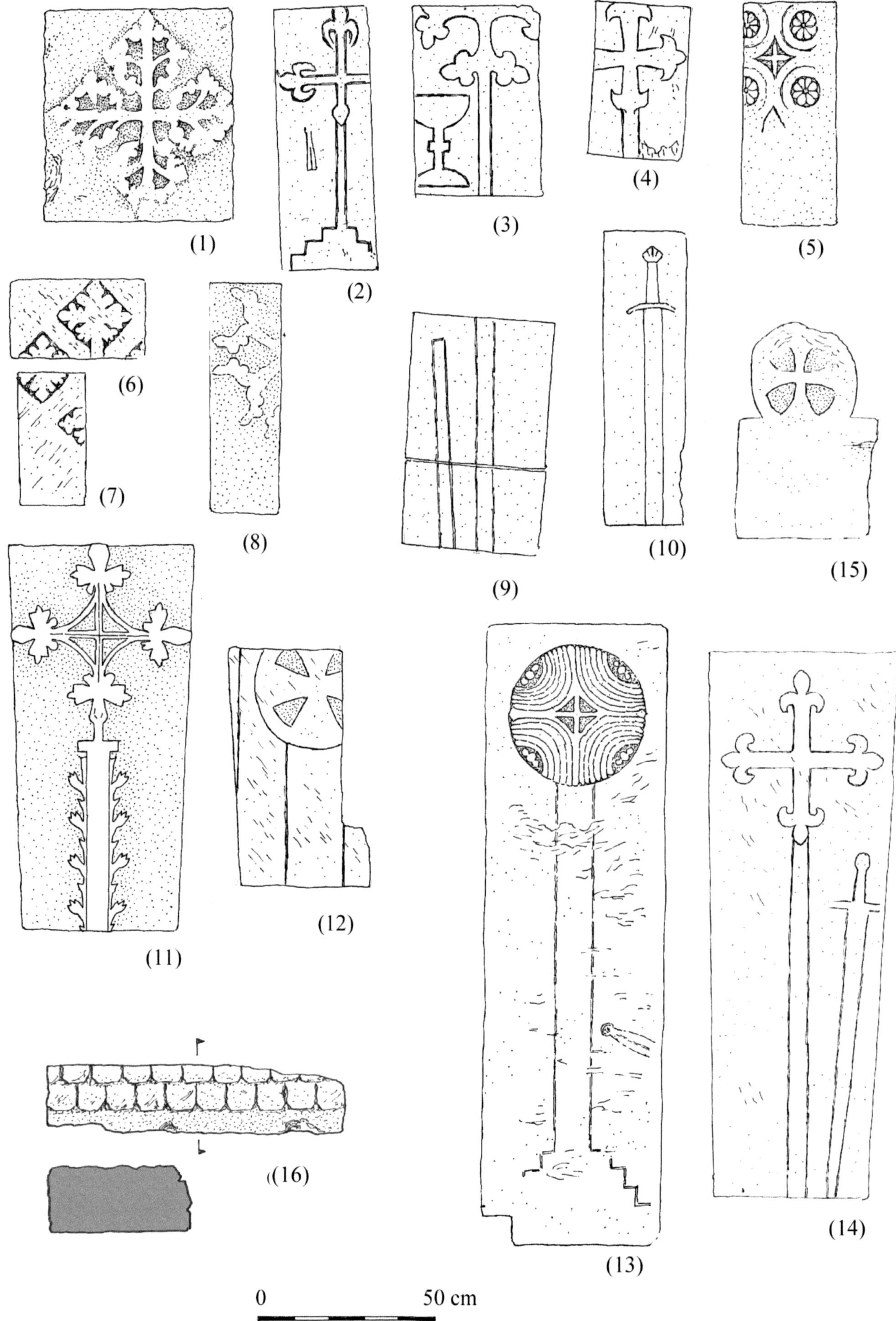

Skelton

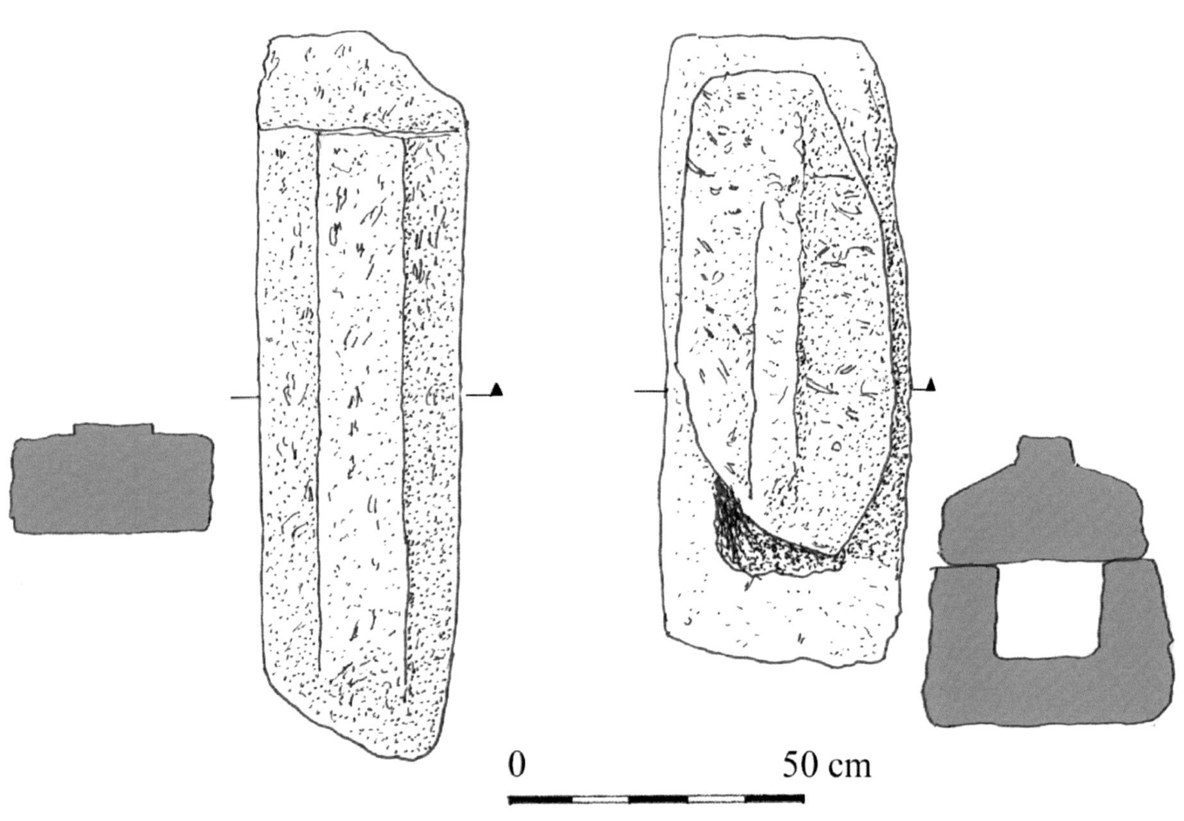

Stokesley Osmotherley Thornaby

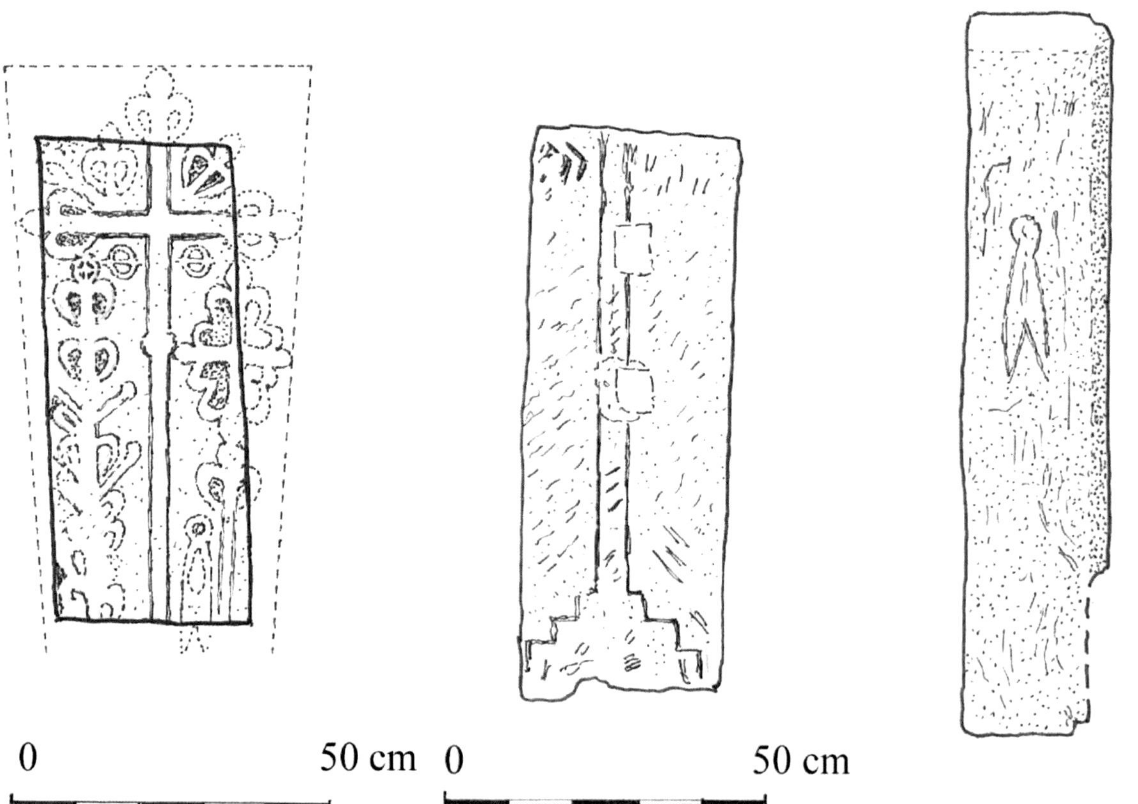

Upleatham

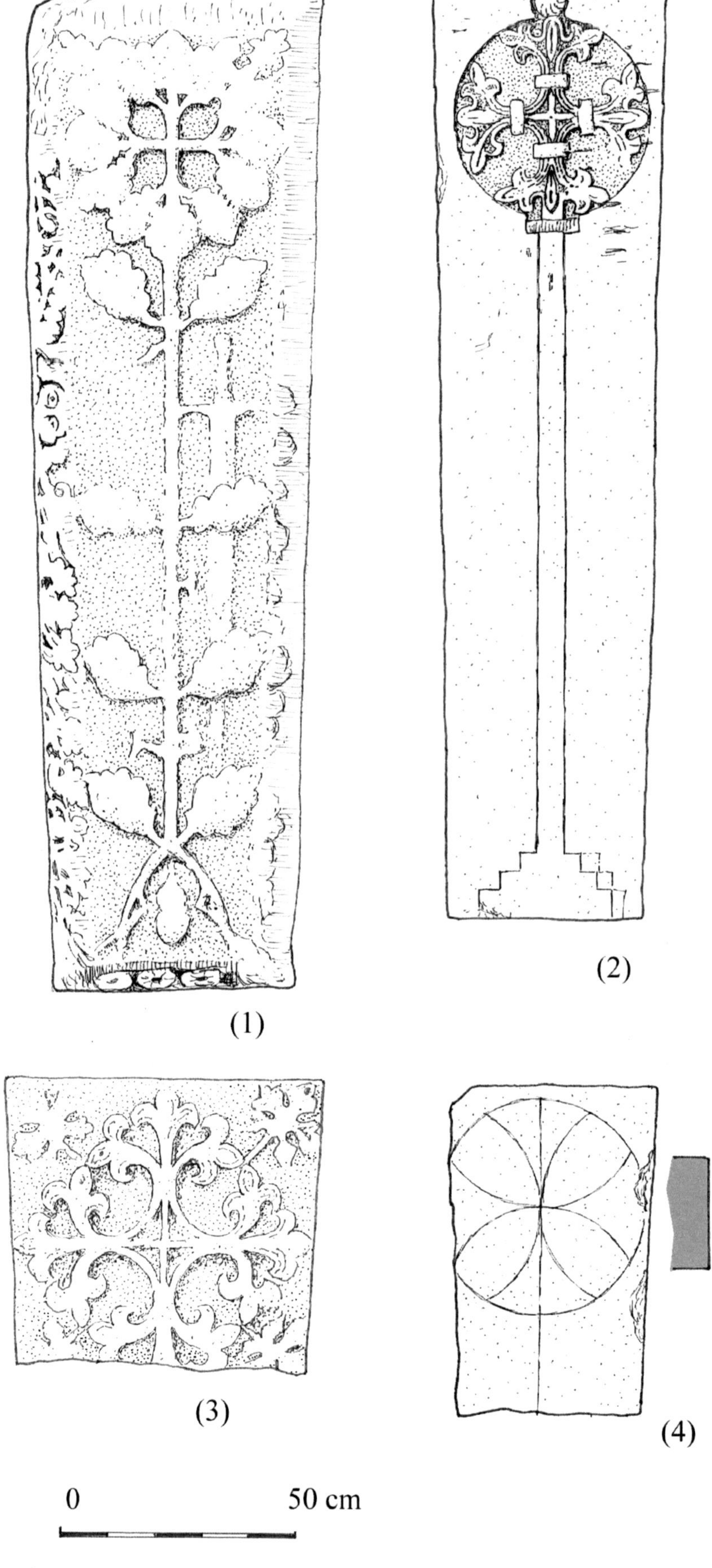

Upleatham Old Church.
Slabs from 1970s excavations.

redrawn PFR from originals
by Mrs Shirley Knight

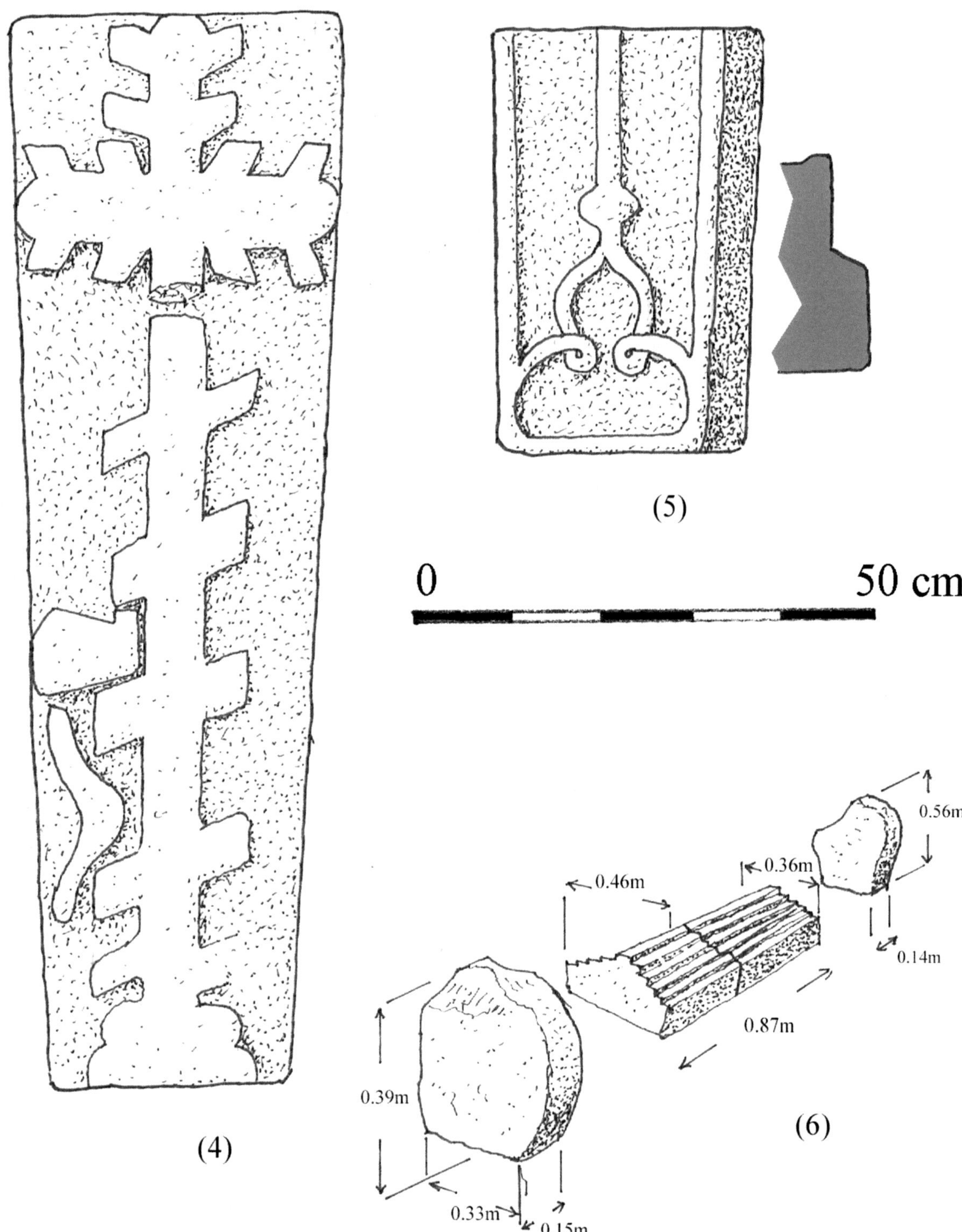

Westerdale

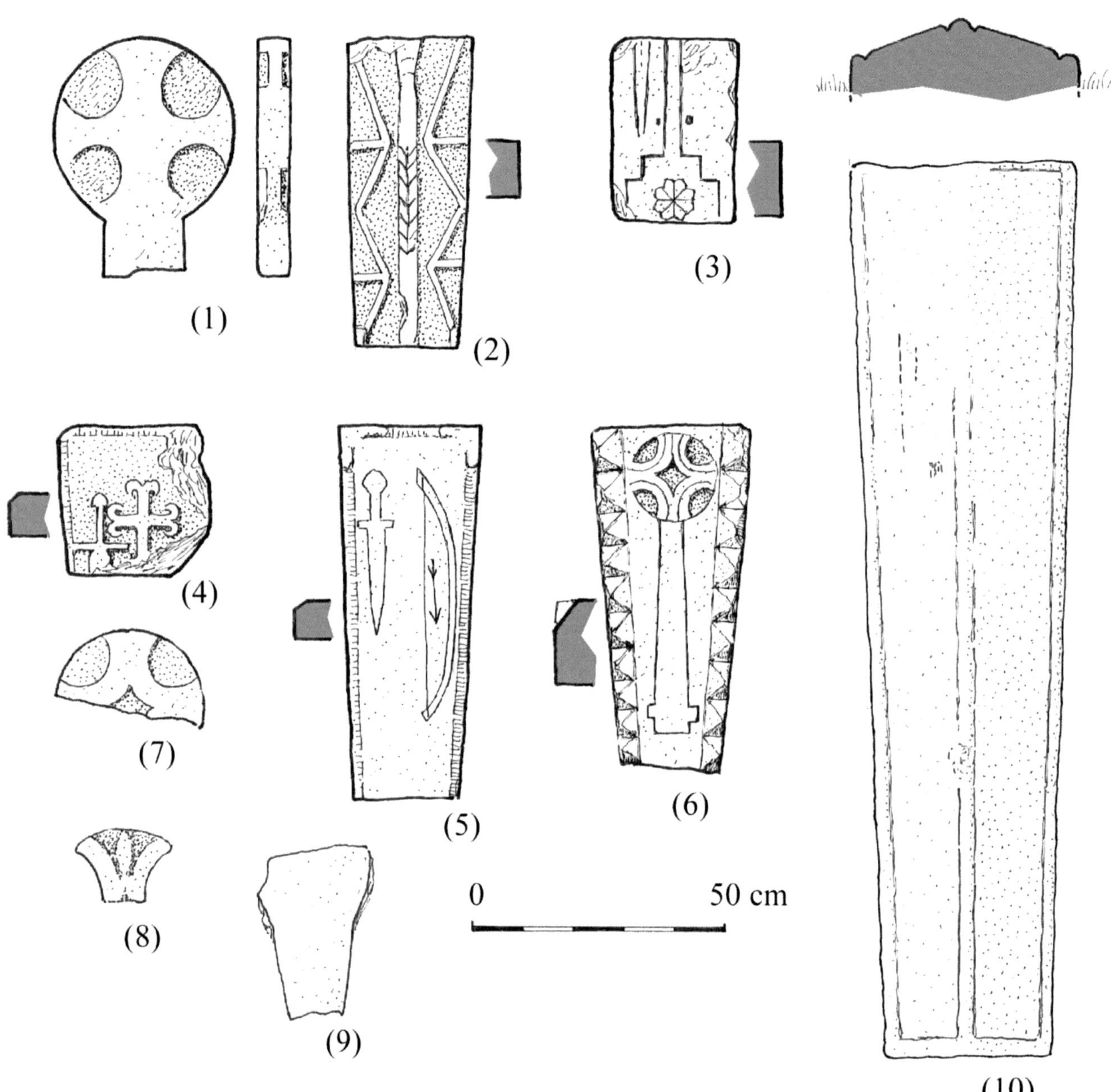

Whitby

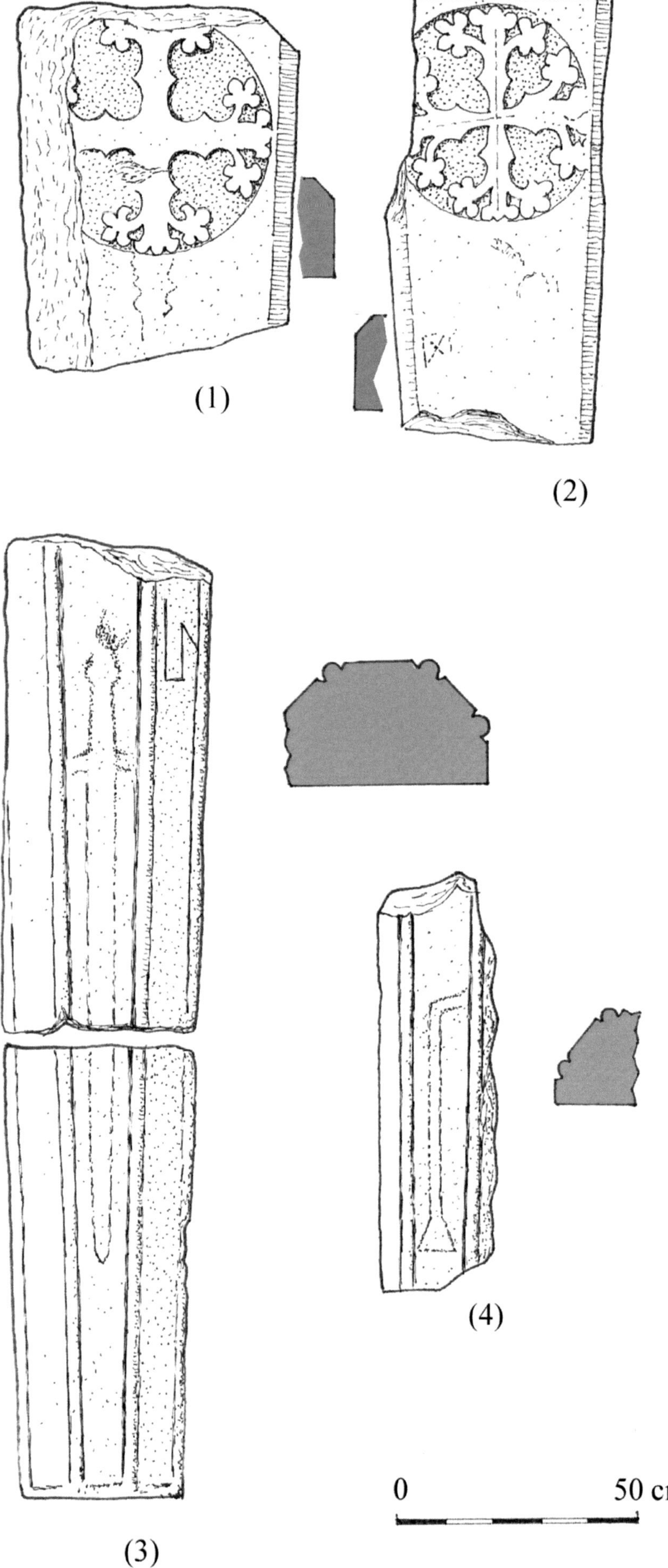

Whorlton

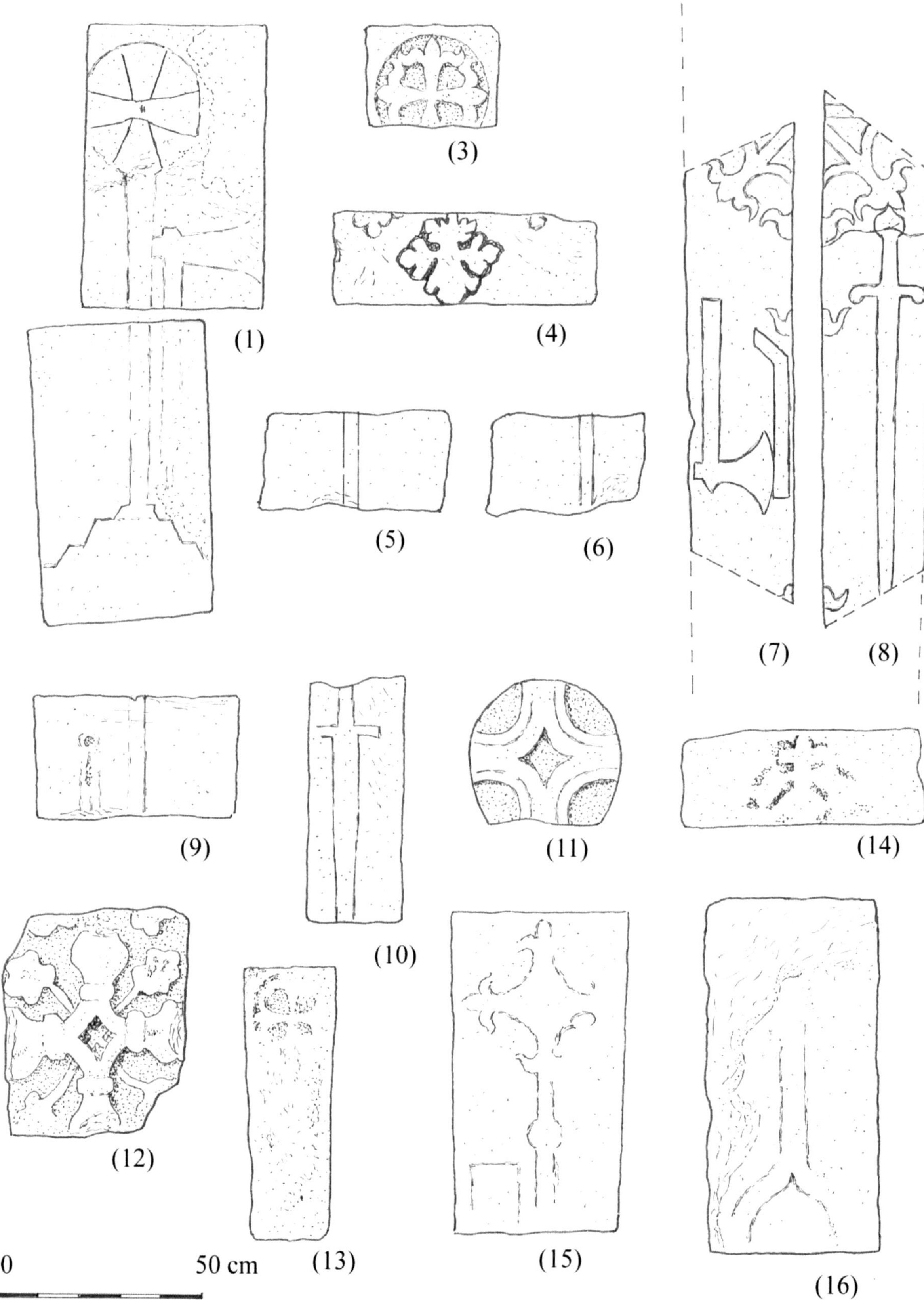

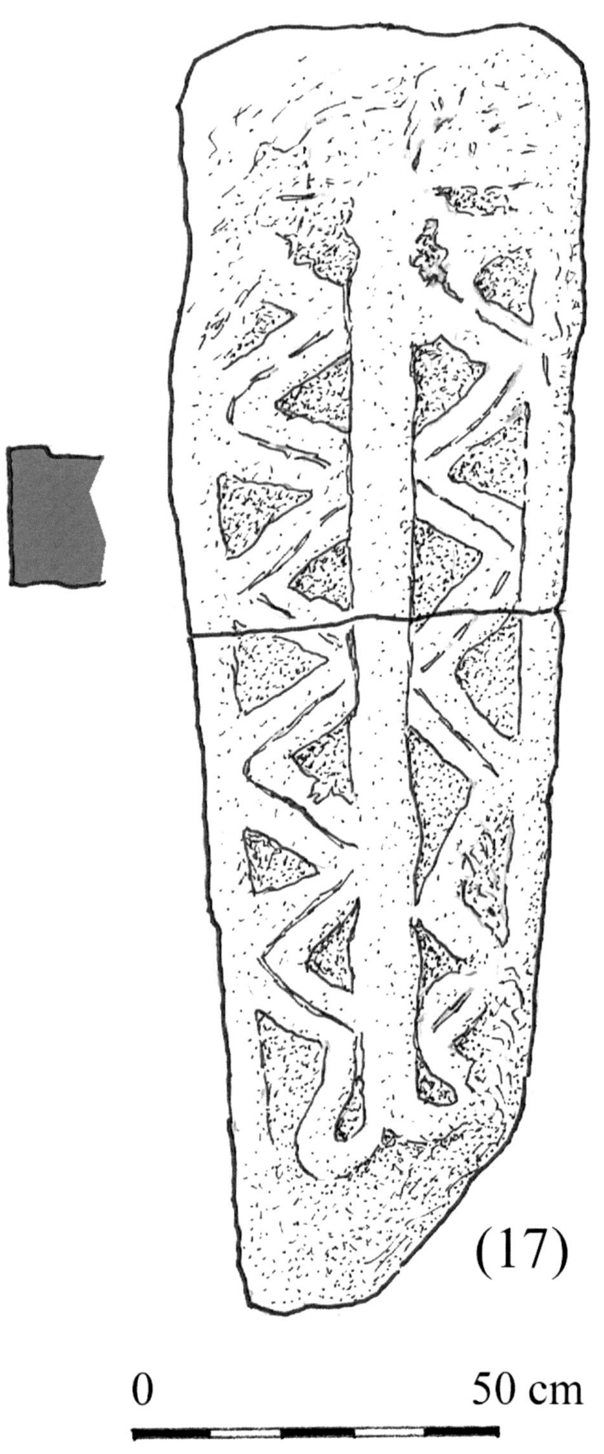
(17)
0
50 cm

Yarm

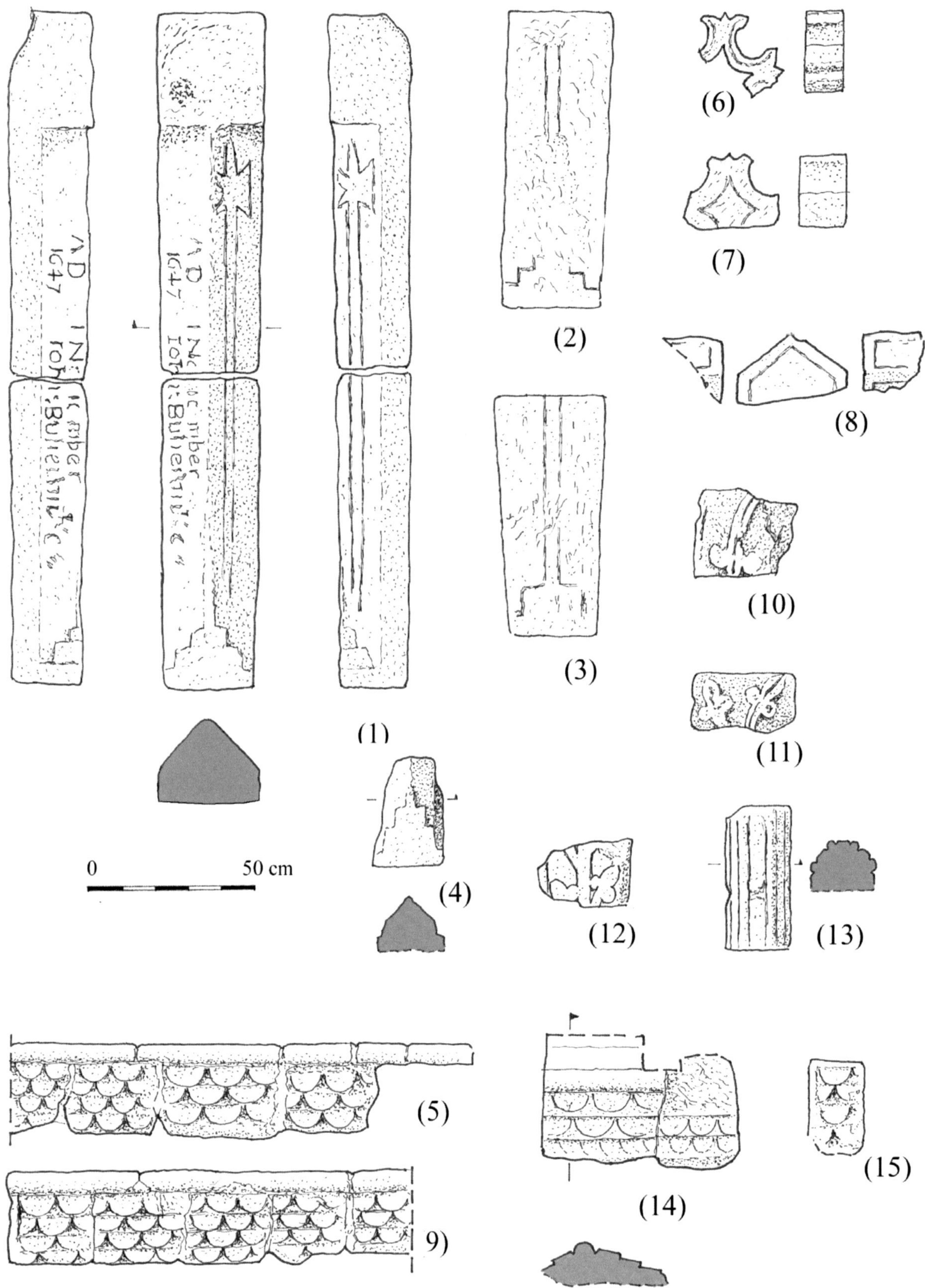

Yarm. Slab in floor at east end of north aisle
drawn 2 5 1986 PFR

(1888 drawing below from Mountford, W.J. c1900
'Summer Saturdays with Country Churches,
unpub MS in Darlington Library Local History Section

(16)

Locations of slabs

This is simply a brief guide to the locations of slabs (when drawn), with additional notes.

Bilsdale (Chop Gate) St Hilda

3 headstones inside 1851 church, 2 lost since c1985

Brotton

(1) In chancel of medieval church, excavated in 1980s, now filled in again
(2) In porch of present church of St Margaret of Antioch

Crathorne

(1) Interior W wall nave S of tower arch
(2) Interior W wall nave N of tower arch
(3)-(4) Internal face S wall tower
(5) (8) Internal face N wall of tower
(9) External face N wall nave m up to W of two-light window

Danby

(1) Internal lintel of inner door of porch
(2) In porch
(3) Lying outside W wall tower (1990)
(4) Lying outside S side tower (1990); perhaps a headstone
(5) E side tower stair just inside lower door
(6) Lintel at top of tower stair
(7) Above chancel arch

Easington

(1) Floor on N of Sanctuary
(2) W wall of nave N of tower arch
(3) Base of tower W wall
(4) Base of tower NW corner
(5) Base of tower N wall
(6) Churchyard outside SW corner tower

Egton

(1) Sanctuary floor
(2) Sanctuary floor
(3) Lying loose in chapel

Great Ayton, All Saints

(1) In recess on internal face of western blocked gallery door on N of nave
(2) Above (1)
(3) In two pieces in centre of external face of W end
(4) External face S wall porch 2.5 m up.
(5) Internal face E wall porch near N end, low down
(6) Internal face N wall nave below eastern of blocked gallery doors
(7) Same wall 2.5 m up 0.5 m E of central window
(8) Internal face E wall porch N end 1.8 m up
(9) Loose on internal sill W window porch
(10) External face E wall porch N end 1 m up
(11) External face E wall porch S end lowest course

Guisborough

(1) Internal face of E wall S aisle

Hutton Rudby

(1) In recess in S aisle
(2)-(4) In recess on N side chancel
(5) External face of W wall nave, high up in gable

Ingleby Arncliffe

(1) Loose in W porch

Ingleby Greenhow

(1)-(6) Set in S side of plinth of priest's effigy under N arcade
(7)-(12) N side –plinth of same monument
(13) Beside civilian monument under N arcade
(14)-(17) Lying loose beneath civilian monument
(18) Internal face N wall N aisle 2.5 m up
(19) Beneath (18)
(20) External face W wall N aisle

Kildale

(1)-(4) Set against the internal walls of the S porch, all to members of the local branch of the Percy family
(5)-(6) Against S face of churchyard wall just W of entrance
(7) Under tower by font
(8) Against external S side tower
(9)-(12) Under tower beside font
(13)-(18) All built into gable of S porch. (16) not necessarily a sepulchral monument
(18) Lying (1985) close to W side churchyard roughly opposite mid-point of path between churchyard gate and church

Kirkby in Cleveland, St Augustine

(1)– (2) Internal face of E wall of S chancel chapel, with other old stones
(3) In pavement at E end nave
(4) Loose in upper tower room (1986)
(5) Finial at W end N chancel aisle
(6) Finial W end S chancel aisle

Kirkleatham

(1) In chancel
(2) Internal lintel of window in N wall tower ringing chamber
(3) External S wall of tower stair turret 5 m aboveground
(4)–(6) In churchyard (1991) not found (2015)

Kirklevington

(1) W internal wall S porch
(2) E internal wall S porch
(3) Internal face N wall chancel, W end
(4)-(8) Internal face W wall vestry
(9)-(15) Internal face N wall vestry
(16)-(22) Internal face E wall vestry
(23)-(24) External face E end below windows

(25) External face N wall vestry high up
(26)-(30) External face W wall vestry
(31)-(32) In S porch in 1991, since then removed by persons unknown

Liverton

(1) In floor on N of sanctuary; probably late 13th century, the arms are Fitz Conan

Lythe

The church has a very large collection of lapidary material, much of it Pre-Conquest. Of the stones drawn, only (1), (2), (4) and (12) are clearly medieval; the others may be earlier.

(1), (12) and (13) in display at SW end of church
Remainder in stone store in tower basement

Marton

(1) In floor N transept

Newton-in-Cleveland

(1) Head of external opening of S porch
(2) Lying outside S wall nave
(3) Head of recess on S of sanctuary
(4) Back wall of recess on S of sanctuary
(5) Finial to S porch
(6) Finial on SE corner nave

Ormesby

(1)-(3) Exterior S chancel vestry
(4) S exterior chancel
(5)-(12) S exterior nave
(13)-(14) S exterior SW nave vestry
(15) Outside N wall chancel
(16) Windowsill in N aisle

Osmotherley

(1) Exterior N nave plinth near W end

Skelton

(1) On floor N side chancel
(2) On floor S side chancel

Stokesley

(1) Internal face of N wall chancel.

Upleatham

(1)-(3) In nave
(4) On W wall Lowther vault (1986) Not found 2015

Whitby

(1)-(4) In 'Museum Corner' in South Transept

Westerdale, Christ Church

(1)– (7) All in the S porch
(8) and (9) In porch 1991, not seen 2016
(10) In churchyard 9 m W of tower

Whorlton, Holy Cross

(1) Internal face of W wall tower, S end 1.5 m above floor
(2) Internal face of W wall tower, centre, 2 m up (1 and 2 halves of same stone)
(3) S splay of first floor window in W wall of tower
(4) Internal face of E wall just below first floor window
(5) Internal N splay of first floor window on E
(6) Internal S splay of first floor window on E
(7) Internal lintel of E first floor window
(8) Internal lintel of W first floor window (7 and 8 halves of same stone)
(9) Internal face of N wall above door
(10) Internal face of S wall 3 m up near SE corner
(11) Headstone loose in chancel
(12) In buttress on N of chancel arch above '1891' date stone
(13) External face E wall tower 1 m up
(14) External face of 2=W wall tower 3 m up
(15) External face W wall tower 1.5 m up
(16) External face W wall tower 1.5 m up
(17) In chancel fixed against S end W wall (drawn 26 2 16)

Yarm

(1) In churchyard 16 m S of E end S aisle
(2) S face of S wall tower (internal) 4 m above ground floor.
(3) N face N wall tower 3 m above first floor
(4) SE corner vestry E wall
(5)-(8) S wall vestry, eastern panel of re-used stones
(9)-(15) S wall vestry, western panel of re-used stones
(16) In floor at E end N aisle, now under fitted carpet